From Tutor Scripts to Talking Sticks

Ms. Mitchell ☺

W9-AWE-513

From Tutor Scripts to Talking Sticks

100 Ways to Differentiate Instruction in K–12 Inclusive Classrooms

by

Paula Kluth, Ph.D.

and

Sheila Danaher, M.S.Ed.
Chicago Public Schools

PAUL·H·
BROOKES
PUBLISHING Co.®

Baltimore • London • Sydney

Paul H. Brookes Publishing Co.
Post Office Box 10624
Baltimore, Maryland 21285-0624
USA

www.brookespublishing.com

Copyright © 2010 by Paul H. Brookes Publishing Co., Inc.
All rights reserved.

"Paul H. Brookes Publishing Co." is a registered trademark of
Paul H. Brookes Publishing Co., Inc.

Manufactured in China by JADE PRODUCTIONS.

The individuals described in this book are composites or real people whose situations are masked
and are based on the authors' experiences. In all instances, names and identifying details have been
changed to protect confidentiality.

Cover and illustrations by Barbara Moran. Ms. Moran is a graphic artist, a presenter, a self-advocate,
an advocate for people with disabilities, and a person with autism. Her artwork has been displayed
across the country. Her unique and captivating drawings are available for purchase from
http://www.karlwilliams.com/moran.htm

Library of Congress Cataloging-in-Publication Data

Kluth, Paula.
     From tutor scripts to talking sticks : 100 ways to differentiate instruction in K-12 inclusive classrooms / by
Paula Kluth and Sheila Danaher.
       p.   cm.
     Includes bibliographical references.
     ISBN-13: 978-1-59857-080-9 (pbk.)
     ISBN-10: 1-59857-080-3
     1. Individualized instruction.   2. Inclusive education.   I. Danaher, Sheila.   II. Title.
LB1031.K48 2010
371.39'4—dc22   2009051345

British Library Cataloguing in Publication data are available from the British Library.

2013   2012   2011

10   9   8   7   6   5   4   3   2

Contents

Communication & Participation

Behavior & Motivation

Teaching & Learning

Literacy

About the Authors

Paula Kluth, Ph.D., is one of today's most popular and respected experts on autism and inclusive education. Through her work as an independent consultant and presenter, Dr. Kluth helps professionals and families create responsive, engaging schooling experiences for students with disabilities and their peers, too. An internationally respected scholar and author, Dr. Kluth has written or cowritten several books for Paul H. Brookes Publishing Co., including *"A Land We Can Share": Teaching Literacy to Students with Autism* (2008), *"Just Give Him the Whale!": 20 Ways to Use Fascinations, Areas of Expertise, and Strengths to Support Students with Autism* (2008), and *"You're Going to Love This Kid!": Teaching Students with Autism in the Inclusive Classroom, Second Edition* (2010). Her popular web site can be found at http://www.paulakluth.com.

Sheila Danaher, M.S.Ed., is Assistant Principal and Inclusion Facilitator at John J. Audubon School, Chicago Public Schools, where she has worked for more than 20 years. She has also served as a special education teacher and an inclusion facilitator. Her areas of expertise include inclusive schooling, curricular adaptations, and autism. Since 2003, Sheila has supported students with autism in an inclusive setting with support from The Gust Foundation, a private organization that partners with Chicago Public Schools. Sheila has completed many certification trainings including Relationship Development Intervention, which she has used in her work as a consultant for families and school districts in the Chicago area.

Preface

Because we work almost exclusively in inclusive classrooms and so often with students with autism, learning disabilities, emotional disabilities, and cognitive disabilities; students needing enrichment; English language learners; and those labeled as at risk; we know that "something different" is sometimes required in order to reach and teach effectively every day. In other words, for the students we spend our time thinking about every day, differentiation is key. Together, we have been in the field nearly 50 years and have collected a lot of tips and tricks for meeting the needs of all students. For this reason, we sat down together to share some of our favorite ideas for differentiating in K–12 classrooms.

But, this is not a book of new ideas.

This is a book of tried-and-true, teacher-created supports and strategies that have been dusted off, collected, borrowed, and, in some cases, redesigned specifically for the visual learner in all of us. It is—for lack of a better way of framing it—a "show and tell" for teachers.

In our work in K–12 schools, we have found so often that educators who—at first glance may appear uninterested in changing their practices or in trying new things—are often quite enthusiastic when we clearly demonstrate or *show* them the technique, method, or materials that we are suggesting. For example, we once consulted with a Ms. M., a middle school teacher who insisted that she could not adapt her literacy lessons for students with disabilities or for her English language learners. We explained the dozens of strategies she could employ to improve performance for all students. We brought articles on the latest research in literacy. And we told her stories of how we, as educators, had successfully used the same strategies in our own teaching. None of these approaches seemed to have an impact on her practice.

Then we visited a second time and came up with examples of the suggestions. We brought 10 different adapted books; software that would help all of her students learn faster and more easily; graphic organizers; and novelty pencils, portable word processors, and mini-wipeboards to motivate her reluctant writers. She not only used the materials (and suggestions) immediately but also started developing her own differentiated products.

We did not set out to write a book with new information, novel concepts, or groundbreaking ideas. Instead, we came to this project with teachers like Ms. M. in mind and with the idea that if differentiation is needed for students, it is needed for teachers, too; so for every educator who learns best visually, this book is for you!

Acknowledgments

This book would never have been written without the support, encouragement, and creativity of Christopher and Susan Gust. The Gusts had a dream to bring teachers, administrators, families, and researchers together to make schools more inclusive and responsive. We are so grateful to be a part of the reality that came out of that dream. Thank you for all you do to make us think bigger, for pushing past perceived problems, and for providing Costello's whenever we need inspiration!

So many teachers helped us create this book, and 99% of them work at the John J. Audubon School in Chicago, Illinois. These teachers allowed us (on several occasions) to come into their classrooms, observe, take photos, ask questions, and interrogate them about their practice. They tried ideas we proposed and shared new ones we had never used before. So thank you to not only the teachers at Audubon but also to the paraprofessionals; building staff; and, of course, the leader of the school (and champion of all things differentiation), John Price. In particular, we have to acknowledge the following staff members who so graciously helped us create new products: Jennifer Larry (who can adapt her way out of a cardboard box) and Margaux Tuck (a co-teacher's dream partner).

A few other districts were particularly helpful in assisting us in designing and testing differentiation techniques: Stoughton School District, Wisconsin; Berwyn South School District 100, Illinois; and West Aurora School District 129, Illinois. Many in these districts have helped us think "outside of the box" as we plan for diverse learners in inclusive classrooms.

All other contributors are far too numerous to mention by name, but those who went above and beyond in trying new strategies in their classrooms or in helping us create the materials you see in the following pages deserve our gratitude: Sam Crane (a willing and very apt guinea pig), Aria Kinch (preschool teacher and child care guru extraordinaire), Amber Looney (tech wizard and patient assistant), and Kaitlynn Philbin (who makes the most challenging task seem effortless).

The content in this book was informed, in part, by the ideas and the writings of several other colleagues and researchers. We would be remiss if we did not acknowledge the work of Kelly Chandler-Olcott, Christopher Kliewer, Patrick Schwarz, and Alice Udvari-Solner. These ideas would not be possible without the many contributions you have made to the field.

Nearly last, but never least, our families supported our work on this project. We love you all and do not take your patience or your support for granted. Erma and Willa, we appreciate the "field testing" you did on the materials. You are both so helpful!

Finally, we are grateful to those at Paul H. Brookes Publishing for the time and care they invested in this project. Rebecca Lazo, as always, was enthusiastic from start to finish; Steve Plocher helped with every emergency (real and imagined); and Leslie Eckard was patient and helpful even when last-minute (and last-second) changes were proposed. We could not have been in better hands and we know it.

To Christopher and Susan Gust for their vision
and to Nicholas, who inspired it all

Organization

Contents

1 Homework Binder

Materials

- Three-ring binder
- Dividers
- Binder folder for each subject
- Sticky notes
- Thick markers
- Three-hole-punched zipper pouch

Description

For students with poor organizational skills, managing homework can be a constant struggle (Betts, Betts, & Gerber-Eckard, 2007; Bos, Nahmias, & Urban, 1999). Even if students manage to copy the right assignment in a notebook, they may fail to bring the correct work home or misplace their sheets or notebook on the way back to school. Wendy Lawson, a woman on the autism spectrum, recalls that her secondary school experience in particular was one big jumble of papers, schedules, and expectations: "I would get class timetables and rooms muddled and was often unprepared for lessons. Homework was usually forgotten or badly done. School was a confusing place to be and I dreaded having to go" (1998, p. 55).

Learners like Lawson often profit from systems that help them stay on top of their work and manage materials (Biddulph, Hess, & Humes, 2006). A homework binder is one such system. A well-organized homework binder will not only help students keep track of their assignments and materials but also teach them good skills and habits such as mindfully putting materials away, purging unneeded papers, and sorting work by subject area.

Directions

Start with a 1-inch binder, keeping in mind that a larger binder may be necessary for an older student. (The inches here refer to the spine width.) Add a three-hole-punched binder folder for each subject, and label it with the content area (e.g., math, science). Label the left inside pocket of the binder as "Homework" and the right side as "Finished Work." Add another folder for permission slips, school–home communication, report cards, and other related papers. Call this folder "Home." In this folder, label one pocket "Read or Respond" and the other pocket "Read or Responded." Students may also want to carry a pencil bag and sticky notes in their binders so they can jot quick messages to themselves or to teachers.

Initially, you should demonstrate where to place items in the homework organizer. When students arrive at school, provide time for them to check their folders and to retrieve papers from both the home folder and from the content area folders. Then, throughout the school day, teach students to look at their work and other papers (e.g., lunch menu, permission slip, important notes to the parent) and decide in which binder folder in the homework organizer they should go. Also, students should be shown how to place finished work in the proper pocket. Over time, students can become very independent when they have time to learn and use the system.

Example

In one middle school, all students created their own homework binder during the first week of sixth grade. Because the students switched rooms three times a day, learning and practicing organizational skills is one area the team of teachers targeted for the entire grade level. Every morning, the teachers gave students 5 minutes to clear out and organize their binders. Every afternoon, they repeated the process. Students with learning disabilities often got assistance from a fellow student or made slight adaptations to their binders. One student, for instance, asked a peer to double-check his binder before he went home. Another student put a sticky note on some of his papers to remind himself of any special directions given by the teacher. He also added notes to indicate which assignments had the highest priority.

Keep in Mind

Older students can add new pockets to their binders that are labeled "Work in Progress" in which they can keep any important notes, study guides, or ongoing projects. These can be added to every subject area and, if necessary, a 3-inch binder can be used instead of a 1-inch binder.

References/ Recommended Reading

Betts, S.W., Betts, D.E., & Gerber-Eckard, L.N. (2007). *Asperger syndrome in the inclusive classroom: Advice and strategies for teachers.* Philadelphia: Jessica Kingsley Publishers.

Biddulph, G., Hess, P., & Humes, R. (2006). Help a child with learning challenges be successful in the general education classroom. *Intervention in School & Clinic, 41,* 315–316.

Bos, C.S., Nahmias, M.L., & Urban, M.A. (1999). Targeting home–school collaboration for students with ADHD. *Teaching Exceptional Children, 31,* 4–11.

Lawson, W. (1998). *Life behind glass: A personal account of autism spectrum disorder.* London: Jessica Kingsley Publishers.

Moss, S., & Schwartz, L. (2007). *Where's my stuff? The ultimate teen organizing guide.* San Francisco: Orange Ave.

Rief, S. (2003). *The ADHD book of lists: A practical guide for helping children and teens with attention deficit disorders.* San Francisco: Jossey-Bass.

Vendors

Extra Packaging, Corp.
http://www.extrapackaging.com/parentteacher
Durable homework folders with one side labeled "Work" and one side labeled "Assignment"

OnlineOrganizing.com
http://www.onlineorganizing.com/ProductsPage.asp?name=HomeworkPad
Forms on which students can write down their assignments as they are given throughout the day and the supplies they will need for each class; includes room for tracking due dates and the student's top priorities for the day

Web Sites

TeacherWebsite.com
http://www.teacherwebsite.com
Teachers can create their own free web sites using the tools provided here. Teachers with web sites can easily post all homework assignments as well as examples of written work and grading information.

Homework Spot
http://www.homeworkspot.com
A portal that features many different homework-related sites for K–12 students

Adapted Agenda

2

Materials

- Agenda book
- Preprinted labels
- Alligator clips
- Blank labels
- Stickers
- Sticky notes
- Page tabs
- Highlighter tape or markers

Description

Adapted agenda books not only serve to help students feel more relaxed and prepared for and aware of the day's events but also they tend to encourage both teachers and students to add structure, stay organized, and maintain helpful routines. In some cases, they may also inspire students to become more independent and skilled at self-management and planning (Goldberg & Zwiebel, 2005).

Students might use adapted agenda books in any number of ways, including to

- Keep aware of the daily schedule
- Keep track of a daily or ongoing "to-do" list
- Record assignments
- Manage key pieces of information (e.g., schedule of who will pick student up after school, dad's number at work)
- Store learning tools (e.g., page tabs, highlighter)

Directions

Some students will be able to use agenda books without any changes at all or may need only slight modifications (e.g., using highlighter tape or markers to help students identify key events or sections). Many students, however, will need more extensive adaptations to their books to be able to use them more independently, more efficiently, or at all. For example, the teacher (or the teacher along with the student) may do any of the following:

- Create preprinted labels with assignments already recorded for students who cannot write independently or for those who struggle to do so in a timely fashion.
- Record key dates such as holidays, school breaks, special assemblies, and testing days for the student (or, if possible, with the student) far in advance so he or she can prepare or simply be aware of the schedule changes.

- Fasten pages that are not being used with an alligator clip; this way, the student can easily find the correct page and will not make errors by recording information in the wrong section.
- Adapt with stickers; add a musical note to the days when students have choir practice or add a sticker to each gym class day indicating what game the student can expect to play (e.g., tennis ball, basketball).
- Add page tabs (either sticky notes or page tab stickers) to help the student quickly find and access the various sections of the book.
- Use highlighter tape or markers to help students identify key events or sections of the book.

Be sure to educate the learner about how to use the supports or adaptations and work with him or her to use the book efficiently. For instance, if you want a student to use stickers as reminders for special days, place a few in the book and then, if possible, supervise as the student finishes the task.

Examples

Emiko, a sixth-grader on the autism spectrum, used her agenda book to keep track of daily activities. When she came into the classroom each morning, she immediately copied the daily schedule into her agenda book. She kept the book with her all day long to help her stay calm and keep focused. One of the adaptations Emiko used was a set of pastel highlighters. Emiko's large middle school used a block scheduling format; to allow larger chunks of time for each of the main subject areas, students only have classes in those subjects on alternating days (specified by the school as "yellow" days and "green" days). Emiko remembered this schedule by coloring her agenda pages to match the daily schedule format. Yellow days were shaded in yellow. Green days were shaded in green.

Jessi, a young woman with cognitive and physical disabilities, needed help from a paraprofessional or teacher to "check out" at the end of each day. The last 5–10 minutes of class were always set aside for updating agenda books, including recording homework assignments and reminders. Because Jessi could not write on her own, an adult had always updated her agenda for her. To help Jessi become more independent, Jessi's teachers created a simple adaptation. Every day, Jessi had two assignments to record in her agenda; one assignment was to read for 15 minutes, and the other assignment changed daily. To help Jessi take more responsibility during "check out" time, the teacher made a stamp that reads, "Read for 15 minutes." On her own, Jessi stamped this on her agenda page each day. Then a peer wrote her second assignment on a blank white address label, and Jessi adhered the label to the correct page. Jessi also needed help to locate the school schedule and hot lunch sections of her agenda book, so a peer helped her make durable tabs that she could grab to flip to each of these sections.

References/ Recommended Reading

Goldberg, D., & Zwiebel, J. (2005). *The organized student: Teaching children the skills for success in school and beyond.* New York: Simon & Schuster.

Rief, S. (2003). *The ADHD book of lists: A practical guide for helping children and teens with attention deficit disorders.* San Francisco: Jossey-Bass.

Vendors

Action Agendas
http://www.actionagendas.com
Agendas that include writing space organized by subject, a weekly journal, and a parent–teacher communication area

School Mate
http://www.schoolmate.com
Planners that include a variety of resources such as maps; time management and goal-setting tips; and English, math, and science aids

Student Agendas
http://www.studentagendas.com
Undated 7" x 9" books that can be started or used during any point in the school year, drilled to snap into a three-ring binder

Web Sites

Adolescent Child Specialty Services, Inc.
http://www.georgiachildpsychologist.com/id64.html
Tips from a psychologist on teaching students to use an agenda book

Freminder
http://www.freminder.com
A free online reminder system. Students who regularly use e-mail can store important dates on this site and receive reminders about birthdays, upcoming events, and even important tests and projects.

Teaching Pre-K–8
http://www.teachingk-8.com/archives/articles/and_on_todays_agenda_by_jeff_eccleston.html
A short article by a teacher, Jeff Eccleston, on the "whys" and "hows" of using a daily agenda with students

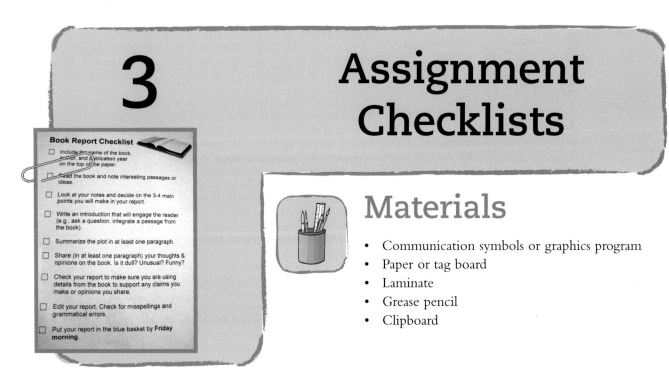

3 Assignment Checklists

Materials

- Communication symbols or graphics program
- Paper or tag board
- Laminate
- Grease pencil
- Clipboard

Description

Many learners feel anxious or frustrated when they need to tackle a big task or assignment. One way to address these feelings is to help students break big tasks down into smaller ones. An *assignment checklist* can make a big task seem smaller and can give students the satisfaction of accomplishment and of managing their own work (Ozonoff, Dawson, & McPartland, 2002).

Checklists can be used for students who struggle to follow multistep directions, who have difficulty sequencing time and order of events, and who would struggle to remember multiple expectations at once (Magnusen, 2005). They can be created for the whole class or for individual students who need more support.

Directions

If the assignment already has been broken down into a bulleted list or individual steps, simply rewrite the list and add a line or check box to each step. If the assignment is not already segmented, assess it and determine how small the tasks need to be for your particular student. Also keep in mind how much your student can handle seeing on each page. Some students may only be able to handle 3 to 4 items on a page, whereas others may be able to tolerate 8 to 10.

Experiment with different visuals to see which ones are most motivating and appropriate for your students. Photographs, color pictures, or line drawings might be incorporated, or even basic symbols and icons might all be used. Consider laminating your list so students can check off items with a grease pencil after each use.

Examples

Even though Liz has to submit a book report twice a month and already knows the required steps, she still uses a visual checklist to manage the work and to help her feel less overwhelmed (e.g., 1. Write the title and author at the top of the report. 2. Write an intro to engage the reader).

Mr. Pratt, a high school English teacher, gave all of his students a checklist to track their progress on a quarter-long research project. Items included:

- Form your team.
- Choose a topic/genre.
- Narrow your topic (with Mr. Pratt).
- Choose your note-taking system.

Two students with disabilities added some color coding, including highlighting all steps requiring extensive reading in yellow and highlighting all steps requiring interaction with the teacher in pink to their checklists to help them pay attention to some of the more challenging requirements.

References/ Recommended Reading

Dyrbjerg, P., & Vedel, M. (2007). *Everyday education visual support for children with autism.* Philadelphia: Jessica Kingsley Publishers.

Magnusen, C.L. (2005). *Teaching children with autism and related spectrum disorders: An art and a science.* Philadelphia: Jessica Kingsley Publishers.

Moore, S.T. (2002). *Asperger syndrome and the elementary school experience: Practical solutions for academic & social difficulties.* Shawnee Mission, KS: Autism Asperger Publishing Company.

Ozonoff, G., Dawson, J., & McPartland, J. (2002). *A parent's guide to Asperger syndrome and high-functioning autism: How to meet the challenges and help your child thrive.* New York: Guilford Press.

Rao, S.M., & Gagie, B. (2006). Learning through seeing and doing: Visual supports for children with autism. *TEACHING Exceptional Children, 38*(6), 26–33.

Sakai, K. (2005). *Finding our way: Practical solutions for creating supportive home and community for the Asperger syndrome family.* Shawnee Mission, KS: Autism Asperger Publishing Company.

Vendors

CleanSweepSupply.com
http://www.cleansweepsupply.com/pages/section0115.html
Over a dozen different clipboards from which to choose

Dick Blick Art Materials
http://www.dickblick.com/categories/markingpencils
Grease pencils in a range of colors

Laminator.com
https://www.laminator.com
Laminators for offices, schools, and for personal use as well

Web Sites

Council for Exceptional Children
*http://www.cec.sped.org/AM/Template.cfm?Section=Home&CONTENTID=9288&TEMPLATE
=/CM/ContentDisplay.cfm*
An article by educator Lisa Marshak featuring several strategies for students with disabilities, including how and when to use checklists

Child-Autism-Parent-Café.com
http://www.child-autism-parent-cafe.com/visual-schedules.html
A variety of visual supports appropriate for students with autism and other disabilities

Project-Based Learning
http://pblchecklist.4teachers.org
Age-appropriate, customizable project checklists for written reports, multimedia projects, oral presentations, and science projects

Success with Supports
http://successwithsupport.com/index.html
A number of support suggestions that include not only descriptions but also photographs

"IRS" Questions

4

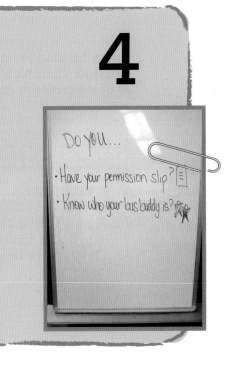

Materials

- Chalkboard or whiteboard
- Brightly colored note cards or sheets of paper
- Marker

Description

If you have students who are forgetful and prone to frustration because of this tendency, the *"IRS" questions* method (Goodman, 1995) may be a good supplement to your other methods of support. This method, as the name suggests, is taken from the federal government. As you have probably noticed, the flap on tax form submission envelopes, as well as on many other kinds of payment envelopes, prompts the user to review materials and double-check certain elements of their forms (e.g., Did you sign your name? Did you include a copy of your W2 forms?). This same type of checklist can be placed near a classroom assignment in-box (e.g., Is your name on the paper? Did you check your work?) or on the door for all to read (e.g., Do you have a pencil? A notebook? Your homework?).

Directions

Write your checklist on a brightly colored note card, sheet of paper, or chalkboard, and post it in the area of the classroom or school where the information is most relevant and hardest for the targeted student or students to miss. For example, "IRS" questions related to test day should be posted on the door of the classroom; "IRS" questions related to personal items might be posted in a student's locker.

Examples

A first-grade teacher, Ms. Hefty, puts brand new "IRS" questions up every day as students leave the classroom. She has the class chant the list (which helps some of the students with reading fluency) and uses the list both to introduce and practice vocabulary words (e.g., permission, retrieve). In addition, the list serves its primary purpose: to help all students leave the classroom with all of their materials and possessions.

Before handing in his math work, Luis, a fifth grader with ADHD, checks the "IRS" note card stuck inside his textbook with the following questions: Is your name on the paper? Are all of the problems completed? Did you check your work?

References/ Recommended Reading

Goodman, G. (1995). *I can learn! Strategies & activities for gray-area children, grades K–4.* Peterborough, NH: Crystal Springs Books.

Peltz, W.H. (2007). *Dear teacher: Expert advice for effective study skills.* Thousand Oaks, CA: Corwin Press.

Rowlands, K.D. (2007). Check it out! Using checklists to support student learning. *English Journal, 96*(6), 61–66.

Vendors

Computer Supplies
http://www.data-labels.com/flnepa.html
A large selection of neon fluorescent paper

Organize.com
http://www.organize.com/todopadknkn.html
Lots of gadgets and materials to motivate learners, including "to do" and "accomplish" notepads

Web Sites

Family Education
http://printables.familyeducation.com/education-and-parents/printable/54417.html
A "Did You Remember?" checklist for kids that can be personalized

The Teacher's Corner
http://www.theteacherscorner.net/classroom-management/index.htm
Teacher-to-teacher tips on managing the classroom and keeping both students and teachers organized

Desk Map

5

Materials

- Paper or index card
- Pen or permanent marker
- Packing tape

Description

Some students need support to find materials and keep their work areas neat. They may have all of the right storage solutions, such as school supplies boxes and pencil bags, but be unable to keep items in any type of order. This disorganization results not only in frustration for the learner (and often for the teacher) but it can also cause students to lose or misplace assignments and inadvertently ruin written work. (We have seen more than one worksheet destroyed by a broken ink pen or upended bottle of glue.)

Desk maps (Goodman, 1995) solve some of these problems for students by helping them to visually see where items belong and where they can, therefore, be found. These tools have the added benefit of familiarizing students with basic mapmaking and map reading, so very young students will hone social studies skills, as well!

Directions

First, have the student organize his or her desk so that supplies are neatly stored and materials have a designated home. Then, draw a diagram of where the different materials are kept in the desk on a small index card or on a sheet of paper. Finally, use clear packing tape to adhere the drawing to the top of the student's desk or to the inside "ceiling" of the desktop.

Initially, you will need to create the desk map so that the student understands what a map looks like and how it is used. After using the map for a few weeks, however, the student may want to change how things are stored in the desk and create his or her own map.

Examples

All of the students in a third-grade classroom made desk maps as part of a social studies lesson on mapmaking. This was a fun introduction to the skill as well as a great organizational support for three students with learning disabilities in the classroom. These students had very chaotic-looking desks and benefited from being able to designate specific spaces for specific materials and having a visual cue to keep items in their "homes."

Walker, a sixth-grader with ADHD, found it hard to find materials in his desk until his teacher worked with him to create a small desk map. The map, no larger than a small index card, indicated space for just three things—textbooks, glasses, and notebooks—but Walker found it was enough of a system to keep the space manageable.

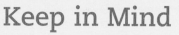

Keep in Mind

Maps are not just helpful in keeping desks organized. Try creating them for students' lockers too.

References/ Recommended Reading

Goodman, G. (1995). *I can learn! Strategies & activities for gray-area children, grades K–4.* Peterborough, NH: Crystal Springs Books.

Lawson, W. (1998). *Life behind glass: A personal account of autism spectrum disorder.* London: Jessica Kingsley Publishers.

Moss, S., & Schwartz, L. (2007). *Where's my stuff? The ultimate teen organizing guide.* San Francisco: Orange Avenue Publishing.

Vendor

OnlineOrganizing.com
http://www.onlineorganizing.com
Advice, newsletter, "tip of the day," and other materials to use with individual students and in the classroom, such as portable desk drawers and pencil trays

Web Sites

Peter Walsh Designs

http://www.peterwalshdesign.com

Although this site may not be completely relevant to students, teachers may find it helpful in organizing the classroom for their students. Walsh is known as a designer and home organizer, but he offers a "tip of the day" on his site that can be helpful to teachers and their middle school and high school students.

Print Free Graph Paper

http://www.printfreegraphpaper.com

Site that allows you to print a variety of types of graph paper (e.g., isometric, hexagonal) for free (you choose the paper size and measuring units); great tool for teaching kids to make their own maps

6 Illustrated School Map

Materials

- Floor plan of the school
- Graphics program
- Paper or tagboard

Description

Many students, especially those on the autism spectrum, are comforted, calmed, and motivated by visual supports (Cohen & Sloan, 2007; Dyrbjerg & Vedel, 2007; Savner & Myles, 2000). Some of these same students struggle mightily with making transitions, navigating large spaces, and dealing with the unknown in general. One way to honor these needs and preferences is to create *illustrated school maps* to help students learn new environments, navigate new spaces, and even become comfortable with new people (Cohen & Sloan, 2007; Myles, 2005).

Directions

Using the available floor plan of the school, create a map for an individual student, adding the following, when necessary

- Arrows or lines to show the path the learner will walk to get to various rooms or spaces
- Pictures to illustrate the uses of various spaces or the people who work in those spaces (e.g., picture of the principal in his or her office)
- Small reminders of what to do in certain environments

Example

Brianna, a fifth-grader with autism, loves visuals of all kinds but especially loves to read and study maps. Maps often are used to help her with transitions (e.g., she holds a map of Minnesota as her family drives from St. Paul to Winona) and with novel situations in general. When Brianna moved from one school to another, the new staff created an illustrated map of the school for her. She studied it before getting to the school and kept it in her homeroom folder all year.

References/ Recommended Reading

Cohen, M.J., & Sloan, D.L. (2007). *Visual supports for people with autism.* Bethesda, MD: Woodbine House.

Dyrbjerg, P., & Vedel, M. (2007). *Everyday education: Visual support for children with autism.* Philadelphia: Jessica Kingsley Publishers.

Myles, B.S. (2005). *Children and youth with Asperger syndrome.* Thousand Oaks, CA: Corwin Press.

Savner, J.L., & Myles B.S. (2000). *Making visual supports work in the home and community.* Shawnee Mission, KS: Autism Asperger Publishing Company.

Vendor

Plan 3D
http://www.plan3d.com
Allows users to create their own three-dimensional floor plans for a nominal monthly fee

Web Sites

Community Walk
http://www.communitywalk.com
A useful resource for creating a variety of maps (e.g., a community, a walking route to or from school, a field-trip itinerary)

PrintFreeGraphPaper.com
http://www.printfreegraphpaper.com
Site that allows you to print a variety of types of graph paper (e.g., isometric, hexagonal) for free (you choose the paper size and measuring units); great tool for teaching students to make their own maps

7 Stay-Put Stations

Materials

Materials for the stay-put station will vary for each student depending on the class. Some of the materials that may be used include the following:

- Pencil cup or pouch
- Extra copy of textbook
- Laminated checklist of what materials belong in the station
- School supplies box
- Magazine holder
- Notebooks

Description

For many students, transitions—especially those required at the middle school and high school levels—are an enormous challenge. For those who struggle with organizational problems, the work load of secondary schools can pale in comparison to the logistics of simply getting from one class to the next and being prepared with the materials necessary for lessons! *Stay-put stations* can help to alleviate stress by allowing learners to make fewer trips to their lockers and giving them one less thought to manage throughout the day (Stevens, 1997).

A stay-put station consists simply of a box, bin, or magazine holder that holds a student's supplies (e.g., textbook, notebook, pencil, calculator) for a given class. In most secondary classrooms, students are expected to tote these types of supplies with them, but if a particular learner finds doing so overwhelming, this adaptation can make a world of difference in the student's stress level and in his or her overall success.

Directions

Determine whether your student requires one, two, or more stay-put stations. (Most classes requiring a textbook or supplies that must be transported daily will need one.) Then consider the student's learning needs and the demands of the classwork with individual teachers to determine what types of materials will be required in each of their classrooms.

In each space, work with individual teachers to determine where to keep materials. Some learners may require an actual desk to store their items, whereas others may need only a small drawer, crate, or cubby.

Do not forget to teach students to store their materials neatly and leave behind only the items designated for that station. If necessary, add a laminated checklist as a cue to the learner about what belongs at a particular station.

Examples

Particia Howlin shares a story about stay-put stations in her book, *Children with Autism and Asperger Syndrome: A Guide for Practitioners and Carers* (1999). As Howlin explains, Guy was a capable young man who needed some simple adaptations to make it through the school day. Without any support, Guy was disruptive; he arrived late to his classes, struggled to find a place to sit, and often did not have the necessary course materials. Guy's teachers then suggested a version of a stay-put support station. After discussions between his mother and the administrator, it was suggested that Guy be allowed to have a fixed desk at which to sit in each classroom. The desk would contain the minimum equipment necessary for Guy to participate in the lessons being taught in that particular class (e.g., paper, pens, ruler). Guy's behavior improved rapidly after these simple changes were implemented.

Peter, a young man with learning disabilities, struggled to transition from class to class on time in his large junior high school building. During the first month of school, Peter was so overwhelmed with transitioning from one classroom to the next, learning to open a new locker, and navigating around an unfamiliar building, that he was late for more than half of his classes. To ensure that Peter was prepared for each of his lessons, his teachers created stay-put support stations for him. In each of his six classrooms, he kept a notebook, a pouch of pencils and pens, any equipment necessary for that particular class (e.g., compass and protractor for math class), an extra textbook (another was kept at home), and a folder.

References/ Recommended Reading

Howlin, P. (1999). *Children with autism and Asperger syndrome: A guide for practitioners and carers.* Philadelphia: Jessica Kingsley Publishers.

Stevens, S.H. (1997). Adjustments in classroom management. In *Classroom success for the LD and ADHD child.* Winston-Salem, NC: John F. Blair.

Vendors

Russel + Hazel
http://www.russellandhazel.com
Binders and supply containers in fun colors and styles; a variety of storage options as well

Teachers' School Supply
http://www.teacherssupply.com
Supplies, study tools, and a large variety of storage solutions for classrooms including different types of trunks, bins, and carts

8 Color-Coded Supplies

Materials

- Colored sticker dots
- Folders in a range of colors
- Notebooks in a range of colors
- Textbook covers in a range of colors
- Binders in a range of colors
- Index cards in a range of colors
- Sticky notes in a range of colors

Description

As students get older, they have more materials to manage. For some learners, this is not an issue; but for others, more materials can mean more mess, chaos, and confusion. One easy and low-cost way to keep these learners organized is to *color code* all of the supplies they use during the day.

Directions

Either assign colors to subjects yourself based on, perhaps, the colors of the textbooks or colors already associated with a subject area (e.g., green for biology, brown for earth science) or ask the student which colors he or she associates with particular subjects and use those as a starting point. Carry the color coding through as much as possible to all or at least most of the materials the student uses to make the task of organizing as worry-free as possible. For example, green materials for that biology class might include a green folder, green notebook, green textbook cover, green binder, and even green index cards or sticky notes.

Examples

Arlo, a teenager with a lot of organizational challenges, asked his teacher for help in managing his class materials. His teacher helped him color code his supplies as a first step in the process of keeping things orderly and making transitions more seamless. Because it was mid-year when he sought help, Arlo was reluctant to switch to new notebooks; instead, he used colored dots to code the supplies he already owned (e.g., blue for math, red for science).

At the beginning of the school year, a fourth-grade teacher asked her students' families to purchase supplies in certain colors. She then designated a particular color for each subject area so students could easily find their own materials or look around the room if they needed a reminder of what to take out. For instance, all of the students' social studies notebooks and book covers were orange; in addition, mini-atlases that were used during social studies were coded with an orange circle sticker.

References/ Recommended Reading

Brower, F. (2007). *100 ideas for supporting pupils on the autistic spectrum.* New York: Continuum.

Landon, T., & Oggel, L. (2002). Lazy kid or executive dysfunction? *Innovations & Perspectives, 5*(2), 1–2.

Reif, S. (2008). *The ADD/ADHD checklist* (2nd ed.). San Francisco: Jossey-Bass.

Vendors

Highlighter Tape
http://www.highlightertapes.com
Highlighter tape that is translucent and easily removable; available in several colors

Identi-Tape, Inc.
http://www.identi-tape.com
Tape in a variety of colors and patterns

Staples
http://www.staples.com
A range of supplies that can be used to code student supplies—dots of different sizes, notebooks, folders, and so forth

Web Site

Sandra Rief
http://www.sandrarief.com
A host of ideas for supporting students in the diverse classroom; many tips, in particular, for teachers of students with learning disabilities

9 Luggage Tag Reminders

Materials

- Luggage tags with see-through windows
- Tag board or blank business cards

Description

You have probably heard real estate agents emphasize, "Location, location, location" when discussing selling points of property. This same mantra could be applied when considering how to teach students to get organized. In other words, put reminders such as luggage tags where they are most likely to be useful! For example, if students need help remembering what to pack in their backpack at day's end, it is probably best to attach a reminder to the backpack itself. If students need help remembering what goes in their gym bag, attach a checklist to it.

Directions

Keeping in mind that less is more, create a short list of what students need to keep in any bag, backpack, supply box, or locker. Cut the list so that it fits into the address window of a luggage tag, and attach the tag to the bag, backpack, box, or locker. Then, demonstrate to the student how to go down the list, item by item, and load up or unpack using the reminder as a guide.

Example

Terri, a high school sophomore, created her own luggage tag reminders for both her music bag and her book bag. Her book bag tag reminds her to pack her Blackberry, her telephone, her electronic reader, and her multi-subject binder. Her music bag tag reminds her to pack her music, flute, and portable music stand.

Reference/ Recommended Reading

Morgenstern, J., & Morgenstern-Colon, J. (2002). *Organizing from the inside out for teenagers: The fool-proof system for organizing your room, your time, and your life.* New York: Holt Paperbacks.

Vendors

Crew Tags
http://www.crewtags.com
A variety of luggage tags in different shapes, colors, and sizes

OnlineOrganizing.com
http://www.onlineorganizing.com/ProductsPage.asp?name=Activitiy_Bag_Tags
Heavy duty, waterproof cards that list the supplies that students use most during the day, which can be attached to a student's backpack or bag. The backs of the tags have spaces for a student to write in any additional items that he or she would like to remember.

Tag My Bags
http://tagmybags.com
Luggage tags in a large variety of themes and styles (e.g., Disney, music, sports)

Web Site

The Old Educator
http://www.oldeducator.com/book_bag.htm
A checklist of items you may want to add to your luggage tags; don't reinvent the wheel if you don't have to!

10 Sticky-Tape Guides

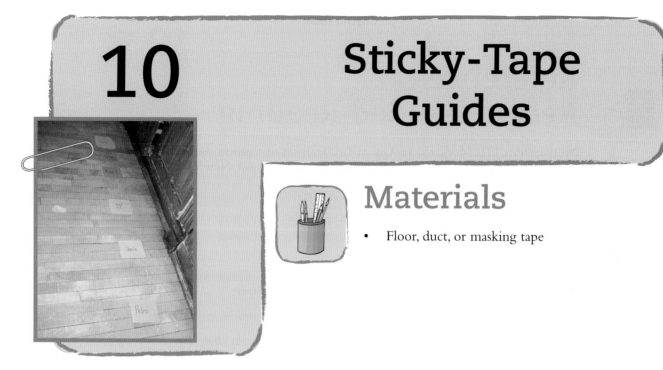

Materials

- Floor, duct, or masking tape

Description

Some students are disorganized because they struggle not only with tracking their materials but also with creating space for those materials and returning materials to their designated spots. Providing a clear visual guide such as a *sticky-tape guide* for frequently used items can help students both find materials they need and become more independent in managing their materials (Dyrbjerg & Vedel, 2007). They can also help students figure out where to walk, stand, or sit (Rao & Gagie, 2006).

Directions

Using tape that is appropriate for the surface with which you are working (e.g., masking tape for the inside of a desk, floor tape for cement), create guides or cues to help the student see

- Where to place materials
- Where to stand or sit
- Where to walk

Examples

Rory, a third-grader with learning disabilities, created his own sticky-tape guides inside his desk. He taped off an area for his supply box, his cell phone, and even his eraser!

Ms. Rochelle, a preschool teacher, taped off 12 small squares down one side of her classroom so that all of her twelve 3- and 4-year olds have a designated waiting spot as they are getting in line at the door.

References/ Recommended Reading

Dyrbjerg, P., & Vedel, M. (2007). *Everyday education visual support for children with autism.* Philadelphia: Jessica Kingsley Publishing.

Eckenrode, L., Fennell, P., & Hearsey, K. (2003). *Tasks galore: Making groups meaningful.* Raleigh, NC: Tasks Galore Publishing, Inc.

Rao, S.M., & Gagie, B. (2006). Learning through seeing and doing: Visual supports for children with autism. *TEACHING Exceptional Children, 38*(6), 26–33.

Vendors

The Empire Tape Company
http://www.empiretape.com
Glow tape, duct tape, floor tape, and more

FindTape.com
http://www.findtape.com
Removable tape, carpet tape, and many other types of tape

Web Site

Success with Supports
http://successwithsupport.com/index.html
A number of visual support suggestions that include descriptions and photographs

Environment & Sensory

Contents

11 Seating Supports

Materials

- Tie-on cushions
- Rocking chairs
- Beanbag chairs
- Wooden bead cushions
- Lawn chairs
- Office chairs
- Director's chairs
- Exercise ball
- Exercise bands
- Reading pillow

Description

Appropriate seating may not be the first thing a teacher considers when planning for a student with disabilities, but, for some, comfortable classroom furniture is pivotal to success. Having a few different seating options in the classroom can potentially boost the educational experiences of all learners. *Seating support* options to try include the following:

- Beanbag chairs
- Rocking chairs
- Reading pillows (large cushions with arms that prop the user upright)
- Floor/exercise mats (individual mats can be made cheaply by sewing a stack of newspapers in between two large sheets of vinyl) or large floor pillows (also easy to make with stuffing from a fabric store and a few yards of material)
- Carpet squares
- Couches, loveseats, arm chairs, or large footstools
- Stadium chairs for sitting on the floor
- Video game chairs

Students with and without disabilities also may prefer to sit on the floor for some part of the day. Teachers even can design instruction that calls for students to sit on the floor, or students might be given the option to sit on the floor or at their desks. Those who prefer to sit on the floor or in a chair without a desk can use clipboards or lap desks for written work.

Directions

Introduce a range of options and observe how and if students' behavior, work habits, or comfort level seem to change. You can also interview students about their seating preferences. As with other sensory issues, work with your occupational therapist to determine what kinds of supports your students need.

Examples

A high school teacher with a very small classroom clustered desks together in groups of four and cleared nearly half of the classroom for a community area. This section of the room contained an old coffee table, two loveseats, an old turntable, stacks of records, and a huge upholstered footstool.

Jimmy, a student with autism, has several different seating options in his fifth-grade classroom. Throughout the day, he moves from his desk, to a small table, to a rocking chair, to the floor—depending on the task, his needs, and the time of day.

Keep in Mind

Some students may prefer to stand for some part of the day. Students can be provided with a lectern and a desk at the back of the classroom and they can alternate between the two as needed.

References/ Recommended Reading

Berkey, S.M. (2009). *Teaching the moving child: OT insights that will transform your K–3 classroom.* Baltimore: Paul H. Brookes Publishing Co.
Schilling, O.L., Washington, K., Billingsley, F.F., & Deitz, J. (2003). Classroom seating for children with attention deficit hyperactivity disorder: Therapy balls versus chairs. *American Journal of Occupational Therapy, 57,* 534–541.

Vendors

Adaptive Mall.com

http://www.adaptivemall.com

Many adaptive seating options to choose from including their own "multi-positioning seat" and a large selection of therapy balls

AllCushions.com

http://www.allcushions.com

A variety of beaded seat cushions

The Bean Bag Chair Outlet
http://www.thebeanbagchairoutlet.com
Beanbag chairs in many sizes and fabrics

Web Site

Suite 101
http://student-health-issues.suite101.com/article.cfm/no_more_classroom_chairs
Learn how and why teachers are choosing to use exercise balls instead of chairs

More Ideas

Tennis Ball Soundproofing

12

Materials

- Tennis balls
- X-Acto knife

Description

Although any person may have a hard time hearing and retaining focus when the room is noisy, young people will likely have an even harder time when desks are slamming and chairs are screeching. Students with language problems or sensory differences, English language learners, and individuals with low hearing will have an especially difficult time. Using tennis balls on the bottoms of chairs to soundproof the room is one way to create a more peaceful classroom for students with and without special needs.

Directions

This adaptation requires nothing more than a number of used tennis balls. (Used tennis balls can be obtained at no or low cost from local tennis clubs, by placing a donation bin at the front of the school, through a PTA drive, or by placing an ad on an electronic bulletin board or an article in the community newspaper; students may also be asked to contribute them in addition to the supplies on their regular supplies list.) Use a blade of some kind to cut an X-shaped incision into each of the tennis balls. Then, attach the balls to the legs of the students' chairs and desks. (Because this task involves the use of a sharp tool, you will most likely want to do this yourself. Also, see Vendors for companies that offer pre-cut balls and a tool that makes the proper incisions.) This will muffle the sound of furniture being moved, causing less distress to students with sensory problems and making communication (e.g., giving directions, assigning homework) at the end of the day (when desks are most likely being shuffled around) easier.

Recycling tennis balls is not only a good idea for supporting students with auditory sensitivity but it is also "green" because it provides a use for equipment that would otherwise be tossed in the trash. Teachers report that, in most cases, the balls last for at least 2 years before losing their effectiveness; therefore, the process need not be repeated every year and may, in fact, last up to 3 years.

Example

Because of its program for deaf and hard-of-hearing students, a middle-school principal decided to use tennis ball soundproofing in all of the rooms of the school. The school sponsored a used tennis ball drive at their back-to-school night. Parents were encouraged to bring balls collected from their own family and friends or from their health clubs. The school collected enough tennis balls to put on the legs of all of the chairs in the classrooms and half of the 600 desks.

Keep in Mind

If you set your classroom up in rows or groups of desks and students, you might want to color coordinate the tennis ball sliders by row or group. For example, one row could be green tennis balls and the next could be yellow.

References/ Recommended Reading

Brown, E.L. (2002). Mrs. Boyd's fifth-grade inclusive classroom: A study of multicultural teaching strategies. *Urban Education, 37*(1), 126–141.

Grandin, T. (1998). *Frequently asked questions about autism.* Retrieved July 31, 2009, from http://www.togetherforautism.org/articles/about_autism.php

Kluth, P. (2010). *"You're going to love this kid!": Teaching students with autism in the inclusive classroom* (2nd ed.). Baltimore: Paul H. Brookes Publishing Co.

Vendors

School Fix
http://www.schoolfix.com/product/5501/flooring_savers_floor_buddy
A resource for purchasing the FloorBuddy, an alternative to tennis balls

Spangler Enterprises
http://www.precuttennisballs.com
Pre-cut tennis balls in a wide range of colors including blue, black, purple, and gray

Tennis Ball Cutter
http://www.tennisballcutter.com
Don't want to risk cuts and scrapes? This device creates the incision for you.

Web Site

Alexander Graham Bell
Association for the Deaf and Hard of Hearing
http://www.agbell.org/DesktopDefault.aspx?p=Teaching_Tips

Study Carrels

13

Materials

- Refrigerator box or other large piece of cardboard
- Scissors
- Markers

Description

A *study carrel* is an inexpensive and handy tool for helping students who are easily distracted or for those who get overwhelmed by a lot of visual stimuli (Conroy, Stichter, Daunic, & Haydon, 2008). Although one or two students in the classroom may find carrels helpful on a regular basis, it is a good idea to have several available. It is likely that all of your students will find the use of a carrel beneficial at some point, especially for test days or for long periods of independent work. Carrels may also be used for the following:

- Silent reading
- Peer tutoring
- Test taking
- Makeup work
- Playing games (e.g., hiding your answers from other teams)

Directions

You can certainly buy carrels for the classroom (prices range from a few dollars to several hundred dollars each), but you can also easily make or create them in minutes. One of the simplest ways to make a carrel (and one that many students will find irresistible) is to get a large refrigerator box, cut out just one side, and place the student's desk in the three-sided "room." You can also simply cut the top and bottom and one side out of a cardboard shipping box. This will give you a three-panel folded cardboard piece to prop up as needed. Students can then decorate the outside of their "office" and even post directions or visual cues on the inside of the box (e.g., 1. Put your name on your paper. 2. Ask for help if you need it.).

Examples

All students in a high school Spanish class are given the choice of taking their final exams with or without a cardboard study carrel.

In a fifth-grade classroom, Jolee, a student with learning disabilities, uses a teacher-created study carrel for independent math work and for all tests and quizzes.

References/ Recommended Reading

Conroy, M.A., Stichter, J.P., Daunic, A., & Haydon, T. (2008). Classroom-based research in the field of emotional and behavioral disorders: Methodological issues and future research directions. *Journal of Special Education, 41*(4), 209–222.

McFarland, J. (1998). Instructional ideas for social studies teachers of inclusion students. *Social Studies, 89*(4), 150–153.

Vendors

Biz Chair
http://www.bizchair.com/studycarrels.html
Carrels, tables, and other types of classroom furniture in addition to office furniture

Classroomproducts.com
http://www.classroomproducts.com/study-carrels.html
Carrels that are priced right at about $1.99 and sold in packs of 20, 30, or 40

Packaging & Design Co.
http://www.packaginganddesign.com/studycarrels
Corrugated study carrels—inexpensive, lightweight, and highly portable

School Outfitters
http://www.schooloutfitters.com/catalog/default/cPath/CAT6_CAT55
A variety of carrels including a few that are portable and cost under $100

Web Site

The Classroom
http://www.gradebook.org/Classroom Seating.htm
Tips on classroom seating

Lighting
Supports

14

Materials

- Lamps
- A variety of bulbs: incandescent, compact fluorescents, full-spectrum, halogen
- Other lighting options: holiday lights, colored lights
- Dimmer switches

Description

The right lighting can soothe, calm, energize, or inspire students. The wrong lighting, however, can be annoying, distracting, and even painful for some learners (Attwood, 2007; Crowther & Wellhousen, 2003; Heller, 2003). Children and adults with disabilities have reported problems, in particular, with fluorescent lights. Fluorescent lighting can affect learning, behavior, and the comfort level of students with autism and learning disabilities and of some individuals with anxiety and other related problems.

Teachers often believe they can do little to alter the lighting in their classrooms, but this is not necessarily true. Not only can the lighting itself be changed (even if you don't have funding for a full room makeover) but also *lighting support* adaptations can be made for individual students.

Directions

To determine whether fluorescent lights are problematic for students in your classroom, you may want to turn off the overhead lights for a few days and see if the change has any effect. If the lighting does seem to be a concern for one or more students, you may need to experiment with different ways of using light. For example

- Try lower levels of light.
- Take advantage of natural light as much as possible. Sit students with sensory problems close to the windows. Be aware that during certain points in the day (e.g., late morning, mid-day), even natural light may be overpowering for some, so be open to feedback from the students regarding any adjustments that need to be made.
- Use upward-projecting rather than downward-projecting lighting.
- Experiment with different types of lighting. Turn on the front bank of lights but not the back, or turn on alternating banks of lights. In one classroom, teachers strung white holiday lights around their whiteboards and plugged night lights into different sockets around the room to give the classroom a more calm and peaceful feeling.

- Try different colors of light. Experiment with a pink or yellow lamp in a corner of the room, for instance.
- Replace fluorescent lights with incandescent bulbs (perhaps not for the entire classroom but maybe for just one lamp that is close by a learner with sensory problems).
- Try LED lights.
- Suggest sunglasses. Glasses might be worn during recess or even indoors (especially near fluorescent lighting). Wearing baseball caps can also help students avoid direct exposure to light.
- For a student with this type of sensitivity, move his or her seat. Sometimes the problem is not the lights themselves but the reflection of light on a wall or other surface.
- Change the lights. Fluorescent bulbs tend to flicker more as they age, so use the newest bulbs possible.
- Use colored overlays on white paper to minimize or eliminate glare from fluorescent lights.
- Move students who are distracted by the noise of fluorescent lights as far away from the lights as possible. It may be helpful for these students to use earplugs while studying.

In sum, teachers should introduce a range of lighting options and observe how (and if) student behavior, work habits, or comfort level seem to change. Some educators even interview students about their lighting preferences as a way to gather information and design appropriate adaptations. As with other sensory supports, work with your occupational therapist to determine what kinds of lighting your students need.

Examples

Ms. Worman teaches fifth grade in an urban school and has worked hard to make her aging classroom homey and comfortable. She does not like the sterility of the fluorescents and usually lights her classroom with a collection of table and floor lamps, some of which are covered with darker shades to make the lighting softer.

Rick, a student with Asperger syndrome, complained often of the flickering lights in his classroom. Mr. Deprey, his teacher, talked to the school engineer who suggested installing newer bulbs. When these were installed, Rick was more comfortable and less distracted. After learning that Rick was this sensitive, Mr. Deprey also allowed Rick to take tests and do independent work at a back table where the lighting was less intense.

Keep in Mind

For children with sensitivity to light, consider the colors and tones used in the rooms. Avoid yellows, reds, and bright whites, if possible. Also avoid finishes that reflect a lot of light (e.g., semigloss and high gloss).

References/ Recommended Reading

Attwood, T. (2007). *The complete guide to Asperger's syndrome.* Philadelphia: Jessica Kingsley Publishers.

Crowther, I., & Wellhousen, K. (2003). *Creating effective learning environments.* Florence, KY: Delmar Cengage Learning.

Heller, S. (2003). *Too loud, too bright, too fast, too tight: What to do if you are sensory defensive in an over-stimulating world.* New York: Quill.

Smith-Myles, B. (2001). *Asperger syndrome and sensory issues: Practical solutions for making sense of the world.* Shawnee Mission, KS: Autism Asperger Publishing Company.

Veitch, J.A., & McColl, S.L. (2001). A critical examination of perceptual and cognitive effects attributed to full-spectrum fluorescent lighting. *Ergonomics, 44*(3), 255–279.

Vendors

BLI Lighting Specialists
http://www.budgetlighting.com
Light fixtures, lamps, different types of bulbs, and lots more; this company also specializes in energy-saving products.

Super Bright LEDs, Inc.
http://www.superbrightleds.com
A huge range of lighting options for classroom or personal use

The LED Light.com
http://www.theledlight.com/index.html
Light bulbs, light bars, task lights, and other related products

Web Site

Donna Williams's Blog
http://blog.donnawilliams.net/2007/02/20/heres-looking-at-you-kid
Donna Williams in one of the most well-known women on the spectrum in the world. She has a great web site (http://www.donnawilliams.net/) and a very informative and provocative blog. The link here connects to an interesting blog entry on fluorescent lighting.

15

Sensory Box

Materials

- Large container (e.g., bin, box, laundry basket)
- Any items that can be used to calm, comfort, and support, such as the following:
  - A weighted animal such as a stuffed snake to be placed on a student's lap or shoulders
  - Slant cushions to be place on student's chair
  - "Fidget" items, such as beaded balls or Koosh balls
  - Sensory writing tools (e.g., lap tray)
  - Vibrating pillows
  - Mp3 player, walkman, or other portable devices for listening to calming music while working

Description

Many students follow a sensory diet (i.e., a collection of activities specifically designed for a student's body and schedule) or have sensory breaks listed as accommodations on their individualized education programs (IEPs) (Smith-Myles et al., 2001). Some sensory breaks require students to engage in some sort of physical activity, but others may simply involve providing materials that help learners relax or energize. One way to provide these materials in a way that is accessible and easy to manage is to create a *sensory box* for everyday use. Having a box in the classroom alleviates the need for learners with disabilities to leave the classroom for sensory breaks and gives them ideas for meeting sensory needs across contexts and environments.

When the sensory box is first introduced, many students will want to use all of the materials and may even act silly or misuse the objects. As with any new classroom materials, students will need to be taught to choose and use the items from the box appropriately. In most cases, this teaching procedure will need to be repeated more than once. You will also want to pay attention to which items work best for which students and, eventually, cue certain learners to use certain items at particular times.

Directions

The first step in this project is finding a container. (A plastic laundry basket is inexpensive and works well.) Working with an occupational therapist, if possible, stock your box with materials from therapy catalogs, or talk to the therapist about teacher-created sensory supports (e.g., sand-filled weighted lap desks, homemade fidget toys).

Examples

While students are taking their standardized state tests, Ms. Haney, a sixth-grade teacher, reminds all of the students in her inclusive classroom about the items in the sensory box. She tells students which items may help them relax (e.g., weighted lizard) and which may help them "stay put" in their seats for longer periods of time (e.g., tactile cushion) and which can help them relieve tension (e.g., stress ball).

John, a child with autism, has difficulty transitioning and remaining seated during large-group activities. He uses the sensory box often. His favorite item is a teacher-made sensory toy—a plastic bottle filled with water, red food coloring, and oil to create a lava lamp effect. The bottle has a calming effect on John and serves as a visual mini-escape for him when he needs a break. Now, John can walk from activity to activity and relax by turning and watching the water bottle.

References/ Recommended Reading

Keane, E. (2004). Autism: The heart of the disorder? Sensory processing and social engagement: Illustrations from autobiographical accounts and selected research findings. *Australian Journal of Early Childhood, 29*(3), 8–14.

Prestia, K. (2004). Incorporate sensory activities and choices into the classroom. *Intervention in School & Clinic, 39,* 172–175.

Smith-Myles, B., Tapscott Cook, K., Miller, N.E., Rinner, L., & Robbins, L.A. (2001). *Asperger syndrome and sensory issues.* Shawnee Mission, KS: Autism Asperger Publishing Company.

Vendors

One Stop Sensory Shop
http://www.onestopsensoryshop.com
Sensory boxes, weighted lap pads, weighted vests, and more

Sensory Comfort
http://www.sensorycomfort.com
Products for children and adults with sensory processing differences (e.g., socks without seams, tactile towels)

Toys Tools and Treasures
http://www.toystoolsandtreasures.com
Thereputic equipment, "stress buster" toys, and a selection of weighted critters such as frogs and lizards

Web Sites

Indiana Resource Center for Autism
http://www.iidc.indiana.edu/irca/Sensory/sensoryIntegrate.html
A handout titled "Sensory Integration: Tips to Consider," created by Kim Davis and Melissa Dubie, two seasoned autism consultants

Sensory Processing Disorder
http://www.sensory-processing-disorder.com
Tons of activity ideas, stories from teachers and families, and answers to common questions about sensory needs

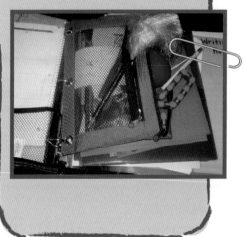

Fidget Bag

16

Materials

- Pencil bag
- Any items that can be used to calm, comfort, and support, such as the following:
  - Small toys (mini-Slinky, little car)
  - Manipulatives (Unifex cubes, counting bears)
  - Squeeze toys (stress ball, water tubes)
  - Textured objects (smooth rock, strip of hook and loop tape, ribbons, shoe laces)
  - Bendable objects (straws, paper clips, rubber pencils)

Description

If students in your classroom do not need the amount of support provided by the items in a sensory box (see adaptation 15), but do need some help to stay focused on daily lessons, a *fidget bag* can be a good alternative. The fidget bag is different from a sensory box not only in the size and type of items included but also in the fact that it is portable. Bags are small and kept either in a student's desk or inside his or her binders.

Items that therapists or teachers commonly call "fidgets" are small manipulatives that provide sensory input and keep the student occupied. These little toys often allow restless students to listen to teacher lectures, attend events such as concerts and assemblies, and get through test days without disrupting others or needing excess movement. As a teacher from a study by Kasa-Hendrickson explains, using this simple support can make the difference between a student's presence in the classroom and his participation in an activity:

> At the beginning of the year Sam could not stay seated through morning meeting and his mom suggested that we give him something to hold. She sent in the Koosh ball. Ever since then he [sits] through meeting just fine. (2002, p. 134)

Directions

When working with an occupational therapist, if possible, stock a pencil bag with materials from therapy catalogs, or talk to the therapist about teacher-created sensory supports. Some of the best fidgets will be items you have around the house or classroom. Try, for starters, balloons filled with sand (and knotted securely), smooth stones, seashells, combination locks, textured ribbon, and straws.

In addition to working with your therapist, you can also observe across environments to determine what to put in an individual student's bag. Pay attention to what he or she does when no fidget toy is available. Does he twirl a pencil? Does she draw on her desktop? Does he pick at his Band-Aid? These simple observations will help you determine what fidgets to provide.

Example

Cullen, a third-grader with an emotional disabilities label, keeps a fidget toy on his desk almost constantly. His teacher is always on the lookout for new gadgets for him to try. She has had fun, in particular, looking for content-related gadgets such as a globe-themed bean-bag ball and a U.S. Presidents slide rule.

Keep in Mind

Giving a child fidgets will only work to a certain extent. Providing a stress ball will help a child stay seated longer, but it won't be a replacement for active learning, movement breaks, or responsive instruction.

References/ Recommended Reading

Kasa-Hendrickson, C.R. (2002). Participation in the inclusive classroom: Creating success for non-verbal students with autism. *Dissertation Abstracts International, 63*(3), 903A. (UMI No. 3046836).

Rotz, R., & Wright, S. (2005). *Fidget to focus: Outwit your boredom: Sensory strategies for living with ADD.* Bloomington, IN: iUniverse.

Vendors

Autism Shop
http://www.autismshop.com
A large selection of fidget toys and sensory items—often small enough for a pouch or a pocket—including wiggle pens, Wikki Stix, cushions, tangle toys, and more

Office Playground
http://www.officeplayground.com/fidgettoys.html
A fun array of fidget toys appropriate for both children and adults

Toys for Autism
http://www.toysforautism.com
Several little toys appropriate for a fidget bag; check the sensory integration section of the site to view smaller items

Web Site

ADDitude: Living Well with ADD & Learning Disabilities
http://www.additudemag.com/adhd/article/1975.html
A link to a useful article on fidgeting as well as an entire web site of resources, tips, and stories related to learning disabilities.

17 Desktop Cheat Sheet

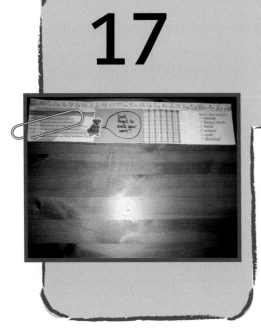

Materials

- Tagboard, cardstock, or desktop name tags
- Permanent marker
- Computer and printer to create cheat sheet
- Book or packing tape

Description

Students can reference personal information, multiplication facts, the alphabet, and measurement equivalents easily when these data are placed on a *desktop cheat sheet*. Sheets can be individualized easily for each student and can include any number of facts or ideas including the following:

- Number lines
- Equivalency charts
- Color or number words
- English, Spanish, or vocabulary in another language
- Commonly misspelled words
- Personal reminders (e.g., wear your glasses!)

Directions

Using either a commercially available name tag or a piece of tagboard or cardstock, design a visual support that will help your student work independently and learn new content. If you are adding to an existing tag, it may be easiest to simply cut out and attach the new content with packing tape. If you are creating a new tag, it is probably best to create the content on the computer (using a graphics program) and print it on the tagboard. Then, attach the cheat sheet to the student's desk with packing tape or book tape.

Example

Derek, a child with cognitive disabilities, has a hard time remembering all of the letters in cursive. His desktop cheat sheet, therefore, includes the alphabet. He is also working on reading a clock face; therefore, images representing different hours of the day also are featured on his sheet.

References/
Recommended Reading

Broun, L., & Oelwein, P. (2007). *Literacy skill development for students with special learning needs.* Port Chester, NY: Dude Publishing/National Professional Resources.

Bulloch, K. (2004). *How to adapt your teaching strategies to student needs.* Retrieved March 1, 2009, from http://www.readingrockets.org/article/370

Vendor

Homeroom Teacher
http://www.homeroomteacher.com/nametagsplatesandhallpasses.aspx
Several types of tags, including more than one with letters, numbers, shapes, and other tools for study and review

Web Sites

ABC Teach
http://www.abcteach.com/index.html
Free printable name tags

Have Fun Teaching
http://www.havefunteaching.com/teacher-tools/desk-name-tags
Many different themed (e.g., farms, rainforests, dinosaurs) name tags that can be printed for free

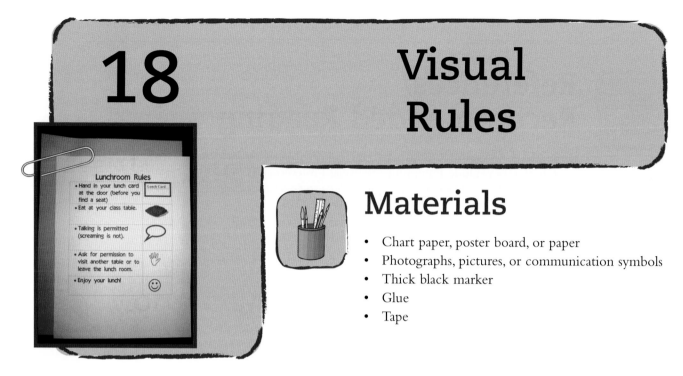

18 Visual Rules

Materials

- Chart paper, poster board, or paper
- Photographs, pictures, or communication symbols
- Thick black marker
- Glue
- Tape

Description

Many students, even those who do not struggle with reading, respond better to *visual rules* and directions than to those in print alone. For some, graphics or pictures are simply easier to decode and understand; for others, pictures actually provide more information. For instance, a picture that shows a student clasping his hands, holding a fidget toy, or standing with his arms at his side potentially provides more information than saying, "Keep your hands to yourself."

Visually supported communication is helpful, in particular, for students with communication and behavior challenges. Among other benefits, visual rules can help students learn effective communication, appropriate social interaction, and positive behavior.

Directions

Write your rules or directions on paper, poster board, or chart paper, leaving room at the end of each line for a drawing or photograph. Glue or tape one or more images next to each rule or direction, making it clear which graphic belongs with which line of text.

Example

Ms. Kasey, a third-grade teacher, found that her students often were confused about lunchroom rules and procedures, especially the one that required students to hand in their lunch cards before finding a seat. She created a set of visual rules and, in doing so, involved the students in selecting the pictures and helping to create the poster. Eric, a student on the autism spectrum, was very interested in the visual procedures and even asked the teacher to make him a smaller copy that he could take home and "study"!

References/ Recommended Reading

Arwood, E., & Kaulitz, C. (2007). *Learning with a visual brain in an auditory world: Visual language strategies for individuals with autism spectrum disorders.* Shawnee Mission, KS: Autism Asperger Publishing Company.

Hodgdon, L.A. (1999). *Solving behavior problems in autism.* Troy, MI: Quirk Roberts Publishing.

Vendor

Use Visual Strategies
http://www.usevisualstrategies.com
Picture cards, CDs of images, videos, and books related to visual strategies. This site features articles on using visual supports as well as examples of schedules, teaching materials, and behavior supports.

Web Sites

Science NetLinks
http://www.sciencenetlinks.com/lessons.cfm?DocID=293
A useful lesson plan on how to create classroom rules with students

Using Graphics in the Classroom
http://www2.drury.edu/dswadley/graphics/index.htm
List of web sites teachers can use to find new graphics for classroom materials and curricula

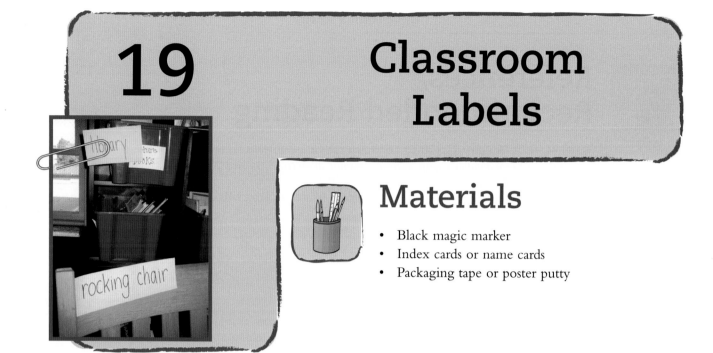

19 Classroom Labels

Materials

- Black magic marker
- Index cards or name cards
- Packaging tape or poster putty

Description

Labeling the classroom is a technique that is easy to implement and beneficial for many learners. Putting labels, captions, and other print around the classroom encourages organization and also helps students learn common words and expand their vocabularies. *Classroom labels* can be used to introduce or reinforce words in English or can be used to teach another language (e.g., sign language, Spanish).

Directions

Determine the words that would be most helpful to your student or students, and print them on individual index cards or name cards. To provide more challenge to students and to encourage reading (versus just labeling), write sentences on your labels, such as "This is the chalkboard." If the cards will be accessible to students, considering laminating them. Labels can be attached to your furniture, walls, or other surfaces with tape or poster putty.

Once the labels are in place, you can either leave them up for students to read and learn from or you can play games and organize activities around them. For instance, Carol Leuenberger (2004), a teacher of young children, recommends "pointer activities" such as having students use magic wands, fly swatters, or special gloves to find words in the classroom or to point out parts of the words (e.g., point to a letter in your name).

Examples

A high school chemistry teacher used classroom labels to introduce his students to vocabulary words that were new to most of them. For example, he posted a label on a pipette, a ring stand, and a tubing pinch clamp.

A sixth-grade teacher labeled her classroom objects to help her four Spanish-speaking English language learners. To create a learning experience for other students, however, she also added the same word in Spanish.

Keep in Mind

Look around the room and find objects or features that might be used to teach words that are new to many students. In other words, look beyond "door," "chalkboard," and "desk." "Credenza," "sill," "plaque," "register," "monitor," "processor," and "terrarium" are all good possibilities.

References/ Recommended Reading

Cunningham, P., & Allington, R. (2006). *Classrooms that work: They can all read and write* (4th ed.). Boston: Allyn & Bacon.

Leuenberger, C. (2004, August). "Reading the room" with pointers: Make the most of your print-rich classroom with playful pointers that motivate students to practice important literacy skills. *Instructor* (1990). Scholastic, Inc. Retrieved November 12, 2009, from HighBeam Research: http://www.highbeam.com/doc/1G1-121150481.html

Vendors

Grade Expectations
http://gradeexpectations.com/cd-3440.html
Classroom labels in Spanish; each set contains 56 classroom cards

Label & Learn, LLC
http://www.labelandlearn.com
Adhesive sign language labels appropriate for use around the classroom

Web Sites

Environments
http://www.eichild.com/r_pages.cfm?ID=232
Free customized labels that can be used for organization or literacy lessons

TeAchnology.com
http://www.teach-nology.com/worksheets/misc/labels
A great set of illustrated labels ready to post in your classroom; labels available for a wide range of classroom objects including paper supplies, teacher materials, and audiovisual items

20 Picture and Object Daily Schedules

Materials

- Communication symbols or other graphics related to daily activities
- Objects related to daily activities
- Poster board or tagboard
- Tape
- Sweater holder, shoe tree, or container to house objects

Description

It often is helpful to create visual tools to give students the information they need to participate successfully in the routines and activities in their lives. Daily *picture and object schedules* often are very comforting, particularly for learners with autism who prefer routines, but other students may profit from this strategy as well.

The primary purpose of a picture or object schedule is to help prepare a learner for what happens next in a sequence of events and to ease transitions. Schedules, however, also can be used to teach academic skills. Text can be included along with symbols or on objects to support student's literacy skills. Concepts such as *before, after,* and *next* can be taught or reviewed as well.

Directions

To create a picture schedule for a learner in your classroom, follow these instructions:
- Divide the day up into hours, classes, or periods and give each time period or activity a name (e.g., the bus and locker segment might be called *arrival*).
- Select a representation system (e.g., communication symbols, photographs, line drawings, objects).
- Pick the format for the schedule (e.g., laminated strip on desktop, spiral notebook) and gather the appropriate materials. If the student requires an object schedule, you will need a sweater holder, shoe bag, or other such container to house artifacts.
- Create or select the images or objects you will use and put them in the appropriate order.
- Once the schedule has been assembled, decide how you want the student to use it: Is it just to use as a reference? Will the student interact with it? Will he or she be in charge of assembling the schedule each day or will you? Once you have answered these questions, teach the student how to use the schedule. For instance, some students may want to take objects off their schedule as related activities are completed.

Examples

Simon has a personal picture schedule that he uses to navigate his day. He starts the day with seven laminated Boardmaker symbols (available from DynaVox Mayer-Johnson; see Vendors) across the top of his desk. After each activity or class, Simon is responsible for taking the corresponding symbol off the schedule and putting it in a box inside his desk. At the end of the day, he then replaces all the symbols.

Whenever Ryder's class lines up to leave the room, he takes an object from his schedule (e.g., a paint brush for art class), carries it to his destination, and hands it to the teacher. When the class is finished, he retrieves the object from the teacher, carries it back to his classroom, and deposits it in a "finished" box near the schedule.

Ms. Ochoa uses a visual schedule in her classroom, even though all but one of her students can easily read and understand the schedule without the images. Using graphics helps the student who has multiple disabilities and also serves as a useful support for ELL students and those students who are visual learners.

References/ Recommended Reading

Chen, D., & Downing, J. (2006). *Tactile strategies for children who have visual impairments and multiple disabilities: Promoting communication and learning skills.* New York: American Foundation for the Blind.

Dettmer, S., Simpson, R.L., Myles, B.S., & Ganz, J.B. (2000). The use of visual supports to facilitate transitions of students with autism. *Focus on Autism and Other Developmental Disabilities, 15*(3), 163–179.

Feldman, J. (1995). *Transition time: Let's do something different.* Beltsville, MD: Gryphon House.

Fittipaldi-Wert, J., & Mowling, C.M. (2009). Using visual supports for students with autism in physical education. *Journal of Physical Education Recreation and Dance, 80*(2), 39–43.

Kluth, P. (2005). *Getting ready for school: Transition tips for students with autism.* Retrieved June 30, 2009, from http://www.paulakluth.com/articles/transitions.html.

Savner, J.L. (2000). *Making visual supports work in the home and community: Strategies for individuals with autism and Asperger syndrome.* Shawnee Mission, KS: Autism Asperger Publishing Company.

Vendors

DynaVox Mayer-Johnson
http://www.mayer-johnson.com/products/boardmaker-plus/
Boardmaker software and other materials for creating curriculum adaptations

Miniatures
http://www.miniatures.com
Most items for an object schedule will be easy to find around the school, but occasionally, teachers find they need to shop around to find a physical representation of an activity or event. This web site of dollhouse fixtures has everything from miniature electronics to miniature birthday cakes!

Web Sites

Do2Learn
http://www.do2learn.com/picturecards/printcards/index.htm
You can assemble and print your own visual supports on Do2Learn for a fee, but this part of the site has free black and white drawings that can be downloaded separately and used for schedules or other tools.

Using Graphics in the Classroom
http://www2.drury.edu/dswadley/graphics/index.htm
List of web sites teachers can use to find new graphics for classroom materials and curricula

More Ideas

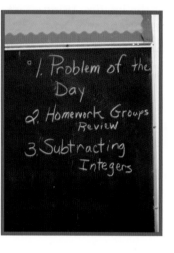
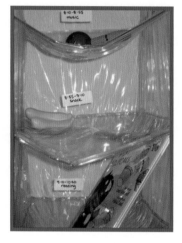

Technology

Contents

21 Microsoft Word

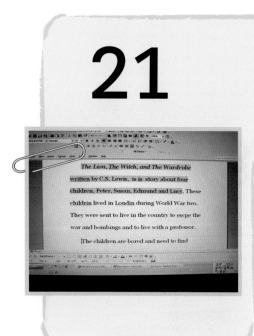

Materials

- Microsoft Word
- Computer

Description

Teachers often use *Microsoft Word* for personal purposes, making lesson plans, and creating products for the classroom. Students also use it to write, create artwork, and complete assignments. These are all appropriate uses, but Microsoft Word can do so much more. This software has many features that can be used to teach new skills, adapt written materials, and support diverse learners as they work onscreen.

Directions

To create products that diverse learners can use, teachers can do the following:

- Highlight key words or phrases.
  [FORMAT > BORDERS AND SHADING > SHADING > FILL]
- Shade key words or phrases.
  [FORMAT > BORDERS AND SHADING > SHADING > FILL]
- Change the size of the text or change the font itself to emphasize ideas, words, or phrases.
  [FORMAT > FONT > SIZE] or [FORMAT > FONT > FONT]
- Use **bold** type or *italicize* key words.
  [FORMAT > FONT > FONT STYLE]
- Add graphics (e.g., clip art, photographs, symbols, autoshapes, graphic organizers).
  [INSERT > PICTURE > CLIP ART] or [INSERT > PICTURE > FROM FILE] or
  [INSERT > PICTURE > AUTOSHAPES] or [INSERT > SYMBOL]
- Use borders so students can see exactly where to attend or where to put an answer.
  [FORMAT > BORDERS AND SHADING > BORDERS > SETTING]
- Increase s p a c i n g between characters to improve visibility and make visual tracking easier.
  [FORMAT > FONT > CHARACTER SPACING]

If students are working on the computer, teachers can do the following:

- Adjust the background color of the document to increase visibility and attention to text.
  [FORMAT > BACKGROUND and then select color]
- Enlarge the toolbar icons.
  [TOOLS > CUSTOMIZE > OPTIONS and select "large icons"]
- Magnify the text on the monitor.
  [Click on the ZOOM option on the standard toolbar; this allows you to change text size from 10% to 500%]

Other ways a teacher can use Microsoft Word to create adaptations include the following:

- Create a writing sample with mistakes and have students correct the mistakes to teach grammar.
  [TOOLS > SPELLING AND GRAMMAR]
- Insert tables into documents to make complex content easier to understand.
  [TABLE > INSERT]
- Add word banks or reminders.
  [INSERT > TEXT BOX]
- Add an organizational chart or diagram.
  [INSERT > DIAGRAM OR ORGANIZATIONAL CHART]

Students can use Microsoft Word as a support for their own work by using the following:

- Spelling and grammar check
  [TOOLS > OPTIONS > SPELLING AND GRAMMAR]
- Autocorrect
  [TOOLS > AUTOCORRECT OPTIONS]
- The thesaurus
  [TOOLS > LANGUAGE > THESAURUS]
- The FIND feature (to see how often they are using certain words and to encourage them to expand their vocabulary)
  [EDIT > FIND]
- The TRACK CHANGES feature (keeps a visual record of text that is added or deleted)
  [TOOLS > TRACK CHANGES]
- The OUTLINE creation feature to create an outline for a writing project
  [FILE > NEW > BLANK DOCUMENT VIEW > OUTLINE]

Examples

Rae, a student with learning disabilities, uses Microsoft Word to write papers for her high school classes. Her teacher has coached her to use the thesaurus to refine her writing as well as to expose her to new vocabulary words.

Students with poor spelling skills often have difficulty using a dictionary because good spelling instincts and a command of common rules and patterns are needed to find hard-to-spell words. Therefore, Ms. Van Ark, a resource room teacher, teaches all of her fifth-grade students how to use the spell check function in Microsoft Word to edit their work.

When printing tests for his sixth-grade students with learning disabilities, Mr. Edwin highlights important key words in the directions (*add, subtract, estimate, round*) in yellow.

References/ Recommended Reading

The Alliance for Technology Access. (2005). *Computer resources for people with disabilities: A guide to assistive technologies, tools, and resources for people of all ages* (4th ed. rev). Alameda, CA: Hunter House.

Barbetta, P.M., & Spears-Bunton, L.A. (2007). Learning to write: Technology for students with disabilities in secondary inclusive classrooms. *English Journal 96*(4), 86–93.

Vendor

Microsoft

http://office.microsoft.com
Microsoft Office can be purchased from many different vendors as well as straight from the Microsoft web site.

Web Sites

Michigan's Integrated Technology Supports

http://dev.cenmi.org/mits/ProductsView.asp?id=657
Want a handy worksheet to remember all of the ways to use Microsoft Word to support your students? Look no further. Go to this link and click on the downloadable file titled, *Using Microsoft Word Tools to Differentiate for Diverse Learners.*

Microsoft

http://www.microsoft.com/ENABLE
Demos, examples, and tips for personalizing Microsoft Word and making it accessible

Curriculum Commercials

22

Materials

- Video camera
- Television or computer

Description

In these standards-driven times, teachers are constantly searching for innovative ways to get students to learn new content or remember key concepts. One of our favorite strategies is to use *curriculum commercials,* which are short, teacher-created videos that help learners remember a concept, idea, or fact. The videos, like commercials, are meant to be memorable and even entertaining.

Directions

To make a curriculum commercial, simply determine what concepts or information you want students to know. Then, consider a fun and unforgettable way to communicate this to your student or students. You might create a jingle or chant, show some compelling graphics, act out a scene or skit, or simply present your content in a humorous or interesting way. No matter how you choose to craft your commercial, make sure that you keep it simple and short (about 2–3 minutes). This way, it is easy to capture the attention of every learner and you can play it several times without taking up much class time.

When it is time for students to view the commercial, think about how you will present it. You might use it to introduce a unit. Have it playing on a "loop" as they come into class. Or pretend that they are going to see a television program, press "play," and let them be surprised by the "character" onscreen! If the content will be helpful for students to see several times (most will be), consider putting your commercial on your classroom or school web site or on http://www.teachertube.com.

Examples

Ms. Frisk, a high school English teacher, made a commercial for all of her ninth-grade English students. Using posters, music, and even some rhymes, she created a 2-minute message about using more vivid word choices in writing. She titled her commercial "Said Is Dead" and shared a list of alternatives in the 120-second clip.

Damien, a young man with fetal alcohol syndrome, loves to listen to his classroom teacher read *Owen* (Henkes, 1993), one of his favorite books. He carries the book with him in the classroom and regularly asks her to read it to him. To give him more opportunities to hear the book, Ms. Crane videotaped herself reading the book and ended the clip by unraveling a banner that read, "READ 20 MINUTES EACH NIGHT!" She e-mailed the clip to Damien's father, who put it on the family computer. Damien was not only able to watch the clip daily but also was soon able to read the book on his own.

References/ Recommended Reading

Henkes, K. (1993). *Owen.* New York: Greenwillow.

Risinger, C.F. (2001). Teaching elementary and secondary history using the Internet. *Social Education, 65,* 297.

Tarr, R. (2006). Using video in the history classroom. *History Review, 54,* 35.

Vendors

School Videos
http://www.schoolvideos.com
Each educational video from this company is researched and evaluated in the areas of subject matter, content, and curriculum compatibility. All products meet national and state curriculum standards.

Walt Disney Studios Home Entertainment (Schoolhouse Rock Videos)
http://disneydvd.disney.go.com/schoolhouse-rock-special-30th-anniversary-ed.html
These 3-minute educational vignettes combine animation, fun music, and catchy lyrics to tackle lessons in American history, grammar, multiplication tables, science, and government.

Web Sites

Education World
http://www.education-world.com/a_lesson/01-1/lp226_05.shtml
Visit this site for a short lesson plan on how to make a music video. The plan helps teachers support students in creating a video; however, educators could also use the plan to create their own tapes.

TeacherTube
http://www.teachertube.com
An online community for posting and sharing videos, documents, and photos. A good site for housing your own videos as well as finding good material from other teachers that can be used in your classroom.

PowerPoint Books

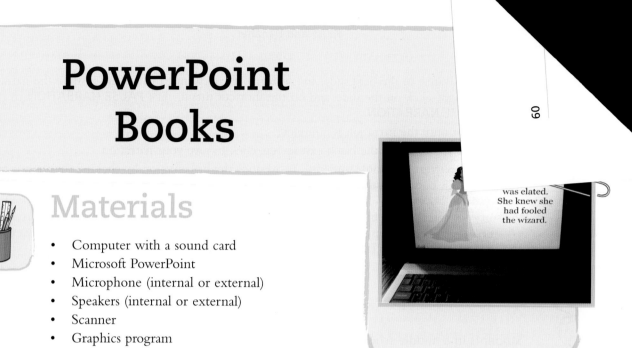

Materials

- Computer with a sound card
- Microsoft PowerPoint
- Microphone (internal or external)
- Speakers (internal or external)
- Scanner
- Graphics program
- Book or story

Description

PowerPoint is an ideal way to adapt a book for a myriad of reasons. It is widely available, user-friendly, and very easy to adapt for different learning styles. *PowerPoint books* are especially appropriate for students who do not read print or who are emerging readers. They are also appropriate for those who struggle to turn pages, hold pages open, or otherwise manipulate a book because they enable individuals to read or explore on their own with the touch of a mouse or the tap of a switch.

Directions

To create a PowerPoint book, follow these simple steps:
- Select a book and scan its illustrations into the computer. Check with the book's publisher for permission if you plan on widely distributing the PowerPoint presentation.
- If the book has a lot of pictures, it is not necessary to include every image. Instead, choose pictures that the student likes or those that best communicate the meaning of the story.
- Open up a new PowerPoint file and use the **INSERT** function to add the pictures to the electronic book. If the book does not have many illustrations, you may need to add related clip art to some of the pages or you can have students create illustrations for it.
- Next, copy the text from the book, or if you need to adapt the text to make it less complex, simplify the story using familiar words and lower level vocabulary. As you are typing, remember that you can change the text to meet the needs of your students. Text can be enlarged, the color of the print can be varied, and fonts can be changed.
- To begin recording, open the PowerPoint presentation.
- On the Slide Menu, click **RECORD NARRATION**. Click **SET MICROPHONE LEVEL**. Follow the instructions to set the level. Then click **OK**.
- In the **SLIDE SHOW VIEW**, speak the narrative text for the first slide into the microphone, then click on the slide to advance to the second slide. Speak the narrative text for that

slide, advance to the next slide, and so forth. If you want to pause and resume the narration, right-click on the slide, and on the shortcut menu, click **PAUSE NARRATION** or **RESUME NARRATION**.

- Repeat until the narration is complete.
- When you come to the black exit screen, click to save your narration.

To actually use the book, students can advance the presentation by clicking the mouse, pressing the **ENTER** button on the computer, or hitting a switch connected to the computer. Students may read the books individually, or you may choose to use a projector so that students can read the story together on the big screen.

Be sure to keep a copy of the book with the presentation both for legal (copyright) reasons and so students can enjoy both versions.

Examples

Students in a middle school technology club worked with second-grade teachers to create a library of PowerPoint books for students in the primary unit of their school. The older students learned about writing for different audiences and honed their computer skills, and the younger students were able to enjoy a wide array of grade-level books.

Three students in a blended first-grade classroom struggle to use books independently. One has physical disabilities, one has Down syndrome, and one has autism. The teaching team (i.e., general education teacher, special education teacher, speech-language pathologist, reading specialist) worked together to create 25 PowerPoint books for the classroom computers. These stories are used mostly by the three learners with disabilities, but the team has discovered that they are also favored by students who are English language learners (ELLs) and also by reluctant readers who love computers.

Keep in Mind

Sound effects can also be added to PowerPoint books to motivate a student and boost his or her comprehension. For instance, you can add dog howls to Sounder (Armstrong, 1969) or a train whistle to *The Little Engine that Could* (Piper, 1961).

Other options for audio include singing, incorporating music, and using multiple voices (possibly for different characters in the book). Depending on the specific preferences of the learner, these strategies may enhance comprehension and interest in the text.

References/ Recommended Reading

Armstrong, W.H. (1969). *Sounder.* New York: HarperCollins.

Copeland, S.R., & Keefe, E.B. (2007). *Effective literacy instruction for students with moderate or severe disabilities.* Baltimore: Paul H. Brookes Publishing Co.

Erickson, K., & Koppenhaver, D. (2007). *Children with disabilities: Reading and writing the four-blocks way.* Greensboro, NC: Carson-Dellosa Publishing Company, Inc.

Piper, W. (1961). *The little engine that could.* New York: Platt & Munk.

Vendors

The CLCD Company, LLC

http://www.childrenslit.com

With a subscription to the Children's Literature Comprehensive Database (CLCD), teachers can use a variety of search options to help find books by subject, age level, and genre and can gain access to teaching tools and more than 145,000 links to web pages featuring authors and illustrators.

Microsoft

http://office.microsoft.com/en-us/powerpoint/default.aspx

PowerPoint 2007 for purchase

Scholastic

http://www2.scholastic.com/browse/home.jsp

Full of resources including books, magazines, and information on guided reading programs

Web Site

Computer Supported Literacy

http://aac.unl.edu/csl/litdev.html

Useful to anyone looking for research related to the literacy development of augmentative and alternative communication users. It also features several links to other literacy sites and resources.

24 Keychain Tutor

Materials

- Keychain tape recorder
- Icons, stickers, or labels
- Tape

Description

If you have students who are forgetful, need help with organizing, or struggle with writing, a *keychain tutor* or tape recorder might be a useful adaptation. Students can be taught to record any number of reminders including homework assignments; facts or information (e.g., spelling words); or simple "to dos," such as "Bring my permission slip tomorrow" or "Union is North and Confederate is South." This adaptation is also a good one for students who are blind or have low vision; instead of copying assignments off the board, for instance, these learners can record them into their keychain and play them back at home.

Directions

Once you have decided on the reminder or content your student needs, write it out for him or her in simple language and demonstrate how to record the message on the device. Then, supervise the learner as he or she records the message. For students who are nonverbal, record the message yourself or have another student record the message. Finally, tape a word, phrase, or icon on the keychain if you are trying to teach the connection between the spoken words and a written word or message.

Example

J.J., a student with learning disabilities, records one or two different vocabulary words each day on his keychain. At dinner, he discusses the words with his mother. By the end of the week, he has studied the entire list of words and is prepared for the test.

References/ Recommended Reading

Mooney, J., & Cole, D. (2000). *Learning outside the lines.* New York: Fireside.

National Center for Technology Innovation and Center for Implementing Technology in Education. (2006). *On the go: What consumer products can do for you (if you know where to look!).* Retrieved July 2, 2009, from http://www.ldonline.org/article/9705

Vendors

Improvements
http://www.improvementscatalog.com/home/improvements/792927071-keychain-memo-recorder.html
This keychain memo recorder can record and play back multiple messages, up to a total of 20 seconds.

Genaldi
http://www.genaldi.com/digital.html
Cell-phone-shaped digital voice recorder

Web Sites

ADDitude: Living Well with ADD and Learning Disabilities
http://www.additudemag.com
An online resource for those with ADD, ADHD, and learning disabilities; includes information on assistive technology as well as a listserv to share and get ideas for children and adults

Hands On Assistive Technology
http://www.teleschool.k12.hi.us/hoat/default.htm
A collaborative distance-learning project designed by the Hawaii State Department of Education and the University of Hawaii Center on Disability Studies. This web site includes a variety of resources such as guidelines for using assistive technology and lots of suggestions for tools that can be used for various challenges and needs.

25 Adapted Keyboard

Materials

- Keyboard
- Large print keyboard stickers
- Colored dots

Description

For most students today, using a keyboard is as easy as using a pencil, but for others, the challenges involved make typing or even pushing keys difficult or even impossible. As Lazzaro (2001) pointed out, to operate a keyboard effectively, a lot of skills need to come together: "You must have significant coordination and finger control. You must be able to strike the desired key without accidentally striking others and also be able to release the key quickly enough to prevent the key's action from repeating" (p. 55).

For students who do not have these skills or abilities, teachers may need to explore *adapted keyboards* or even different types of keyboards.

Directions

Adaptations that may be made to the keyboard include the following:
- Adding colored dots to one or more keys to help students identify them (e.g., to the **ENTER** key)
- Adding large-print keyboard stickers to the keyboard
- Providing an enlarged keyboard
- Providing an alternative keyboard (e.g., ABC board instead of QWERTY board)
- Using a key guard

Two adaptations can be made to your computer that affect how your keyboard works: Key Repetition Control and Sticky Keys.

Key Repetition Control (Ignores brief or repeated keystrokes; slows repeat rate)
- Go to the **CONTROL PANEL.**
- Open **ACCESSIBILITY OPTIONS.**
- Go to **KEYBOARD.**

- Turn on **FILTER KEYS**.
- Press **APPLY**.
- For Windows Vista, go to the **CONTROL PANEL**; click on **EASE OF ACCESS**; click on **CHANGE HOW YOUR KEYBOARD WORKS**; and click the checkbox for **TURN ON FILTER KEYS**.

Sticky Keys (single key typing–use **SHIFT**, **CONTROL**, or **ALT** key by pressing one key at a time):
- Go to the **CONTROL PANEL**.
- Open **ACCESSIBILITY OPTIONS**.
- Go to **KEYBOARD**.
- Turn on **STICKY KEYS**.
- Press **APPLY**.
- For Windows Vista, go to the **CONTROL PANEL**; click on **EASE OF ACCESS**; click on **CHANGE HOW YOUR KEYBOARD WORKS**; and click the checkbox for **TURN ON STICKY KEYS**.

Work with your occupational therapist, if possible, to determine what types of adaptations your student requires. Once you select one or more adaptations, be sure to give the learner plenty of time to acclimate to the new materials or supports. You may even take data on the student's performance on the keyboard before and after adding the adaptations.

Example

Ricky, a young man with cognitive disabilities, requires just two simple adaptations to the keyboard. His teacher puts a green dot on the ENTER button and a red sticker on the BACK-SPACE button so that he can find them easily when signing into the computer, playing games, or completing basic exercises in his keyboarding class. Because he has low vision, his machine was also outfitted with large print keyboard stickers.

References/ Recommended Reading

Case-Smith (2005). *Occupational therapy for children* (5th ed.). St. Louis: Mosby.
Cook, A.M., & Hussey, S.M. (2002). *Assistive technologies principles and practice.* St. Louis: Mosby.
Lazzaro, J.J. (2001). *Adaptive technologies for learning & work environments* (2nd ed.). Chicago: American Library Association.
Wu, T.F., & Chen, M.C. (2006). Keyboard adaptations for children with cerebral palsy. *Lecture Notes in Computer Sciences, 4061,* 966–972.

Vendors

Enable Mart (Technology for Everyone)
http://www.enablemart.com/Catalog/Keyboards-Mice
Shop for a variety of keyboards including one-handed keyboards, large-print keyboards, and ergonomic keyboards.

Inclusive TLC, Inc.
http://www.inclusivetlc.com
Offers several different models of keyboards

Web Sites

A–T Children's Project
http://www.communityatcp.org/Page.aspx?pid=1309
A helpful table of keyboard problems and solutions for those with disabilities

Better Living Through Technology
http://www.bltt.org/index.htm
This site should be bookmarked as a "favorite" for any teacher working with students who use assistive technology or augmentative and alternative communication. Check this page—http://www.bltt.org/accessibility/keyboard.htm—in particular, for tips on adapting keyboards.

Audio Notepad   26

Materials

- Tape recorder
- Blank cassette tapes

Description

Digital recording is so quick and easy that it has become *the* method of voice recording in many schools today, but old desktop cassette recorders can still come in handy in the classroom. They are cheap and, in some schools, still plentiful.

One of the ways we like to use recorders is to create digital *audio notepads* for our students. Notepads are essentially to-do lists, reminders, or pieces of information that are recorded on cassette tapes instead of on paper. Students tend to find audio notepads easy to use, and the novelty of the exercise makes it fun and motivating as well.

Directions

We have used audio notepads in a variety of ways, including these three:

- *Don't Forget!* In this version of the audio notepad, have students "jot down" reminders to themselves on the cassette recorder at school that they can then play at home. Although we have most often used it for students who struggle with writing, it is also a fun way for any student to get organized.

- *Tell Me a Story:* For students who cannot write independently or for those who just do not write fluently enough, use audio notepad as a tool for composing stories, creating poetry, outlining essays, making lists, or even writing songs. Have learners decide on a topic or concept and then instruct them to dictate their ideas into the tape recorder. This content can then be transcribed or even summarized by a teacher.

- *Talk Show:* Students with and without disabilities often have difficulty coming up with ideas for creative writing. You can, of course, provide writing prompts, have students generate lists, or give learners pictures or photos to inspire ideas. Another technique, however, is the talk show audio notepad. Have the learner interview classmates to get ideas for future assignments. *Talk Show* also can be used for students to develop ideas that they already have. One learner simply interviews another and asks them to elaborate on their topic ideas (e.g., "Tell me more about the story," "What characters will be in your story?").

In his book, *Web Literacy for Educators* (2001), Alan November shares that cassette recorders can also help teachers bridge past and present; he suggests letting students use recorders to practice their podcasting skills!

Example

Jonah, a young man with significant learning disabilities, struggles to get started on any writing assignment. Teachers observed that he was regularly waiting 10 or 15 minutes before writing even a word. To help him with these initiation problems, Ms. Shannahan, his teacher, began using a version of the audio notepad. Ms. Shannahan began by providing Jonah with a prompt (usually a picture but sometimes an object) and then having him record any thoughts, ideas, or observations about it. After he spoke for about 2 minutes, he could invite a classmate to make comments. Then, he listened to the tape once or twice and began writing his assignment.

Keep In Mind

If you want to update this strategy and have the resources to do so, you might want to try speech recognition software as an alternative. Nuance's *Dragon NaturallySpeaking* (see Vendors list) is a good choice, but there are others on the market that also work well. *Dragon NaturallySpeaking* comes in several different versions, depending on the features needed.

References/ Recommended Reading

Cooper, P. (2007). *When stories come to school: Telling, writing, & performing stories in the early childhood classroom.* New York: Teachers & Writers Collaborative.
November, A. (2008). *Web literacy for educators.* Thousand Oaks, CA: Corwin Press.

Vendor

Nuance
http://www.nuance.com/naturallyspeaking
Home site for *Dragon NaturallySpeaking* speech recognition software

Web Sites

Scholastic (Writing Workshop)
http://teacher.scholastic.com/activities/writing/tguide/index.asp?topic=Other#description
A lesson plan on recording oral histories

School for Champions
http://www.school-for-champions.com/fiction/dictation.htm
Tips on using a tape recorder to dictate ideas and stories

STAR Tech Program
http://www.startechprogram.org/technology/midtools.html#
More ideas on using tape recorders in the classroom

27 Video Modeling

Materials

- Video camera, telephone with recording capabilities, or computer camera

Description

Video modeling is a strategy in which a video of one person engaging in a desired behavior or activity is used as a teaching aid for another person. *Video self-modeling* is a strategy used when students are videotaped, and subsequently watch their own tape as a model. Both strategies have been used to teach movements, actions, behaviors, activities, and routines to students with autism. This strategy also can be used with any learner (with and without disabilities). Video modeling can help students develop and strengthen communication skills, academic performance, and social and self-help skills.

According to a study by Corbett and Abdullah (2005), one reason why video modeling works so well for students with autism is because watching a video on screen (versus watching a role play or actual event) restricts a learner's field of focus and does not require face-to-face interaction or the ability to process visual information more readily than verbal information. In addition, it seems to make a novel activity more routine. Students may not actually have tried the activity yet, but through video modeling, they may have "experienced" it several times.

Research on children with autism has shown that video modeling can be very effective in improving the following:

- Social interaction
- Academic skills
- Communication skills
- Daily living skills
- Play skills
- Social initiations

Directions

To create your own movie, decide what routine, activity, or task you want to tape. Get your equipment ready, and wait to catch the student in a successful moment. For some behaviors, you may need to wait an hour or even a few days to get what you need. For instance, if you are hoping to take a video of a student sharing a toy, it may take some time and coaching to get a video of it actually happening.

If the behavior you are targeting seems too challenging to capture, you may need to film familiar peers instead of the learner him- or herself. If students are willing and able, you can teach them how to behave or interact and film it after letting them practice the "scene" a few times. This way, you leave less to chance and are able to get the footage you want faster. If you are unable to get what you need from either the student or from familiar peers, you may try to film either adults or unfamiliar peers. Commercial videos are also available for certain tasks, behaviors, and skills.

After you have finished filming, show the student the clip. Let him or her watch several times. Have him or her watch, in particular, right before being asked to engage in the target activity. For instance, if you are teaching a child to play catch, show him or her the video right before recess. It also can be very helpful to send the video home so parents can review the content with the student.

Example

In a high school business class, the students engaged in role play to practice skills related to job interviews. William, a young man with Asperger syndrome, was taken with the exercise and asked his father to practice the role play with him several times at home. William's father then decided to videotape the role play so that his son could watch it whenever he needed to be reminded of the language and behaviors associated with interviews. When William eventually landed a job interview (with the help of his teacher), he navigated the process with ease and was offered a position as a retail clerk at a music store. William found the role play and videotaping so helpful and was so successful with it that his family and teachers began using it across environments and contexts.

Jason, a kindergartener with a diagnosis of Pervasive Developmental Disorder, struggled to walk through the hallway with his classmates. He often ran ahead of the group or walked in a zigzag motion, moving from one side of the hall to the other. Because of these difficulties, teachers had to hold Jason's hand during daily transitions outside the classroom. To fade this adult support and create more independence for Jason, the special education teacher created a video of Jason walking a few feet on his own without adult support. She showed the short clip to Jason several times, and he then brought it home to watch on his own. After a few weeks, Jason was able to walk without holding a teacher's hand as long as he could be at the beginning of the line (his position in the video tape).

References/ Recommended Reading

Bellini, S., & Akullian, J. (2007). A meta-analysis of video modeling and video self-modeling interventions for children and adolescents with autism spectrum disorders. *Exceptional Children, 73,* 261–284.

Bellini, S., Akullian, J., & Hopf, A. (2007). Increasing social engagement in young children with autism spectrum disorders using video self-modeling. *School Psychology Review, 36,* 80–90.

Charlop-Christy, M.H., & Daneshvar, S. (2003). Using video modeling to teach perspective taking to children with autism. *Journal of Positive Behavior Interventions, 5,* 12–21.

Corbett, B.A., & Abdullah, M. (2005). Video modeling: Why does it work with autism? *The Journal of Early and Intensive Behavioral Intervention, 2*(1), 2–8.

Hine, J.F., & Wolery, M. (2006). Using point-of-view video modeling to teach play to preschoolers with autism. *Topics in Early Childhood Special Education, 26,* 83–93.

McCoy, K., & Hermansen, E. (2007). Video modeling for individuals with autism: A review of model types and effects. *Education & Treatment of Children, 30,* 183–213.

Nikopoulos, C., & Keenan, M. (2006). *Video modelling and behaviour analysis: A guide for teaching social skills to children with autism.* Philadelphia: Jessica Kingsley Publishers.

Vendor

Model Me Kids, LLC

http://www.modelmekids.com

Model Me Kids videos help students learn social skills at school, at parties, on the playground, and more. These videos were designed for children, adolescents, and teens with autism, Asperger syndrome, PDD-NOS, Nonverbal Learning Disorder (NVLD or NLD), and developmental delays.

Web Sites

TeacherTube

http://www.teachertube.com

Several free video modeling examples for students ranging in age from pre-K through high school. Consider uploading your own video modeling examples (with parent and student permission, of course) to the site to help other teachers and students and to give the student opportunities to watch the video at home, at school, or elsewhere.

YouTube.com

http://www.YouTube.com

As with TeacherTube, search YouTube using key words such as *video modeling* and *autism* and you will find a wealth of examples submitted by parents, therapists, and teachers. Find video examples of getting haircuts, hand washing, greeting people, and sharing, to name a few.

Teacher Radio

28

Materials

- Digital music player
- CDs and portable CD player or audio cassettes and audio cassette player
- Audio files
- iTunes or other digital media player application for Windows or Mac
- Windows 95/98/2000 or NT

Description

Students (especially those in middle and high school) are often seen with iPods or other digital audio players glued to their ears when they are outside the classroom. In some cases, teachers may be able to take advantage of this bond young people have with their music and devices. *Teacher radio* is essentially a "record" you make for your students. It can include music, messages from the teacher, recordings from classroom discussions, or any other material you feel is relevant or interesting. This strategy is especially helpful for learners who have difficulties with transitions or down time (e.g., riding the bus, passing in the hallway).

Directions

Begin by assembling a "playlist" for your station. In other words, decide what you want your student to hear. Music is always a good choice because many students are comforted or inspired by their favorite songs, but consider these options as well:
- Inspirational quotes or stories
- Helpful mantras or affirmations
- Social narratives (such as Carol Gray's Social Stories)
- Small snippets from class lectures or textbooks
- Jokes
- Advice from peers or parents
- Trivia questions
- Tips, information, or facts recited by a favorite person

   Then assemble the station by creating any files of your own and adding in any music or podcasts you have purchased. To create your own audiofiles using Microsoft Word, go to Start and find Sound Recorder in your programs. You will see a red circle (furthest button on the right); click on this to begin recording. You will have 60 seconds to sing a song, recite a poem, record reminders, or recite key facts. This file can be added into your "station" along with your music or other audio files.

Example

During his 45 minutes on the bus each day, Adam, a young man on the autism spectrum, listens to a few different "radio stations" created by his teacher. Each of these selections has favorite songs, calming mantras to help him get through the day, a few fun facts from the social studies curriculum, and a social narrative about riding the bus.

Keep in Mind

If digital audio players and/or related technology are not available, the same technique can be used with audiocassettes and tape recorders or by burning a playlist from iTunes or another digital media player application to a CD.

References/ Recommended Reading

Hagiwara, T., & Myles, B.S. (1999). A multimedia social story intervention: Teaching skills to children with autism. *Focus on Autism and Other Developmental Disabilities, 14*(2), 82–95.

Jensen, E. (2000). *Music with the brain in mind.* Thousand Oaks, CA: Corwin Press.

Myles, B., & Simpson, R. (1998). *Asperger syndrome: A guide for educators and parents.* Austin, TX: PRO-ED.

Vendors

iTunes
http://www.apple.com/itunes
A huge range of songs and podcasts. Many files are free to download. Check out podcasts such as Stuff You Missed in History Class (from HowStuffWorks.com); Leo Laporte (The Tech Guy), and Scientific America Podcast (from Scientific America) for your secondary education students, for example.

LearnOutLoud.com
http://www.learnoutloud.com
LearnOutLoud.com is a great resource for audio and video learning materials. Visit them to browse thousands of audio books, MP3 downloads, and podcasts.

MP3.com
http://www.mp3.com
Files to purchase but plenty of free music too.

Songs for Teaching
http://www.songsforteaching.com
Buy songs to help students learn math concepts, vocabulary, geography, new languages, and so forth.

Web Site

The Gray Center for Social Learning and Understanding
http://www.thegraycenter.org
This is the home site for Carol Gray, the creator of the Social Stories™ model. The web site features a book store, conference information, teaching tips, several examples of Social Stories, and tips on writing quality Social Stories™.

29

PowerPoint Notes

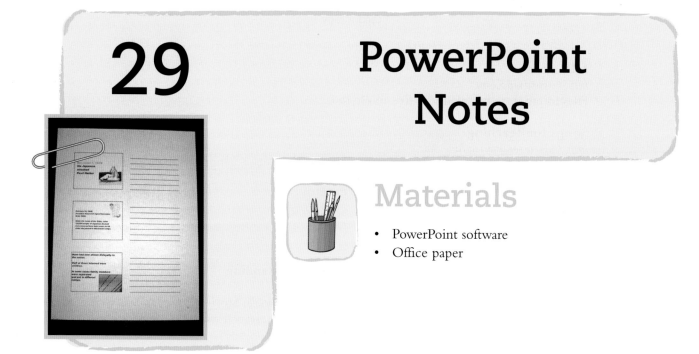

Materials

- PowerPoint software
- Office paper

Description

PowerPoint notes are printed PowerPoint presentations structured for easy note taking. These notes can be created to make following a teacher's PowerPoint lecture easier, or they can be designed for students to use even if the teacher is not using PowerPoint. In this case, a teacher may simply want students to have information and graphics to use as a guide, as information is provided in a lecture or whole-class discussion. For instance, if an art teacher was planning to hold up a series of drawings and comment on them, a student who struggles with traditional notetaking might get a copy of PowerPoint notes complete with the scanned drawings and the main ideas presented.

PowerPoint is a particularly good choice for notes pages because it is very easy to add graphics; material from the web can be imported if needed; and color, fonts, and designs can all be used to make the content memorable.

Directions

To create a PowerPoint document, open the PowerPoint program and you will see a dialog box. In this box, click on **BLANK PRESENTATION**. The New Slide dialogue box will then appear. It will prompt you to choose a format for your slide. You can start with a title slide or with any format you think is appropriate for displaying your content.

Once you are "on" a slide, add text by typing into one of the text boxes on the slide. You can also add graphics to the slide. Simply move your cursor to where you want the picture to be pasted. Then, go to your toolbar and click **INSERT > PICTURE**. You will then have several choices. You can retrieve Clip Art or pictures from a file on your computer or from a camera to name a few. Search for your picture in the location of your choice. When you find the one you want, click on it and it will be inserted into your presentation.

To add a new slide to the talk you can go your toolbar and click **INSERT > NEW SLIDE**.

When you are finished creating your presentation and ready to make a set of notes, go to the toolbar and click on **FILE > PRINT**. A dialog box will pop up. In the bottom left corner of the box, you will see a narrow window titled, **PRINT WHAT**. To change the default setting, open the drop-down menu and you will see a few options. Choose **HANDOUTS**. Then look at the box titled **HANDOUTS** to the right of the **PRINT WHAT** window and click on that drop-down menu. You will have several options again. To create a set of notes with three slides on the left and spaces for writing on the right (see picture), you will choose "3." If you want students to have the material but need the slides to be larger, you can select "2"; this will give you one slide on the top of your page and one on the bottom.

Examples

In a 10th grade American History class, Scott, a student with cognitive disabilities, needs extra help with notetaking. His special education teacher creates PowerPoint note sets for each lecture so that Scott can see the three to five main ideas of the day. Scott then is responsible for adding comments to the right side of the page to personalize the notes. The notes also serve as study guides for Scott because he is responsible for learning each point from his notes set. Whereas other students may be responsible for remembering many pieces of the lectures, Scott must study and recall just those included in his notes. Another way Scott's teachers use these notes to support his learning is to e-mail him each PowerPoint presentation they create. This way, he can review the presentations again and he can search for any web links his teacher may have added such as related music, video clips, or pictures.

A family and consumer education teacher gives six big lectures per semester. Each lecture is supported by a PowerPoint presentation. Every student in the classroom gets a set of PowerPoint notes for these lectures. They take notes on the lecture during the class and then use the pages to study for the tests that follow the lectures.

When students are sick or need extra assistance, the teacher provides an enhanced set of notes; this consists of the same slides others get, but teacher lecture comments are added to each slide. (To create such a set of notes, type your lecture notes on the white strip underneath each PowerPoint slide in VIEW > NORMAL and print *Notes* instead of *Handouts*.)

Keep in Mind

Students can also be asked to take notes using PowerPoint. Pitler, Hubbell, and Kuhn, for instance, suggest a novel approach they call "combination notes." The two-column format they discuss in their book links "essential concepts on the left with multi-media enhancements on the right" (2007, p. 131). This method is not only different enough to pique the interest of many students but allows them to learn in the ways that suit them best (e.g., auditorially, visually). (See photo on page 78.)

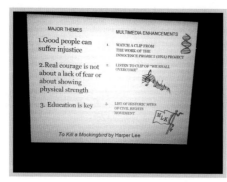

References/ Recommended Reading

Finlekstein, E., & Samsonov, P. (2008). *PowerPoint for teachers: Dynamic presentations and interactive classroom projects.* Jossey-Bass: San Francisco.

Pitler, H., Hubbell, E.R., Kuhn, M., & Malenoski, K. (2007). *Using technology with classroom instruction that works.* Alexandria, VA: Association for Supervision and Curriculum Development.

Vendor

Microsoft
http://office.microsoft.com/en-us/powerpoint/default.aspx
You can buy PowerPoint on the web site or just get a free 60-day trial.

Web Sites

Internet 4 Classrooms
http://www.internet4classrooms.com/msppt_toolbar.htm
Two educators, Susan Brooks and Bill Byles, are behind this great site. Internet 4 Classrooms is a free web portal designed to assist teachers who want to find high-quality, free Internet resources to use in classroom instruction. The link included here takes you right to information on PowerPoint.

PowerPoint in the Classroom
http://www.actden.com/pp
Great tutorials for students and for teachers

The PowerPoint® Blog
http://pptblog.tlccreative.com
This illustrated blog focuses on PowerPoint and multimedia development and would be helpful for novice and experienced users of the software.

Audio Books

30

Materials

- Cassette tapes or CDs
- Internal or external microphone
- Tape recorder or digital recorder

Description

Audio books are recorded books that students can use as a supplement to reading (following along with the audio with the book in front of them) or instead of reading (especially helpful and appropriate for students who are blind or with low vision and for those who are interested in reading materials they themselves could not access on their own). Audio books are used in the classroom for several reasons. They can strengthen a student's fluency (i.e., student's ability to follow print). They can also help learners with comprehension or the ability to understand the meaning of what they are reading because instead of focusing on decoding and the "work" of reading, learners can just listen to and focus on the story or content.

Audio books are especially helpful tools for struggling readers but they can also be used as a novel supplement to whole-group instruction. For instance, a teacher can introduce a novel by playing the beginning chapter as students walk into the classroom or play certain passages to the whole group as a way to generate discussion points.

Finally, audio books can be used for individual instruction. Students can listen to them during silent reading lessons or listening centers can be set up for any student to access. The goal of a listening center typically is to provide students with auditory support during independent reading, so all centers should, of course, have books available so learners can both look and listen.

Directions

Using a tape recorder and an external or internal microphone, read the story with appropriate volume and expression. Cue the listener when it is time to turn the page (either with words or by using an auditory cue of some kind) if the recordings are designed for students to follow along in a book.

Examples

To coax Bryan, a young man with autism, to listen to books on tape, his teacher asked the child's father to make several audio books that Brian could use during the school day. Although Bryan would not listen to audio books recorded by the teacher, he grinned broadly when he heard his father's voice and would listen not just once but several times to the selections his dad had created for him.

Aria, a student with learning disabilities, prepares for her biology classes by listening to her textbook on CDs. Each quarter, her teacher lets her know which tracks will be the most important. She listens to these—sometimes more than once—on the school bus. Her teacher also gives her extra credit for listening to (and talking to her teacher about) one science-related book per quarter (e.g., *A Short History of Nearly Everything,* by Bill Bryson, 2003).

Musslewhite and King-DeBaun (1997), share a story about a young man who "reads" not only with audio but also by using visual supports:

> A macro on Danny's [augmentative communication device] is used to permit Danny to listen to stories that are somewhat above his independent reading level. His speech-language pathologist or parent enters each story into a notebook file, line by line. Danny then presses a message cell where the macro is stored to read each line. The text is available on the [device] display and each line is spoken through the high-quality synthetic speech. This combination of text and speech output supports Danny's learning far better than simply listening to the story read by an adult or on an audiotape (1997, p. 298).

Keep in Mind

Audio books should be used to provide students with more complex or age–appropriate literature or content. It should be a supplement to literacy instruction but should not replace literacy instruction. In other words, it is still important to teach all learners to read! As in the third example (above), the audio also can be supplemented with visuals via computer programs and AAC (augmentative and alternative communication) devices.

References/ Recommended Reading

Boyle, E.A., Rosenberg, M.S., Connelly, V.J., Gallin-Wahburn, S.G., Brinckerhoff, L.C., & Banerjee, M. (2003). Effects of audio-texts on the acquisition of secondary-level content by students with mild disabilities. *Learning Disability Quarterly, 26*(3), 203–214.

Bryson, B. (2003). *A short history of nearly everything.* New York: Broadway.

Lipscomb, G.B., Guenther, L.M., & Mcleod, P. (2007). Sounds good to me: Using digital audio in the social studies classroom. *Social Education, 71*(3), 120–124.

Musselwhite, C., & King-DeBaun, P. (1997). *Emergent literacy success: Merging technology and whole language.* Park City, UT: Creative Communicating.

Van Horn, R. (2007). Online books and audio books. Phi Delta Kappan, 89, 154–155.

Vendors

Amazon.com
http://www.amazon.com
Thousands of books on CD; used and new copies available for most selections

Mighty Book
http://www.mightybook.com
More than 100 animated talking and singing books

Web Sites

Assistive Media
http://www.assistivemedia.org
Assistive Media has hundreds of copyright-cleared magazine articles and books on a wide range of topics.

Audiobooks.org
http://www.audiobooks.org
Free audio books and links to many books for purchase

AudioBooksForFree.com
http://www.audiobooksforfree.com/home
Public domain books and stories in MP3 format; preburned CDs are also available for a charge

LibriVox
http://librivox.org
The goal of LibriVox is to convert every book in the public domain to digital audio. The books are read by volunteers and saved as MP3 files for download.

Project Gutenberg
http://www.gutenberg.org
Project Gutenberg is one of the most comprehensive collections of free audio books on-line. Some are read by volunteers and others are computer-generated.

Communication
&
Participation

Contents

31 Personal Portfolio

Materials

- Photographs
- Artifacts central to the individual's life (e.g., ticket stub, pamphlet from favorite amusement park)
- Work samples
- Notes from family and friends

Description

Students who have unique needs and abilities may want to introduce themselves to a teacher through the use of a portfolio. Portfolios may include photographs, artwork, writing or school-work samples, lists of favorite things, or even video- or audiotapes. Although using a portfolio is a good idea for students with disabilities, it also can be a useful activity for the entire class. At the beginning of the school year, all students can work to create a portfolio to share with classmates and school personnel as a strategy to get to know each other better.

Portfolios can be in paper, audio, or video form; formal or informal; a few pages or dozens of pages; and include only current information and artifacts or serve as a cumulative record of the student's life. One student we know keeps his formal portfolio at home and carries a four-page paper condensed copy with him at all times. Another student, a young woman with Asperger syndrome, developed a creative videotape portfolio complete with clips of her sisters reading poetry that she had written.

Directions

Ask the student (or his or her family) to bring in a range of materials that can be used to complete a personal portfolio. Photographs (e.g., of family members, of the person engaged in their favorite activity); work samples; artifacts that represent favorite places, events, products, and trips; and even messages or notes from friends and family can be used in a personal portfolio. A "typical day" or "typical week" statement also can be very telling and can prompt conversation, connections, and even understanding. Arrange the materials by category (e.g., family, favorite movies, trips I have taken) or chronologically (as a life story) so that anyone viewing it can quickly learn about the person.

Depending on the person's age and how he or she wants to use the portfolio, you also can add a pouch where students can keep business cards (phone numbers, e-mail addresses), class pictures, or any other token to share with peers.

Example

J.D., a young man with autism, assembled a portfolio he would use as he transitioned from high school to the work place. He did not speak, and those who met him for the first time often struggled to connect with him. When his teachers first accompanied him to his new school, J.D.'s peers began asking them questions about him: Did he understand them? Did he have any interests? Why did he flap his arms like that? The teachers decided that J.D. needed a way to represent himself so that they did not need to serve as his voice and liaison. In order to facilitate this process, the teachers worked with J.D. to create a portfolio that he could use to introduce himself to new people and to interact with those he already knew. J.D.'s portfolio included the following items:

- Four pages of photographs (J.D. with family and friends, snapshots of him playing soccer at a community park, J.D. working with peers on a biology experiment, vacation photos from the Rock and Roll Museum in Ohio)
- A short "résumé" outlining some of the classes he took in middle school
- A list of his favorite movies and CDs
- A "Learning About Autism" pamphlet that J.D. got at a conference
- A glossy picture of the Green Bay Packers, J.D.'s favorite football team

Although it took a few weeks, J.D. soon became comfortable initiating "conversations" with his classmates using his portfolio. Individuals who saw J.D.'s portfolio now had a way to interact with him and learn more about his life. Two of J.D.'s classmates even developed their own portfolios to share with him.

In addition, all of J.D.'s new teachers had opportunities to review his book before he started their classes; this helped them become acquainted with J.D. as an individual and begin to understand his needs and strengths. One of J.D.'s teachers even used one of J.D.'s favorite movies in her English class as a result of reviewing his portfolio; another teacher helped him to create some watercolor landscape paintings to include in his growing album.

Keep in Mind

A portfolio can be an especially helpful tool for students who do not speak or use a reliable communication system.

References/ Recommended Reading

Campbell, P.H., Milbourne, S.A., & Silverman, C. (2001). Strengths-based child portfolios: A professional development activity to alter perspectives of children with special needs. *Topics in Early Childhood Special Education, 21*(3), 152–161.

Keel, P. (1998). *All about me.* New York: Random House.

Krebs, C.S. (2002). Self-advocacy skills: A portfolio approach. *Re:View, 33*(4), 160–163.

Vendors

Random House

http://www.randomhouse.com/catalog/display.pperl?isbn=9780767902052

Random House is the publisher of a 1998 book called *All About Me,* by Philipp Keel. This is a very unique resource for older learners who are looking for ideas for telling their story to others (a special teen edition is also available). You can purchase this book on the Random House web site by following the above link or from most major booksellers.

Take a Look at Me Portfolio

http://www.strengthsbased.com

The *Take a Look at Me Portfolio* is a book designed to engage individuals and their family members as they identify student strengths, interests, and preferences. It is available in English, French, Spanish, Vietnamese, and Korean.

Portfolios-and-Art-Cases.com

http://www.portfolios-and-art-cases.com

An online shop for art portfolios and portfolio cases

Web Sites

FolioLive

http://www.foliolive.com

An electronic portfolio tool that aids in the creation of fully customized electronic portfolios

KidPrintables.com

http://www.kidprintables.com/allaboutme

A great place to visit to generate ideas for portfolios for young children. Kids can color in a variety of worksheets and fill in information about themselves and their lives. These sheets can be used as the portfolio itself or can be used as part of a larger product.

Starfall.com

http://www.starfall.com/n/level-b/me/play.htm?f

This site allows small children to enjoy a virtual game of "All About Me." Students will enjoy sharing information about themselves and their favorite things. This may be a good introduction to creating a portfolio.

Question Jar

32

Materials

- A container (e.g., cookie jar, coffee can)
- Small slips of paper or index cards

Description

The *question jar* is simply a container of some sort (a cookie jar or coffee can works well) that holds a variety of general questions or prompts for the teacher. The question jar can be used in any classroom for any number of purposes, including the following:

- To "shake up" a long or potentially dry lecture
- To get shy or reluctant learners to participate
- To give students unique opportunities to contribute to teacher-led lessons

The question jar is also great to use as a support for students with moderate and significant disabilities. Often, these learners struggle to participate in whole-class instruction and remain passive during discussions and lectures. Giving them one or two opportunities to draw from the question jar inspires their participation and gives them a simple way to communicate with the teacher.

Directions

The questions are folded up, so they cannot be read by simply gazing into the jar. At different points in a lecture or whole-class discussion, ask one or any number of students to reach into the jar, grab a question, and interject it into the discussion or lecture. You can choose to answer the question when it is asked or at any point during the lecture or discussion.

Create a variety of questions for a certain activity or class period. Some examples of questions include the following:

- "Tell us a joke related to this topic."
- "Act out one piece of the lecture today."
- "What do you think is the most interesting part of today's lecture?"
- "Call on one of us to teach for 3 minutes."

Example

Ava, a student with cognitive and physical disabilities, was included in a ninth-grade biology class. Although her teachers were able to find many ways to include her in the more active parts of the lesson (e.g., using adapted equipment in the lab), they struggled to generate ideas for boosting her participation in class discussions and demonstrations. The question jar served as a solution to this problem. Ava's teachers created two jars. One jar contained the names of all of the other students in the classroom. Ava used this jar to choose classmates to answer teacher questions that were posed during discussions. The other jar was filled with questions. At the end of the teacher's explanation of an upcoming lab, Ava would select a question and the teacher would answer it. Questions in the jar ranged from "Do you have any other tips for us before we begin?" to "What is one piece of information we should all take away from this lab?"

Keep in Mind

You may need to use the question jar during a specific time each day. This will make the questions easier to write. For instance, you could make a jar for discussing a piece of literature (e.g., "Which character is the most interesting to you and why?") or to use after a new math concept has been introduced (e.g., "Can you share a real-world application?")

References/ Recommended Reading

Kliewer, C., & Biklen, D. (2001). School's not really a place for reading: A research synthesis of the literate lives of children with severe disabilities. *The Journal of the Association for Persons with Severe Handicaps, 26,* 1–12.

Udvari-Solner, A., & Kluth, P. (2008). *Joyful learning: Active and collaborative learning in the inclusive classroom.* Thousand Oaks, CA: Corwin Press.

Vendor

The Container Store
http://www.containerstore.com
A variety of canisters, jars, and bins that can be used to make your own question jar

Web Site

Low Tech Methods of Augmentative Communication by **Janet Scott**
http://www.acipscotland.org.uk/Scott.pdf
A nice, short review of low-tech augmentative and alternative communication (AAC)

33

Talking Spinner

Materials

- Spinner from an old board game, blank spinner, or spinner template
- Cardstock
- Laminate
- Sticker paper
- Word/phrase/picture or number stickers or a magic marker

Description

Teachers of students with moderate and significant disabilities are constantly seeking new ways to encourage students to communicate and to help them participate more fully in activities and lessons. Spinners with phrases, words, or even sentences on them are one novel way to motivate learners while providing another way to augment their communication. By using a *Talking Spinner,* you can have students play adapted games, participate in whole-class discussions or small-group activities, ask and answer questions, learn new vocabulary words, or simply encourage conversation and socialization.

Directions

The easiest way to construct a spinner is to adapt an existing one. By either purchasing a blank spinner and writing selections on the individual spaces or by covering the spaces of a board game spinner with sticker paper or construction paper, you can create a fully functioning Talking Spinner in minutes. You can also download templates off of the web and make your own spinners. To create a sturdy spinner of your own, you can either print on cardstock and laminate the spinner or print your spinner on sticker paper and apply it to a thin piece of cardboard.

Examples

In a high school drama class, students were working on an improvisation game called Time Machine in which players act out the same scene over and over again from different eras and settings. Patrick, a young man with multiple disabilities, was the emcee for the activity and was, therefore, responsible for dictating the era for each pair or trio. As groups of students got on stage to act out a scene, Patrick would flick the talking spinner and students would act out the scene from the era printed on the spinner (e.g., 1950s American living room, yesterday in math class, on the trail with Lewis and Clark in 1806).

In a tenth-grade biology class, students learned a new "power word" each week. The teacher introduced the word and then Nate, a young man with cognitive disabilities, would use a talking spinner to determine how the class would learn about the new concept or process. Depending on Nate's spin, the teacher would have to either draw a picture of the concept or process, act it out, sing about it, tell a story about it, or ask a student to read about it from the textbook.

References/ Recommended Reading

Aronson, J. (1999). *25 super-fun math spinner games.* New York: Scholastic.

Musslewhite, C., & King-DeBaun, P. (1997). *Emergent literacy success: Merging technology and whole language for students with disabilities.* Park City, UT: Creative Communicating & Southeast Augmentative Communication Conference.

Vendors

Ablenet
http://www.ablenetinc.com/Store/tabid/205/Default.aspx?CategoryCode=90
Students with severe disabilities can be active participants in many commercially available games using this switch-activated device, the All-Turn-It Spinner. Accessory packages are available for golf, bowling, and bingo and for creating your own spinner games.

EAI Education
http://www.eaieducation.com/531806.html
Blank spinners, spinners with color blocks, and more

Web Site

The Home School Hutt
http://www.webeans.net/hutt/gamespinners.htm
Free spinners that can be printed on card stock

34

Remnant Books

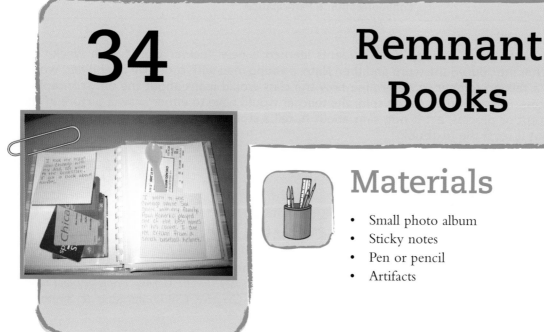

Materials

- Small photo album
- Sticky notes
- Pen or pencil
- Artifacts

Description

Remnant books are a visual/tactual way of helping students record events in their lives and communicate with others about these events. These books can then be used as tools for choosing topics for face-to-face communication (Beukelman & Mirenda, 2005), selecting writing topics (Musselwhite & Hanser, 2003), or even embellishing stories and conversations.

To create such a book, remnants or artifacts from activities are saved and inserted into a small photo album. The remnants should be things that are, in some way, meaningful to the student such as an ad from the newspaper, a paper coaster from a favorite restaurant, a token from a carnival, a plastic admission bracelet from the local water park, a coupon for a favorite food, a photograph of Grandma's farm, a "Good job" sticker from a dentist visit, a business card from the new occupational therapist, or a Lego piece from a new set.

Directions

Whenever possible and appropriate, take objects, pictures, or other artifacts from the different events the student attends and appointments or experiences in which he or she engages. Place these remnants in the photo album.

Then, with a sticky note, write the date and details of the event in first person (e.g., "I went to the football game. We had a great time. Our team [Spartans] scored one touchdown. Ella spilled hot chocolate on me"). If possible, include several details because this will help any partner talk about the remnant and the event with the student, ask better questions, and even inspire new ideas for using the book.

To use the book with a student, simply let the student choose a remnant. Then, have a conversation about the place, event, or activity that the remnant represents. Or, get the book and look through it with the student (as you would a photo album) for the purpose of getting "caught up" with the person and finding out about his or her recent experiences. The book can also be used in an academic context; students can choose remnants to write about in a story or journal. Finally, remnant books can be used during social time when students chat about the past weekend or experiences over the summer. The student with disabilities can pass his or her book around or point in response to questions from peers.

Following are some helpful tips for working with remnant books:

- Make the interactions fun and informal (more like a conversation than a lesson).

- Encourage the student to vocalize or use AAC (e.g., sign language, device) as he or she looks at the book with teachers or peers.

- Make the book available so that the student can initiate interactions by adding remnants or pointing to existing ones.

To make constructing the book easier, keep a pack of sticky notes in the book. Blank labels or strips of double-sided tape can also be stored inside the last page of the album and used as an on-the-spot adhesive when needed.

Example

Ricardo, a young man with multiple disabilities, used his remnant book to choose writing topics in his daily journal. During journal time, Ricardo would point to a remnant and his teacher or a peer would then paste it on to his journal paper. A peer would then help Ricardo write a sentence about the remnant (using the sticky note to get more information). Ricardo would then choose stickers and stamps related to his artifact to complete his journal entry. For example, when Ricardo brought a brochure from the Sears Tower, his entry read, "I went to the Sears Tower and rode an elevator." He then used a skyscraper stamp to complete the journal entry.

Keep in Mind

The artifacts do not have to be things the student necessarily likes or has good feelings about. As long as the items are meaningful in some way, the artifacts can also be things the student connects with an unpleasant experience. For instance, a student included a photo of the Golden Gate Bridge in his remnant book even though riding over it with his family was frightening for him. He was eager to share the experience even through it had been a difficult one.

References/ Recommended Reading

Beukelman, D.R., & Mirenda, P. (2005). *Augmentative & alternative communication: Supporting children and adults with complex communication needs* (3rd ed.). Baltimore: Paul H. Brookes Publishing Co.

Ho, K.M., Weiss, S.J., Garrett, K.L., & Lloyd, L.L. (2005). The effect of remnant and pictographic books on the communicative interaction of individuals with global aphasia. *Augmentative and Alternative Communication, 21*(3), 218–232.

Musselwhite, C., & Hanser, G. (2003). *Write to talk—talk to write! Supporting language and literacy for AAC users* (2nd ed.). Phoenix, AZ: Special Communications.

Vendor

The Photo Album Shop

http://www.photoalbumshop.com

Retailers of photo albums, from custom-made, matted-page albums to general purpose, dry-mount, slip-in, and self-adhesive photo albums and accessories

Web Sites

Closing the Gap, Inc.

http://www.closingthegap.com

Closing the Gap, Inc., is an organization that focuses on assistive technology for people with special needs through its bimonthly magazine, annual international conference, and extensive web site.

International Society for Augmentative & Alternative Communication

http://www.isaac-online.org

The International Society for Augmentative & Alternative Communication is an alliance to create opportunities for individuals who communicate with little or no speech. Visit their site for information on AAC as well as up-to-date research on supporting students with communication needs.

Art Options Box **35**

Materials

- Box
- A variety of art supplies including, but not limited to, stamps, stickers, stencils, markers, crayons, pencils, charcoal, chalk, clay, pencil grips, paint, paper punches, adapted scissors, sticky notes, glue sticks, paper scraps, photos, and magazine pictures

Description

So many students cannot easily cut, draw, paste, or color. For these learners, it is important to provide a collection of materials and adapted materials that they can access not only during art projects but also when completing worksheets, writing stories, and engaging in projects. One way to do this is to create an *art options box*.

Directions

Stock your box with anything you think will help your student write, draw, paint, or complete work. It can be helpful to assemble your art box with your occupational therapist, because he or she will be able to make recommendations on the types of materials that should be included for individual students.

Example

Chase, a second-grade student with cerebral palsy, used his adapted art box daily to participate not only in his art class and in art activities but also in academic activities, such as filling in workbook pages, creating class projects, making charts and graphs in math class, and writing in his journal. Some of the items he used most commonly were bingo markers for coloring pictures and creating graphs in math and stickers for decorating his drawings and paintings.

References/ Recommended Reading

Davalos, S. (1999). *Making sense of art: Sensory-based art activities for children with autism, Asperger syndrome, and pervasive developmental disorders.* Shawnee Mission, KS: Autism Asperger Publishing Company.

Flowers, T. (1996). *Reaching the child with autism through art: Practical, "fun" activities to enhance motor skills and improve tactile and concept awareness.* Arlington, TX: Future Horizons.

Vendor

Dick Blick (special needs section of their site)
http://www.dickblick.com/categories/specialneeds
Dick Blick sells adapted drawing and painting materials and furniture that can be used in the art room.

Web Sites

Art Education and Disability Resources on the Web
http://people.unt.edu/~say0005
Created by a doctoral candidate in art education, this site contains links to vendors, ideas for finding and using adaptive equipment, and information on how and why to adapt art activities for students with disabilities.

Art Therapy & Autism
http://www.art-therapy.us/autism.htm
Information about art therapy, links, and materials for further study

Rubber Stamps

36

Materials

- Pen or pencil
- Rubber bands
- Scissors
- Plastic bottle caps or corks
- Cardboard
- Strong glue
- Ink

Description

Rubber stamps can be an effective support for learners with fine motor problems, poor writing skills, or even low motivation. Stamps can be made available to a student to help him or her fill in worksheets or tests. The stamps also are a fun center activity for kinesthetic learners to practice sentence building, counting skills, or their spelling words for the week. Examples of rubber stamps that may be useful in the classroom include the following:

- Name
- Date
- Numbers
- Math symbols (e.g., +, −)
- Letters
- Words
- Pictures

Many different stamps are available commercially and will meet most of the needs that teachers have within and across curricula, but being able to make your own stamps will ensure that you always have the right stamp for a given situation.

Directions

To make your own stamp, follow these instructions:
- Decide on a design, and draw it on a piece of cardboard.
- Using a range of rubber bands, cut out all of the shapes that you need for your design (large bands, such as those you get on the stems of broccoli, work very well).
- Glue all of the pieces onto the cardboard.
- Press down firmly to ensure that all of the rubber pieces are all the same height/level on the board.

- Allow the glue to dry.
- Add a grip. (A plastic bottle cap or piece of a wine cork will work.)
- Ink and test out the stamp.
- Correct any flaws in your design (e.g., loose pieces of rubber).
- Begin using your stamp in the classroom.

Examples

During a writing center in a first-grade classroom, picture, word, and letter stamps were scattered around the table. Children worked with a partner to create books about Martin Luther King. All of the students were invited to use the stamps as a supplement to their written sentences. For Charles, a student with a cognitive disability, the stamps (including a commercial stamp of King and teacher-created word stamps) were used to write his actual sentences. Charles also used a stamp to put his name on his papers and to record the date.

A student with Down syndrome used a rubber stamp to complete a math worksheet. Students had to determine if 25 angles were obtuse, acute, or right. Using three different letter stamps, the student stamped a label for each angle on the sheet indicating if each was obtuse (O), acute (A), or right (R).

Keep in Mind

If you include text in your design, do not forget to use the mirror image of the text (otherwise, the image will come out backwards).

References/ Recommended Reading

Diller, D. (2003). *Literacy work stations: Making centers work.* Portland, ME: Stenhouse Publishers.

Downing, J. (2008). *Including students with severe and multiple disabilities in typical classrooms. Practical strategies for teachers* (3rd ed.). Baltimore: Paul H. Brookes Publishing Co.

Udvari-Solner, A. (1996). Examining teacher thinking: Constructing a process to design curricular adaptations. *Remedial and Special Education, 17,* 245–254.

Vendors

Addicted to Rubber Stamps
http://www.addictedtorubberstamps.com
Many great deals on this site on items ranging from rolling and pre-inked stamps to letter stickers and craft kits

Alison's Montessori
http://www.alisonsmontessori.com/Educational_Rubber_Stamps_s/29.htm
No matter what age or grade level you teach, this site has stamps appropriate for your classroom, including sets appropriate for teaching geometric shapes, weather (e.g., partly cloudy, precipitation), the world map, and anatomy.

theStampMaker.com
http://www.thestampmaker.com
Design a rubber stamp and have it shipped in just one business day.

Web Sites

Learn 2 Stamp
http://learn2stamp.com/home.shtml
A large collection of tutorials, techniques, projects, and information on all facets of rubber stamping

Teacher Stamping
http://www.kinderpond.com/rubber.stamps.html
A teacher-created web site with dozens of ideas for using rubber stamps in lessons

37 Sticky Words and Phrases

Materials

- Blank labels
- Sight words, vocabulary words, and content-related phrases

Description

For many learners, participation in classroom activities is challenging or impossible because of difficulties with communication or writing. Most of these students will need augmentative and alternative communication (AAC) as well as curricular adaptations to be successful. Using *sticky words and phrases* is one such adaptation. Using simple mailing labels as a communication and curriculum support, teachers can print out sight words, vocabulary words, common classroom phrases, lines from textbooks, quotes from literature, and even math phrases and problems for students to use during daily exercises, group activities, and assessments.

Directions

After you have decided on the words students need to study or on the phrases that will be used during a given unit or assignment, print them out on a set of either address labels or return address labels. The smaller labels will work best for single words, and address labels are probably more appropriate for phrases and sentences.

Examples

Kaitlynn, a sixth-grade student, has difficulty with spelling tests both because writing itself is challenging and because she reads and spells at a significantly lower level than her same-age classmates. Her spelling test, therefore, has the same number of words as her peers (10), but instead of spelling from memory, Kaitlynn has to look at all 10 words and place the correct sticker in the corresponding spot on her sheet. Her test, then, becomes a reading task instead of a spelling task, and she is able to participate independently using the stickers as her only adaptation.

Students in a ninth-grade English class were playing a game of Mad Libs in small groups. Students were encouraged to use as many different words as they could generate and to stay away from common words such as *very* or *big*. Luz, a young woman with cerebral palsy, generated her ideas in advance and had them printed on labels. When it was Luz's turn to share, peers peeled her stickers off the sheet and stuck them on the game sheet.

Reference/ Recommended Reading

Kapell, D., & Steenland, S. (1997). *The magnetic poetry book of poetry*. New York: Workman Publishing Company.

Vendors

Oriental Trading
http://www.orientaltrading.com/ui/browse/processRequest.do?sku=65/70197&requestURI= processProductsCatalog
Several sets of common everyday phrase stickers

Sam Flax
http://www.samflaxny.com/browse.cfm/4,3842.html
Assorted word stickers; sets include words such as *cousin, forever, great, let,* and *truth*

Web Site

Magnetic Poetry
http://www.magneticpoetry.com/kidspoetry
A great web site for kids with and without disabilities. This vendor of magnetic poetry sets (and other related materials) offers a handful of games for kids, including a poem builder that lets you drag and drop words and phrases on a virtual refrigerator to create your own literary masterpiece.

38 Writing without a Pencil

Materials

- T-shirts, caps, or signs, each with one letter on them
- Letter and word cards
- Pocket charts
- Pictures and/or images from magazines
- Camera
- Sticky notes

Description

Writing without a pencil involves giving students opportunities to create words and put sentences together without actually putting writing utensil to paper! This strategy works well for students with physical disabilities and those with motor planning problems but, due to its novel and more interactive nature, it is also a good departure from paperwork for all students (especially those in the early primary grades) (Berkey, 2009). Some of the techniques that may be used include Human Scrabble, sticky note letter scramble, letter locomotion, pocket chart compositions, word and story dictation, story graffiti, and photo essay.

Directions

For any of the activities described, start with familiar letters (e.g., the letters of the student's name), words (e.g., those related to the classroom or to a favorite hobby), and pictures (e.g., family photographs, images of sports heroes). Work with your building's reading specialist to make the experiences as appropriate and yet as challenging as possible.

- *Human Scrabble:* Let every student wear a T-shirt or baseball cap, or a sign with a letter on it, and provide opportunities for them to get into different formations and spell various words. This same game can also be played in different ways. Instead of making words using single letters, students can make sentences, poems, and even tongue twisters using word hats, shirts, or signs.

- *Sticky note letter scramble:* Write individual letters of the alphabet on sticky notes and let the student assemble the notes to create words. The same activity can be done with alphabet blocks.

- *Letter locomotion:* Have students hang on to each other and travel as a train as they either "write" a letter from memory or follow lines of tape the teacher has placed on the floor (Berkey, 2009).

- *Pocket chart compositions:* Give students pictures and letter or word cards and let them compose new sentences by switching the order of the cards in the pocket chart.
- *Dictating words and stories:* Ask another student to act as the learner's scribe and write letters, words, and sentences for the learner.
- *Story graffiti:* Give the students pictures, words, and phrases ripped out of different types of magazines and ask the student to assemble them into a story. Then, working with a teacher or peer, have the individual tell the corresponding story or have him pick a peer to do so.
- *Photo essay:* Have the student take a series of pictures, thus writing a "story" with the camera; then, as a class, create captions for each picture.

Examples

Tiani, a third-grade student with autism, has a hard time using a pencil or even typing on a computer. Her teacher, therefore, has her "write" using pocket chart words and phrases. To make the activity compelling for other students in the classroom, the teacher includes interesting words and phrases from new literature selections and social studies and science lessons. Tiani uses the chart during guided reading, independent practice time, and, occasionally, during writer's workshop.

Students in a high school Spanish class use Human Scrabble several times a month to learn and practice spelling new words. Students wear signs around their necks (each with a different letter) and, working in small groups, generate as many Spanish words as they can, using their collection of letters.

Students in a second-grade classroom wrote stories in their journals several times each week. Chris, a student with Down syndrome, brought one or two photo essays to school each week and used these as his journal stories. He worked with his speech-language pathologist to create captions for his pictures to embellish the story.

References/
Recommended Reading

Berkey, S.M. (2009). *Teaching the moving child: OT insights that will transform your K–3 classroom.* Baltimore: Paul H. Brookes Publishing Co.

Rooyackers, P. (2002). *101 language games for children: Fun and learning with words, stories, and poems.* Alameda, CA: Hunter House.

Vendors

Biome 5
http://www.biome5.com
The bioME 5 Animal Alphabet Project was created by two architectural designers. They make a T-shirt for every letter of the alphabet.

Learning Resources
http://www.learningresources.com/category/id/100614.do
A variety of pocket charts and card sets

Web Sites

KinderKorner
http://www.kinderkorner.com/pocketcharts.html
This web site, created by a teacher named Victoria Smith, contains hundreds of teaching tips and resources related to pocket charts.

School Scrabble
http://school.scrabble-assoc.com/main_sublinks.asp?id=65&sid=201
A web site run by Hasbro, the creator of Scrabble; contains a word of the day feature, printable resources, and ideas for using Scrabble in the classroom

More Ideas

Content-Specific Communication Board

39

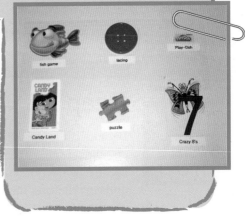

Materials

- Communication symbols
- Tape or adhesive
- Tag board or paper

Description

Content-specific communication boards are graphic representations of language. They serve as an alternative to spoken language, allowing even very young children who do not speak or who have limited speech a method of communicating. Boards are composed of cells that vary in number, shape, color, size, and content; they can be teacher-created or a software program can be used to construct each cell. Content-specific communication boards can be personalized for each student who requires one; one individual's board may consist of an $8\frac{1}{2}$ x 11-inch piece of paper with only one cell on it, whereas another child's board may have 100 cells containing pictures and text.

Directions

Working with a speech therapist, if possible, decide which messages are appropriate and necessary for the student, keeping in mind that different boards may be needed for different topics, subjects, and lessons. Teachers may make general boards that contain messages for communicating across lessons in a content area (e.g., ADD IT, SUBTRACT IT, LET'S CHECK OUR WORK, GET THE CALCULATOR, GOOD JOB) and boards for specific units or lessons (e.g., FLIP THE COIN, MY TURN, WHAT WAS THE OUTCOME? HEADS, TAILS).

Examples

Patrick, a third-grade student with cerebral palsy, uses a communication board for crafts, art class, and group and personal projects. He uses a head pointer to point to one of nine messages, including COLOR IT BLUE, COLOR IT RED, COLOR IT YELLOW, COLOR IT GREEN, COLOR IT ORANGE, CUT IT, MY TURN, PASTE IT, and LET'S ADD STICKERS.

Theresa, a middle school student on the autism spectrum, switches between using an AAC device, sign language, and various content-specific communication boards. She often uses a paper board with six choices during her guided reading group because it serves as a short-cut for communication. Symbols on the board include READ THAT PAGE AGAIN, TURN THE PAGE, I HAVE A QUESTION, I LOVE THIS STORY, I DON'T LIKE THIS STORY, and THAT PART IS FUNNY.

Keep in Mind

Because communication boards typically are very easy and inexpensive to make, teachers should give them to all students in the inclusive classroom (Sonnenmeier, McSheehan, & Jorgensen, 2005). This way, students can have fun communicating in a different way, and the learner with disabilities gets several opportunities to see how to use the augmentative communication tool. In addition, having all students use a board can help all learners remember certain words, ideas, and even behaviors. For example, a WAY TO GO board was created for a student with physical disabilities. He used it in his role as "encourager" during cooperative learning exercises. When he no longer had this role in the group, the teacher passed the board to the new encourager to remind this individual of the possible range of responses (e.g., GOOD IDEA, THANKS FOR YOUR HELP, VERY CREATIVE, KEEP UP THE GOOD WORK, INTERESTING IDEA).

References/ Recommended Reading

Beukelman, D., & Mirenda, P. (2006). *Augmentative & alternative communication: Management of severe communication disorders in children and adults* (3rd ed.). Baltimore: Paul H. Brookes Publishing Co.

McSheehan, M., Sonnenmeier, R., Jorgensen, C., & Turner, K. (2006). Beyond communication access: Promoting learning of the general education curriculum by students with significant disabilities. *Topics in Language Disorders, 26*(3), 266–290.

Mirenda, P., & Erickson, K. (2000). Augmentative communication and literacy. In A. Wetherby & B. Prizant (Eds.), *Autism spectrum disorders: A transactional developmental perspective.* Baltimore: Paul H. Brookes Publishing Co.

Sonnenmeier, R., McSheehan, M., & Jorgensen, C. (2005). A case study of team supports for a student with autism's communication and engagement within the general education curriculum: Preliminary report of the beyond access model. *Augmentative and Alternative Communication, 21*(2), 101–115.

Vendors

Aut 2 Communicate
http://www.aut2communicate.com
This web site contains letterboards for individuals with autism.

Blissymbolics
http://www.blissymbolics.org
This system of 1,400 black and white symbols and text labels was developed as an auxiliary language. Blissymbolics is a symbolic, graphical language that can be combined and recombined in endless ways to create new symbols.

Buddy Speak
http://buddyspeak.com
Buddy Speak is a nonelectronic communication board that can be used for enhancing literacy and communication skills for students with and without disabilities.

Communication Bracelets
http://www.ineedhelpcommunicationbracelets.com
These communication bracelets are good for students who need access to communication symbols as they are on the go. Several versions are available, including one that focuses on needs and another that focuses on feelings.

DynaVox Mayer-Johnson
http://www.mayer-johnson.com/MainBoardmaker.aspx?MainCategoryID=5419
DynaVox Mayer-Johnson is the manufacturer of Boardmaker software products. This web site contains descriptions of and information about the Boardmaker family of products. Boardmaker allows a user to create printed materials using Picture Communication Symbols and other graphics.

Web Sites

Closing the Gap
http://www.closingthegap.com
Closing the Gap, Inc., is an organization that focuses on assistive technology for people with disabilities through its bimonthly magazine, annual international conference, and extensive web site.

Darlene Hanson, MA, CCC
http://www.darlenehanson.com
This is the professional web site of Darlene Hanson, a speech-language pathologist. You will find communication planning formats and tools, articles, links, and product ideas on this site.

40 Talking Sticks

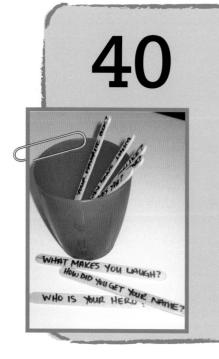

Materials

- Tongue depressors, craft sticks, or popsicle sticks
- Fine-tipped marker
- Plastic cup or tin can

Description

So many learners with disabilities cannot easily start a conversation or interact socially with their peers without adult support. By providing a series of concrete conversation starters using *talking sticks,* a learner can talk to peers without adult interference and can initiate communication instead of only responding to questions or participating in conversations others initiate.

Directions

Create a series of questions that are both appropriate for a student's age group and tailored for the time period or environment you are targeting. For example, questions you design to ask in the lunch room may be different from those you design for students to use at a class party. Provide a range of questions. Some should be thought provoking, such as, "What does it mean to be a good friend?" Others can be just plain fun, such as, "Describe your favorite pair of socks." Still others may be simple questions to open a discussion, "What did you do this weekend?"

Use a fine-tipped marker to print one question on each stick. Depending on the age of the students, you may want to let them participate in developing the questions and even writing them on the sticks. Questions that might be used include the following:

- What's your favorite form of exercise?
- What's your favorite Disney movie?
- What television commercials make you laugh?
- Tell about a time when you could not stop laughing.
- What did you do for your last birthday?
- What's your favorite web site?
- What's the best costume you've ever worn?
- What did you have for breakfast?

- What do you like best about your appearance?
- Who is your hero?
- What is your favorite memory of kindergarten?
- Have you ever been stung by a bee?

Example

A group of seventh-grade girls uses a set of talking sticks to interact, catch up, and socialize during free time in homeroom. Jill, a student with significant disabilities, needs to initiate conversations using the sticks, but the other students enjoy using them too. Therefore, the girls take turns selecting a stick and listening to answers from one another. Jill also uses her DynaVox communication device to participate in the conversations so that she also can answer questions from the group.

References/ Recommended Reading

Gibbs, J. (1995). *Tribes: A new way of learning and being together.* Sausalito, CA: Center Source Systems, LLC.

Poole, G. (2003). *The complete book of questions: 1001 conversation starters for any occasion.* Grand Rapids, MI: Zondervan.

Stock, G. (2004). *The kids' book of questions: Revised for the new century.* New York: Workman.

Vendors

Kwik Crafts
http://kwikcrafts.com/crafts/category/Craft-Sticks.html
Plain popsicle sticks, colored popsicle sticks, craft sticks, and more

The Box Girls
http://www.theboxgirls.com
Boxes of questions that can be used in a variety of situations and environments

Table Topics
http://www.tabletopics.com
Durable plastic boxes filled with questions and conversation starters; different editions are available, including one especially for kids and one focused on pets

Web Sites

Ice Breakers, Fun Games, & Group Activities
http://www.icebreakers.ws/small-group/icebreaker-questions.html
List of questions that can be used for this game and others. Check out their other game ideas as well.

Tribes: A New Way of Learning & Being Together
http://www.tribes.com
Articles and information about the importance of building community and supporting student interdependence

Behavior & Motivation

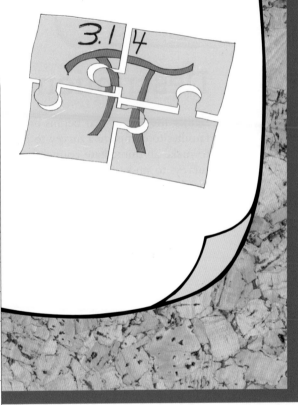

Contents

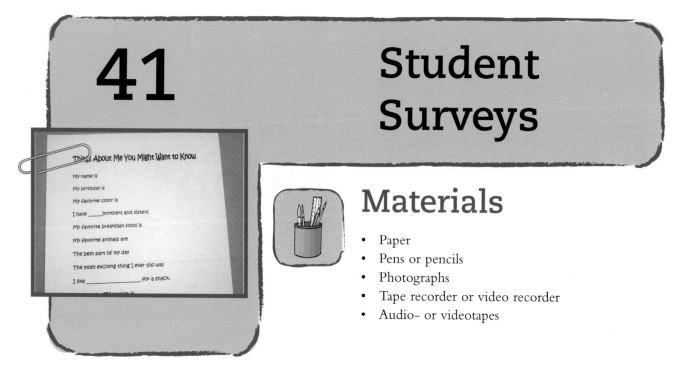

41 Student Surveys

Materials

- Paper
- Pens or pencils
- Photographs
- Tape recorder or video recorder
- Audio- or videotapes

Description

Before the school year begins or during the first few weeks, many teachers ask students and their families to complete a survey to help them become more personally acquainted with learners and to make an immediate connection with them. Some teachers may choose to administer different surveys to students than they give to their parents, whereas other teachers may design a survey that families and students complete together. Although a survey would undoubtedly help a teacher learn more about students new to the school, many teachers choose to use surveys with every student in the class.

A survey can give a student and his or her family an opportunity to provide information that is positive and personal and can give the teacher a unique firsthand account of the student's life. This is especially important if the student's background or experiences are unfamiliar to the teacher (Pascopella, 2004) or if the teacher has a specific goal of connecting classroom experiences to the interests or lives of his or her learners (Pennington & Krouscas, 1999). When educators have only test scores and clinical reports to inform their teaching, they may be puzzled by how to translate that information into practice. Personal surveys can help fill in gaps left by individualized education programs, behavioral reports, or student data files.

Directions

When considering the use of a survey, teachers will want to focus on students' learning styles, interests, needs, and strengths; they may also want to ask students ideas for the classroom. Although questions will vary by age group, possible questions include the following:

- How do you learn best?
- Write about your favorite teacher. What did you like about his or her teaching?
- What do you need to be comfortable in my classroom?
- What hobbies do you have?

- What topics are you an expert on?
- What do you want to learn this year?
- What is your favorite part of the school day?
- How can our classroom be more welcoming to you?
- What is your favorite thing to do at school?
- Describe a perfect school day.
- What do you like to read?
- What words describe you best?
- Tell me about yourself as an expert. What kind of expertise do you have (e.g., skateboarding, karate, babysitting, collecting bugs, meeting people, drawing)?
- What else do you want me to know about you?

If one or more students cannot write, the teacher, parent, or support person may allow learners to submit visual surveys. Students might draw pictures; create a collage; or submit photographs, a videotape, or an audiotape in response to the survey questions.

Examples

Ms. Hamann, a seventh-grade teacher, gives all of her students a survey to complete during the first week of school. The survey contains questions about student learning needs (e.g., "Describe a lesson you would find interesting and motivating"), preferences (e.g., "On a scale of 1–5, how much do you enjoy group work?"), and strengths (e.g., "List three areas of expertise you have"). Sylvia, a student with cognitive disabilities, could not easily answer all of the questions as they were presented; therefore, along with her peers, she submitted photographs of herself engaged in certain activities (e.g., reading to a younger sibling, taking care of tomatoes in her garden) and brought in some of her favorite objects (e.g., cases of favorite DVDs, drawings of her playing with her younger siblings, a cross-stitch hanging she made for her grandmother) to share with the teacher.

On the first day of school in her English classroom, Ms. Kader gives her students a short survey about their writing strengths and needs. She then has them spend most of the hour writing a short essay about the look, feel, and sights of the ideal classroom.

References/ Recommended Reading

Ferguson, D.L., Ralph, G., Meyer, G., Lester, J., Droege, C., Guojonsdottir, H., et al. (2001). *Designing personalized learning for every student.* Alexandria, VA: Association for Supervision and Curriculum Development.

Pascopella, A. (2004). Playing catch-up with Hispanic students. *District Administration, 40*(11), 38–44.

Pennington, T.R., & Krouscas, J.A. (1999). Connecting secondary physical education with the lives of students. *Journal of Physical Education, Recreation, & Dance, 70*(1), 34–39.

Vendor

Teacher Vision

http://www.teachervision.fen.com/students/resource/2878.html

Lots of "getting to know you" activities including a printable survey that will help you learn about students' life experiences, feelings, ideas, and even their dreams (http://www.teachervision.fen.com/classroom-management/printable/6240.html?detoured=1)

Web Sites

International Reading Association (Bio-Cube)

http://readwritethink.org/materials/bio_cube

A neat activity for kids and grown-ups! Students fill out questions on the sides of a virtual cube, entering information such as name, background, and biggest obstacle. The Bio-Cube typically is used as a comprehension tool for exploring main characters or for learning about an individual before or after reading an autobiography, but students can use it easily as a tool for sharing about themselves.

Index of Learning Styles Inventory

http://www.engr.ncsu.edu/learningstyles/ilsweb.html

Created by Dr. Richard Felder, this inventory gives elementary and secondary teachers ideas for questions they might ask their students (e.g., "I am more likely to be considered [a] careful about my work or [b] creative about my work").

See-Me-Strong Book 42

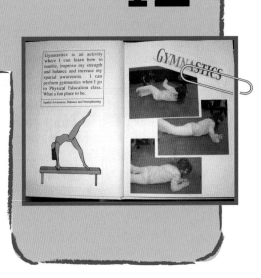

Materials

- Binder or photo album
- Photographs
- Paper

Description

It is often helpful to encourage students verbally and let them know they can succeed. However, actually seeing this success can be even more powerful for some learners. A *see-me-strong book* is a visual record of a student successfully performing a set of actions, engaging in a task, or even simply sitting quietly in certain environments.

Once the books are created, they can also be used as prompts for writing and for encouraging communication and language development. Veksler, Reed, and Ranish (2008) point out that the teacher can ask questions about the photos, elicit comments from the student or even work with the learner to read the constructed book.

Directions

Examine your student's day to determine areas of struggle, confusion, or difficulty. Does your student have difficulties participating in the morning homeroom routine? Does he wander on the playground, not knowing how to join a game? Is getting on the bus the hardest part of the day? Once you have determined problems in the schedule, take photographs of him or her in the targeted areas, activities, or lessons. If the playground is a challenge, take several pictures of him or her playing four-square, climbing on the equipment, swinging on the swing, and shooting a basket. If getting through the homeroom routine is a difficult, take pictures of the student completing each step of the process including coming into the classroom, handing in homework, and choosing a book for silent reading.

Step two is to put your photos into book form so the learner can review the "story" at his or her leisure. Some teachers add a description of what is happening in different photos and others may have their students write or dictate a caption for each page or picture.

Examples

Ms. Dunn, a physical education teacher, used this technique to help Lila, a little girl on the autism spectrum, feel more comfortable during weekly activities. She first took photographs of Lila participating in 10 different physical education activities (e.g., volleyball, running on the track, juggling). She then reviewed the book with Lila, giving her information about each of the photos and the activities. Lila took the book home and brought it to school on days when she had physical education class. After having the book for only a few weeks, Lila was able to participate more fully and recall more of the rules of each activity and felt less nervous and anxious about transitions from one sport or game to the next.

When Ivy, a young woman with Williams syndrome, struggled to move from center to center in her elementary math class, her teacher, Ms. Wix, created a see-me-strong book for her. Ms. Wix took a photograph of Ivy successfully engaging in activities in all six centers . Ivy used the book not only for math centers but also to calm down at other points of the day, as well.

Keep in Mind

A photo book, like the see-me-strong books discussed in this section, also can be configured as a choice book. Students who struggle to make decisions or those who feel overwhelmed when options are too open-ended will profit from having and using photos that represent choices that can be made under certain circumstances and in certain settings (e.g., where to hang out before first period, what to do in study hall, who to work with in art class).

References/ Recommended Reading

Baker, J. (2003). *The social skills picture book: Teaching play, emotion, and communication to children with autism.* Arlington, TX: Future Horizons.

Baker, J. (2006). *Social skills picture book for high school and beyond.* Arlington, TX: Future Horizons.

Veksler, D., Reed, H., & Ranish, A. (2008). The thematic photobook system: A teaching strategy or exceptional children. *TEACHING Exceptional Children Plus, 5*(1). Retrieved July 4, 2009, from http://escholarship.bc.edu/education/tecplus/vol5/iss1/art5

Vendors

Natural Learning Concepts
http://www.nlconcepts.com/autism-pdd-all.htm
Illustrated books for young children that help teach play, conversation, and social skills

Shutterfly
http://www.shutterfly.com
Shutterfly and other sites like it allow users to download pictures and "publish" their own photo albums; a good choice for creating a book that a student will use over a long period of time. A nice feature of the site is that the books you order are stored in your account, so if you need copies in the future, you can easily access them.

UseVisualStrategies.com
http://www.usevisualstrategies.com
Many ideas on using visual strategies, in general, and dozens of related products from which to choose

Web Site

Dr. Jed Baker's web site
http://www.jedbaker.com
Dr. Baker is a national expert on social skills development and supports for people on the autism spectrum. Baker believes that "seeing is learning," and he popularized the idea of using photographs to teach social skills. Visit Dr. Baker's web site to learn about his ideas and his speaking schedule.

43   Cue Cards

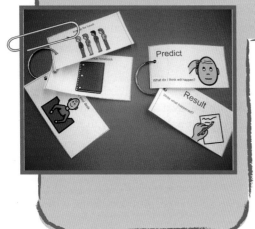

Materials

- Book rings—preferably 1¹/₂ inches in size
- Hole punch
- Computer with graphics program and printer or premade flash cards or index cards

Description

Many students find information easier to process and directions, therefore, easier to follow when they are presented visually as well as verbally (Arwood & Kaulitz, 2007; Faherty, 2000). For these learners, a set of *cue cards* can make life in the classroom easier. Cue cards are simply small, palm-sized visual aids that reinforce what a teacher (or student) is trying to communicate to a learner with a disability. Each card typically consists of a simple phrase and a picture.

Directions

Create your cue cards using any computer graphics program, magazine pictures, photographs, or illustrations. Then, print, laminate, and punch each of the cards in one of the top corners. To make the task easier and so that all the holes line up, use a "punched-hole" card as a guide for punching holes in the remaining cards. Then slide all of the cards onto a book ring. Finally, clasp the book ring shut tight.

Give the student the ring and demonstrate—across situations and environments—how to use the cards. You can show him or her how to use them to supplement communication (e.g., "I'm really hungry"), or they can be used to reinforce directions or messages for the student (e.g., "I think the bus is late").

If you have extra cards that the student does not need on a regular basis, those can be kept (pre-punched) in a box or on a separate ring and then added as needed.

Example

Brecken, a young man on the autism spectrum, often struggles to understand or process his teacher's spoken directions; therefore, the teacher created a ring of cue cards to help him navigate the classroom and the school day. Messages range from "line up for band" to "take out your portfolio" to "clean off your desk."

References/
Recommended Reading

Arwood, E.L., & Kaulitz, C. (2007). *Learning with a visual brain in an auditory world.* Shawnee
    Mission, KS: Asperger Autism Publishing Company.
Charlop-Christy, M., & Kelso, S. (2003). Teaching children with autism conversational speech using
    a cue card/written script program. *Education and Treatment of Children, 26,* 108–119.
Crissey, P. (2005). *Picture directions. Building independence step by step.* Verona, WI: IEP Resources.
Faherty, C. (2000). *Asperger's: What does it mean to be me?* Arlington, TX: Future Horizons.

Vendor

AutismShop.com
http://www.autismshop.com/store/home.php?cat=275
Several sets of visual cue cards appropriate for different situations (e.g., school, home, birthday parties)

Web Sites

Polyxo.com (Let's Get Visual)
http://www.polyxo.com/visualsupport/letsgetvisual.html
An article about visual supports, written by Brian S. Friedlander

Technical Assistance Center on Social Emotional Intervention for Young Children
http://challengingbehavior.org/do/resources/teaching_tools/ttyc_toc.htm
This site contains a PowerPoint presentation detailing how to assemble a set of cue cards. The presentation contains several pages of cue cards that can be used as is or adapted to fit your needs. Even
if the types of prompts provided are not appropriate for your students, watching the presentation
will help any teacher see and understand the variety of ways cards can be used.

44 Partner Puzzles

Materials

- Tagboard
- Photographs or magazine pictures
- Scissors
- Clear plastic baggie

Description

Activities in inclusive classrooms often require collaboration, teaming, and interaction (Dymond, Renzaglia, & Chun, 2008; Udvari-Solner, 2007; Udvari-Solner & Kluth, 2007). Students often are asked to work in pairs or small groups, but typical methods for grouping learners can lead to groans and complaints because students often want to work with their friends. To avoid protests, try making group formation into a game. By creating small jigsaw puzzles, students of any age can learn something new while finding their teammates in a fun, low-risk, and even humorous way.

Directions

For each group you want formed, create a puzzle with 3–6 pieces (depending on how many students you want in each group). Then, paste a picture on a piece of tagboard and laminate it. Finally, cut the pieces apart and store the group of puzzles in a clear baggie. When it is time for a group activity, give each student a puzzle piece and have him or her find partners by seeking others from the same puzzle pieces.

Teachers can turn the game into a learning tool by creating puzzles that match the content being taught. For example, if groups are forming to work on science projects, pictures of famous scientists can be used. If groups are forming for a collaborative writing exercise, puzzle pieces could reveal famous quotations. Students with disabilities and other students who are interested also may want to take these puzzles home if they prove helpful as a teaching tool.

Examples

During her social studies classes, Ms. Chaudoir grouped her students into pairs by having them assemble jigsaw puzzles of famous moments in U.S. history (e.g., signing of the U.S. Constitution, Battle of Gettysburg).

Students in a chemistry class find new lab partners by fitting together puzzles of diagrams from their textbook.

Keep in Mind

Another way to form groups is to make a set of index cards containing several famous pairs, trios, or groups (depending on what size you want the groups to be). Pass out one card to each student and have them find their partners by talking to one another, showing their card, and looking at the cards of others. Ideas for pairs include the following:

- Bart and Lisa Simpson
- Sherlock Holmes and Watson
- Jim and Huck Finn
- Lewis and Clark
- Barack Obama and Joe Biden
- Clifford the Big Red Dog and Emily
- Batman and Robin
- Romeo and Juliet
- Helen Keller and Anne Sullivan
- Peanut butter and jelly

Ideas for trios include the following:
- The Three Musketeers
- Harry Potter, Ron Weasley, and Hermione
- Daddy Bear, Mamma Bear, and Baby Bear
- The butcher, the baker, and the candlestick maker
- The Nina, the Pinta, and the Santa Maria

Some teachers create pairs or trios connected to their content area, so an English teacher might have pairs such as Scout and Jem and Lennie and George, and an American History teacher might pair U.S. presidents with their vice presidents.

References/ Recommended Reading

Dymond, S.K., Renzaglia, A., & Chun, E.J. (2008). Inclusive high school service learning programs: Methods for and barriers to including students with disabilities. *Education and Training in Developmental Disabilities, 43,* 20–36.

Jolliffe, W. (2007). *Cooperative learning in the classroom: Putting it into practice.* Thousand Oaks: Sage Publications.

Udvari-Solner, A. (2007). In M.F. Giangreco, *Quick-guides to inclusion: Ideas for educating students with disabilities* (2nd ed., pp. 151–164). Baltimore: Paul H. Brookes Publishing Co.

Udvari-Solner, A. & Kluth, P. (2007). *Joyful learning: Active and collaborative learning in the inclusive classroom.* Thousand Oaks, CA: Corwin Press.

Vendors

Compoz-A-Puzzle Inc.
http://www.compozapuzzle.com
Several different blank puzzles that can be drawn by teachers or students themselves; use these to create pictures related to content or to write facts relevant to your subject area

Puzzle World
http://www.puzzleworld.com
Get theme or puzzle ideas from this "everything puzzles" web site. Puzzles are organized by brand, theme, and piece count.

Web Sites

The Cooperative Learning Center at the University of Minnesota
http://www.co-operation.org
The Cooperative Learning Center is the home base of Roger and David Johnson, two researchers known around the world for their work in cooperative learning. On this site you will find information on research related to cooperative learning as well as a Q&A on cooperative learning, in general.

Factacular
http://www.factacular.com/subjects/Famous_Pairs
A list of famous pairs

TEFL.net
http://edition.tefl.net/ideas/teaching/putting-students-into-groups
Fifteen ways to put students into groups

Peer Tutor Scripts

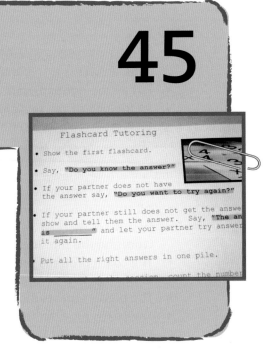

Flashcard Tutoring
- Show the first flashcard.
- Say, **"Do you know the answer?"**
- If your partner does not have the answer say, **"Do you want to try again?"**
- If your partner still does not get the answer show and tell them the answer. Say, **"The an is _____"** and let your partner answer it again.
- Put all the right answers in one pile.

Materials

- Pen and paper
- Photographs or graphics program

Description

Peer tutoring is an instructional strategy that consists of pairing students together to learn or practice an academic task. The pairs of students can be of similar or differing ability and/or age range. One tutoring relationship is peer-to-peer, in which some students may have more skill or experience than others and can share their expertise. In other instances, teachers may want to use cross-age tutors. Tutors may be culled from upper grades within the same school or from different buildings (e.g., high school students tutoring middle school students).

Directions

- Decide on the skills or competencies your student or students need.
- Write a script, keeping in mind the reading level of the potential tutor(s).
- Review the script with the tutor and be sure he or she understands all of the steps. Then, have the student practice with you before tutoring a peer.
- Once the student understands the script and the lesson, pair the students up and observe a tutoring session. Give feedback to help students make the most of their time together.
- Continue to monitor the sessions regularly, checking with both the tutor and tutee to make sure the sessions are productive and enjoyable for both participants.

Examples

Sara, a fourth grader, tutors first-grade students in math, which is an area of struggle for her. This tutoring relationship has boosted her self-esteem in this curricular area. Each week, she works with a different student on a flash card exercise. She uses the following script:
- Ask the child to tell you the answer to the problem.
- If he or she gets the answer wrong, ask him or her if he or she wants to try again.

- If he or she still does not get the answer, show and tell him or her the answer and say, "The answer is ____"; then, let him or her try answering it again.
- Put all the right answers in one pile.
- At the end of the session, count the number of problems answered correctly and record the number on the chart.

In their article "Classwide Peer Tutoring at Work," Fulk and King (2001) describe a peer tutor script that can be used to have peers practice spelling words together. The script is as follows:

- All students neatly write their spelling words on separate 3" x 5" cards.
- Words are checked against models for accuracy. Students write the definitions of the words on the flip side of the cards as needed.
- The coach prompts the player to spell a word either orally (e.g., "Spell *jargon.*") or in print (e.g., "Write *jargon.*").
- The player repeats the word and then spells ("Jargon: j-a-r-j-o-n.")
- The coach provides feedback for an incorrect oral response ("No, *jargon* is spelled j-a-r-g-o-n. Now you spell it.").
- The player repeats the correct spelling and the coach reinforces by saying, "That's right."
- Or, the coach prompts the player to compare his or her spelling to the correct model ("No, *jargon* is spelled j-a-r-g-o-n. Now you spell it.").
- The coach asks for the definition ("What does *jargon* mean?") and provides appropriate feedback for either a correct or incorrect response.
- The students switch roles and repeat the process in their new roles. (p. 50)

References/ Recommended Reading

Fulk, B.M., & King, K. (2001). Classwide peer tutoring at work. *TEACHING Exceptional Children, 34*(2), 49–53.

Herring-Harrison, T.J., Gardner, I.R., & Lovelace, T.S. (2007). Adapting peer tutoring for learners who are deaf or hard of hearing. *Intervention in School & Clinic, 43*(2), 82–87.

Maheady, L. (2001). Peer-mediated instruction and interventions and students with mild disabilities. *Remedial & Special Education, 22*(1), 4–15.

Pressley, A.J., & Hughes, C. (2000). Peers as teachers of anger management to high school students with behavioral disorders. *Behavioral Disorders, 25*(2), 114–130.

Rohrbeck, C.A., Ginsburg-Block, M., Fantuzzo, J.W., & Miller, T.R. (2003). Peer-assisted learning interventions with elementary school students: A meta-analytic review. *Journal of Educational Psychology, 95*(2), 240–257.

Stenhoff, D.M., & Lignugaris/Kraft, B. (2007). A review of the effects of peer tutoring on students with mild disabilities in secondary settings. *Exceptional Children, 74*(1), 8–30.

Topping, K. (2001). *Peer assisted-learning: A practical guide for teachers.* Newton, MA: Brookline Books.

Vendor

The National Tutoring Association
http://www.ntatutor.com/store.htm
The store page on the National Tutoring Association's web site has a few resources that readers may find useful such as games, books, and software.

Web Sites

Kids as Reading Helpers: A Peer Tutor Training Manual
http://www.interventioncentral.org/htmdocs/interventions/rdngfluency/prtutor.php
Jim Wright, the author of this comprehensive manual, is a school psychologist who lives and works in Syracuse, New York. The manual includes helpful materials for teachers and students, including some peer–tutor scripts for reading lessons.

National Tutoring Association
http://www.ntatutor.com
Resources to help your school grow its tutoring programs, including information on the National Tutoring Association's peer tutor training program

Peer Assisted Learning Strategies
http://kc.vanderbilt.edu/pals
Peer Assisted Learning Strategies combines "proven instructional principles and practices and peer mediation so that research-based reading and math activities are effective, feasible, and enjoyable."

Tutor Source
http://www.tutorsource.com
Looking for a tutor for your school or program? Tutor source will help you find qualified tutors in your area in a number of subjects and grade levels.

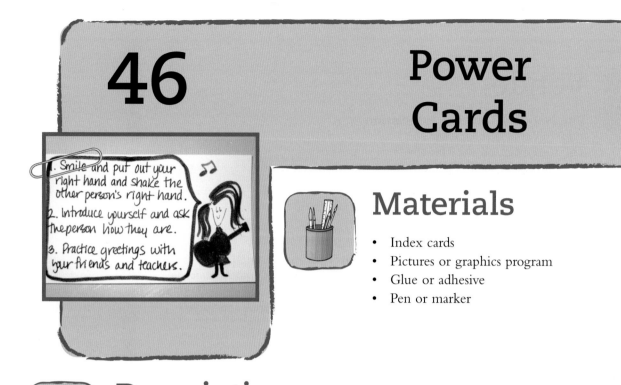

46 Power Cards

Materials

- Index cards
- Pictures or graphics program
- Glue or adhesive
- Pen or marker

Description

Power cards, a strategy developed by Elisa Gagnon (2001), is a tool that teachers can use to motivate and inspire any student who has a passion, fascination, or interest in an object, person, animal, character, or even in an event or hobby. Originally designed to use with students with autism, teachers have found it helpful in supporting students with a whole range of needs, including those with cognitive disabilities, emotional disabilities, and learning disabilities.

The power card strategy can be used in a variety of situations including those in which an individual is confused about the requirements or rules, does not understand choices, is struggling with generalizations, needs visual supports to act, or needs help to remember what to do in a specific setting or context.

Directions

The technique consists of 1) a story about a strategy a student's "hero" has used to solve a problem; this is usually written on a single page, and 2) the power card itself (which is the size of a business or index card), which recaps how the person using the card can use the same strategy to solve a similar problem.

If you find that the power card strategy is particularly effective for one of your students, you might consider additional ways to keep the 1, 2, 3 information handy for that individual. For instance, the same information that appears on a power card can be posted inside a locker or desk. Or, it can be slipped into the front see-through cover of a binder, slipped into an acetate keychain, or even made into a set of stickers (by printing from the computer onto mailing labels) that can be applied to any number of materials or surfaces.

Example

Gagnon (2001) shares a story about Kimberly, a young woman with autism, who usually hugs people when she greets them. Because Kimberly is getting older and meeting a wider range of people, her family wants her to learn to shake hands when she meets new people. Kimberly loves Shania Twain, so a story about the popular entertainer was written for her. In this story, Shania learns that it is not always best to hug everyone. She decides to shake hands with her many fans instead of hugging them (especially those she is meeting them for the first time). At the end of the story, "Shania" shares three tips with the reader:

1. Smile and put out your right hand and shake the other person's right hand.
2. Introduce yourself and ask the person how they are.
3. Practice greetings with your friends and teachers. (p. 43)

Kimberly's power card, then, features a photo of Shania Twain and these three tips. She can review both the story and the card repeatedly and carry the card with her for those times when she may be meeting a lot of new people.

Keep in Mind

Power Cards also can be used for students without disabilities. If this strategy is effective for one of the students in your inclusive classroom, consider introducing it to everyone. Allow all students (those with and without disability labels) to make power cards for themselves. Ask students to think of situations, experiences, and events that make them uncomfortable or nervous. Then ask them to think of one of their passions or areas of special interest. Teach them how to integrate these things into a story and then into a power card that they can keep in their locker, wallet, or desk.

References/ Recommended Reading

Gagnon, E. (2001). *Power cards: Using special interests to motivate children and youth with Asperger syndrome and autism.* Shawnee Mission, KS: Autism Asperger Publishing.

Spencer, V., Simpson, C.G., Day, M., & Buster, E. (2008). Using the power card strategy to teach social skills to a child with autism. *TEACHING Exceptional Children Plus, 5*(1), 1–10.

Winter-Meissiers, M.A. (2007). From tarantulas to toilet brushes: Understanding the special interest areas of children and youth with Asperger syndrome. *Remedial and Special Education, 28,* 140–152.

Winter-Meissiers, M.A., Herr, C., Wood, C., Brooks, A., Gates, M.A., Houston, T., et al. (2007). How far can Brian ride the daylight 4449 express? A strength-based model of Asperger syndrome based on special interest areas. *Focus on Autism and Other Developmental Disabilities, 22,* 67–79.

Vendor

Autism Asperger Publishing Company
http://www.asperger.net
Educators can pick up a copy of Gagnon's *Power Cards* book at AAPC, her publisher's web site. In addition, check out the newsletter with tips from teachers and an example of creating a power card using the Power-Puff Girls as the student's fascination: http://www.asperger.net/newsletter_dec01 keeling.htm

Web Site

Autism Spectrum Institute at Illinois State University
http://www.autismspectrum.ilstu.edu/resources/factsheets/powercard.shtml
A description of the power card strategy and an example about winning and losing

Doodle Notes

47

Materials

- Coloring books or pages
- Crayons or markers

Description

It is not uncommon to walk into an American classroom and see a student who is doodling being redirected or even reprimanded. Kevin Ryan, a graphic designer who found his home at a successful advertising design firm, recalls his experiences trying to covertly doodle during his school days:

> From the first time I was reprimanded for drawing Bart Simpson or a favorite logo during class, I have always said, "Yes, I am paying attention!"…Sketching has always kept me in the moment. Surely I'm not the only person on the planet who has developed the fine art of passive listening while doodling. So, why is it that some people think just because you're not staring directly into their eyes, you must be a troublemaker who doesn't pay attention to anything? (http://www.dday.com/blog/design/kreation/yes-i%E2%80%99m-paying-attention)

Many learners such as Ryan are accused of or seen as being off task. Research, however, indicates that this assumption may be far from the truth. Students who are allowed to doodle, color, or sketch as part of the note taking process may not only be more alert and motivated but may also be more likely to attend to and recall lecture information (Andrade, 2009).

Directions

Using *doodle notes* in the classroom can be as easy as distributing coloring pages to some or all of the students in the classroom and letting them color and doodle on the page as they write down key points or draw graphic representations of the presented content. The pages also can be designed for students to color or fill in pieces of the page as part of the lecture or class discussion. For example, you could give students a coloring page of the Supreme Court building and print a fact about the Supreme Court on each pillar. As you cover each point, you can instruct students to fill in the corresponding pillar and add any other notes they deem to be important.

Examples

As Lucine's teacher lectured about tsunamis, earthquakes, and volcanoes during a middle school unit on natural disasters, Lucine colored pages with images related to the lecture. Using a permanent marker, her teacher wrote lecture points on sections of the sheet and instructed Lucine to add any words or phrases she thought were important and to color in each section as the point was covered.

A high school history teacher gave a mini-lecture to his students on Allies of World War II. During the lecture, he allowed students to take notes in their notebook or to take notes on different coloring pages. Students could choose from a map of France, a map of England, or a map of Europe.

References/ Recommended Reading

Andrade J. (2009). What does doodling do? *Applied Cognitive Psychology, 23,* 1–7.
Budd, J.W. (2004). Mind maps as classroom exercises. *Journal of Economic Education, 35*(1), 35–46.
Golon, A.S. (2006). *The visual-spatial classroom: Differentiation strategies that engage every learner.* Denver, CO: Visual-Spatial Resource.

Vendor

Acorn Naturalists

http://www.acornnaturalists.com/store/Science-and-Nature-Coloring-Books-C447.aspx
A great selection of coloring books for older students, including ones on plants, habitats, reptiles, and mammals

Web Sites

The Coloring Spot
http://thecoloringspot.com
Lots of coloring pages on themes ranging from ocean life to music to The Wonders of the World; in addition, they offer several "sheets" students can color online

Edupics.com
http://www.edupics.com
Hundreds of realistic coloring pages on themes appropriate for K–12 classrooms, including ones on Napoleon, African American history, U.S. presidents, China, Greece, space exploration, latitude, pollution, and natural disasters

USA National Doodle Day
http://www.doodledayusa.org
Check out celebrity doodles, reasons to doodle, and doodles in the news!

Safe Space

48

Materials

- Comfortable seating
- Room dividers

Description

In her book, *Nobody Nowhere: The Extraordinary Biography of an Autistic,* Donna Williams (1992) stated, "Allowing me privacy and space was the most beneficial thing I ever got" (p. 218). Many individuals with autism report a need to retreat into a *safe space* at times. Liane Holliday Willey (1999), another woman with Asperger syndrome, suggests that even college students will need to find a place to unwind and re-group somewhere on campus.

Teachers should make quiet study or relaxation areas available for any student who seems to need to get away. The library might be used, or a few chairs might be set up in the hallway (depending on fire codes of the school) for any student who needs a break from the chaos of the classroom. The most important part of creating a safe space, of course, is ensuring that the area will not be used or viewed as a place of punishment.

Directions

Talk to your school administrators, the building engineer or custodian, and your fellow teachers to find places in your classroom and throughout the school that can function as safe spaces for students who frequently need a break. Possible spaces include the following:

- Nook or corner in the classroom
- Shielded area of the hallway
- Corner of the library
- Area in the school office
- Area near counseling offices
- Foyer area
- Extra meeting room or office space

Once the area has been identified, look for ways to make it welcoming for any learner who will use it. If the area is out in the open, look for some way to make the space more private (e.g., putting up a makeshift cardboard wall). Add seating that is comfortable and perhaps even a poster with tips for relaxation.

In some cases, teachers may even want to model how to ask for and use safe space. A short discussion about the space will likely suffice for older students, but for those in preschool and early elementary classrooms, educators might want to engage in some role play in order to get students comfortable with the idea of safe space and the space itself.

Example

Hedeen, Ayres, Meyer, and Waite (1996) share a story about creating and using safe space for a young woman with behavior challenges. As the authors recall, Becky, a fourth-grader, often needed breaks from her classroom. Teachers, however, were unsure of how to give her time away without stigmatizing her or making her feel punished. In order to create the best possible situation (and space) for Becky, the teachers worked closely with their student to give her a respectable place to take a break and support to learn new relaxation skills as well.

Initially, the staff provided a small room used for testing, but Becky began to throw furniture and destroy materials. Seeing that the space would not work, the team kept searching. Next, the teachers tried a small study space that many students used throughout the day. The teachers also brought music and books into the room because these items often served to calm Becky.

Once this ideal space was found and created, Becky seemed to approve. When she first came to the room, she sat down at the desk, looked at books, listened to music, and returned to class without protesting. According to staff members, Becky seemed to like the space and viewed it as a beak instead of as a punishment, as did her teachers. In explaining the creation of the room, Hedeen and her colleagues share that safe space must be seen as a support and not as a consequence.

> Traditional learning theory assumptions might lead us to interpret what we had done as a reward for Becky's negative behavior, and we might have expected Becky's "loud-in-the-classroom" behavior to escalate in order to obtain this reward. We might have also expected her to refuse to leave "Becky's room." Neither of these things happened. We believe that, to borrow a phrase from [a teacher], Becky had given us the "best behavior she could" under the present circumstances—she wasn't trying to manipulate us directly, although she was telling us that she needed a break. When we responded to her needs by giving her a break rather than a punishment, she was apparently able to recoup and return to work. When we treated Becky as we would want to be treated, her behavior improved. (Hedeen et al., 1996, p. 154–155)

References/ Recommended Reading

Hedeen, B., Ayres, B., Meyer, L., & Waite, J. (1996). Quality inclusive schooling for students with severe disabilities. In D. Lehr & F. Brown (Eds.), *People with disabilities that challenge the system* (pp. 154–155). Baltimore: Paul H. Brookes Publishing Co.

Holley, L.C., & Steiner, S. (2005, Winter). Safe space: Student perspectives on classroom environment. *Journal of Social Work Education, 41*(1), 49–64. Available online at http://findarticles.com/p/articles/mi_hb3060/is_1_41/ai_n29209284/?tag=content;col1

Williams, D. (1992). *Nobody nowhere: The extraordinary biography of an autistic.* New York: Avon.

Willey, L.H. (1999). *Pretending to be normal: Living with Asperger's syndrome.* Philadelphia: Jessica Kingsley Publishers.

Vendors

Ergo in Demand
http://www.ergoindemand.com/child-care-room-dividers.htm?cm_mmc=google-_-shopping-_-n%2Fa-_-n%2Fa
These 4-foot-tall room dividers can help you create a private space while giving you more room to post student work and display visuals.

Teachers' School Supply
http://www.teacherssupply.com/classroomfurniture/roomdividers.htm
A good source for inexpensive room dividers

Web Site

Gentle Teaching International
http://www.gentleteaching.com
Even more ideas on sensitively supporting students who experience challenging behaviors

49

Laptop Lectures

Materials

- Binder or file folder
- Page protectors or laminate
- Icons/pictures/symbols
- Velcro, magnets, or pockets

Description

Some students need more activity and movement than typical whole-class structures allow (Udvari-Solner, 1996; Wehmeyer, Lance, & Bashinski, 2002). In these instances, it may be a good idea to make laptop versions, or *laptop lectures,* of the materials that are being used at the front of the classroom. With these materials, a student with a disability (or a student who is simply fidgety) can be more active than passive and, in some cases, may be able to stay with the lesson longer.

Directions

For most laptop lectures, a three-ring binder works well; however, different materials may be used if desired. Binders with a clear plastic cover work particularly well because the clear plastic cover allows the teacher to put a cover page or label inside and easily communicate the content of the binder to the learner.

To make interacting with the materials easy, laminate the pages or put them inside sheet protectors so the student can mark them with a grease pencil. You can also use small magnets, reusable stickers, plastic pockets, or hook-and-loop tape in your book to create more opportunities for the learner to interact with the materials.

Examples

In a ninth-grade social studies class, the teacher assigned her students five locations to study and memorize each week. During the introduction of these locations, she would point to the locations on a set of maps and use an overhead projector to circle certain cities or areas. The same set of maps was provided to Dominick, a student with attention-deficit/hyperactivity disorder in that classroom. Dominick's maps were kept inside page protectors in a three-ring binder. A grease pencil was attached by a string to the binder so that Dominick could circle the locations along with his teacher.

In a kindergarten class, teachers created two laptop lectures for calendar time and the weather report. While other students watched the teacher and participated by paying attention and listening to the lesson, the learners with autism watched the lesson and followed along with the teacher by placing Velcro numbers (days of the month) on a laptop calendar that looked just like the classroom calendar. On the back of the binder, the teachers had included icons representing different types of weather. The learners were able to follow along with the lesson and participate by placing the correct weather icons in a designated square on the binder.

Keep in Mind

Other students may want to use these materials too, so you may want to make a few copies and pass them around the room, giving a few students at a time the opportunity to "do as the teacher does."

References/ Recommended Reading

Kluth, P. (2007). *Don't lecture me! 5 ways to keep whole class instruction active & memorable.* Retrieved from: http://www.paulakluth.com/articles/lectureme.html on June 1, 2009.

Udvari-Solner, A. (1996). Examining teacher thinking: Constructing a process to design curricular adaptations. *Remedial and Special Education, 17*(4), 245–254.

Wehmeyer, M.L., Lance, G.D., & Bashinski, S. (2002). Promoting access to the general curriculum for students with mental retardation: A multi-level model. *Education and Training in Mental Retardation and Developmental Disabilities, 37,* 223-234.

Vendors

Leaps and Bounds

http://www.leapsandbounds.com/catalog/product.jsp?productId=6742&parentCategoryId=85192&categoryId=85255&subCategoryId=86257

A personal calendar appropriate for young children

TinSnips: Calendar Skills

http://www.tinsnips.org/Pages/calendarskills.html

Calendar templates and materials—many for purchase but some are free to download

Web Site

The Apple (50 Activities that Will Grab Your Students' Attention)

http://www.theapple.com/training/articles/122-50-actions-that-will-grab-your-students-attention

A short article by Julia Thompson featuring dozens of ways to engage students during whole-class instruction.

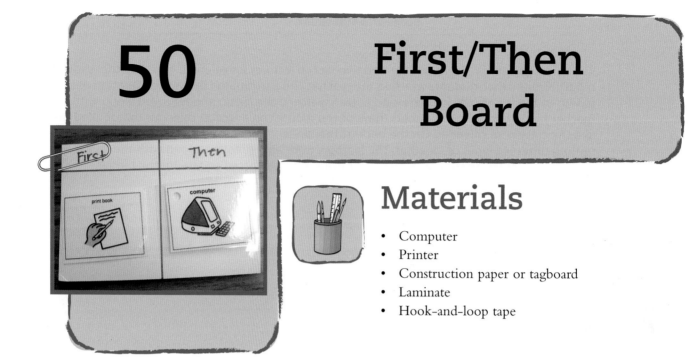

50 First/Then Board

Materials

- Computer
- Printer
- Construction paper or tagboard
- Laminate
- Hook-and-loop tape

Description

A *First/Then Board* is a mini-schedule that is portable and can be used to provide more choices to a student or to reinforce simple instructions. The teacher places a word or picture of what the student has to do under the FIRST (left) section of the card. For the THEN (right) side of the card, the student might choose a preferred activity to engage in for a short period of time or the teacher can select something he or she feels the learner will enjoy or appreciate.

The teacher can create the cards with pictures and words, or just words (use any graphics program or the Internet Picture Dictionary listed listed under Web Sites to find free, usable images).

The First/Then Board and the picture or word cards should be laminated to be used many times throughout the school day.

While First/Then Boards are most often used to provide balance for students and to give them choices throughout the day, they can also be used when a teacher wants to remind a student of two tasks that must be completed in a row. First/Then Boards are helpful for many reasons. They can relieve student anxiety about the schedule; they help teachers avoid repeating a lot of unnecessary verbal instructions; and they can help to ease transitions. Some teachers even choose to use them for the entire class instead of only for individual learners because they can cut down on schedule-related questions such as, "What are we doing next?" and "What can we do when we finish?"

Directions

Using thick paper or tagboard, print out a two-column, two-row table on the computer (or simply create your board and your columns using a thick magic marker). Label the first column "FIRST" and the second column "THEN." Then, use clip art, any graphics program, photos, or illustrations to create cards for activities, tasks, or jobs the student has to engage in, enjoys, and might want to try. Finally, attach hook and loop tape to the back of each card and on each side of the First/Then Board.

Example

Chad, a first grader with an emotional disability, finds center work very overwhelming. There are many different activities, and he prefers some (e.g., listening station) over others (e.g., writing station, letters/sounds station). To motivate Chad to try different centers, the teacher places her center choice under the "First" space (e.g., letters/sounds station), and Chad places his choice under the "Then" space (e.g., listening station).

Keep in Mind

A First/Then Board is often the first schedule that a student will use. As the student learns this concept, you can easily begin to add more choices or pictures to this board, thus creating a visual schedule for the individual. These are also great for parents who are having difficulty getting a child to sit down for homework.

References/ Recommended Reading

Breitfelder, L.M. (2008). Quick and easy adaptations and accommodations for early childhood students. *TEACHING Exceptional Children Plus, 4*(5). Retrieved July 3, 2009, from http://escholarship.bc.edu/cgi/viewcontent.cgi?article=1151&context=education/tecplus

Marks, S.U., Shaw-Hegwer, J., Schrader, C., Longaker, T., Peters, I., Powers, F., et al. (2003). Instructional management tips for teachers of students with autism spectrum disorder (ASD). *TEACHING Exceptional Children, 35*(4), 50–55.

Vendor

Clipart.com
http://www.clipart.com
For a weekly, monthly, or annual subscription fee, you can get a huge range of images that can be used for your adaptations.

Web Sites

The Behavior Guy
http://thebehaviorguy.com/2008/07/14/14readymade-if-then-board
Web site of Darren Tagliarini, a behavior specialist. Scan the site for many classroom management resources including an If/Then Board example.

The Picture Dictionary
http://www.pdictionary.com
Use the flash cards section to print images in several different categories such as musical instruments, school, and sports.

Technical Assistance Center on Social Emotional Intervention
http://challengingbehavior.org/do/resources/teaching_tools/ttyc_toc.htm
The "Teacher Tools" page of this web site contains directions not only for making a First/Then Board but also for creating at least a dozen other supports for students with learning and social needs.

Teaching & Learning

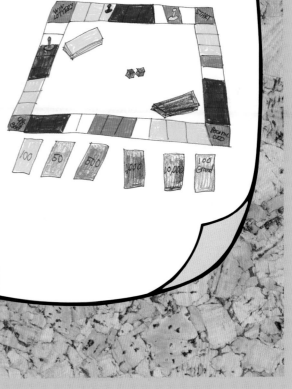

Contents

51 Adapted Worksheets

Materials

- School supplies that might be used to make print materials more accessible, such as the following:
  - Contact paper
  - Page protectors
  - Binders
  - Liquid paper
  - Highlighters
  - Stickers
  - Sticky notes

Description

Many classrooms use worksheets regularly for independent work, centers, or homework. Oftentimes, students with special needs require a different (e.g., more complex content, less complex content, less cluttered format, easier to read) worksheet than their peers or a worksheet with modifications (Downing, 2008).

Directions

There are many different ways to modify a worksheet. Examples include the following:
- Changing a question into a declarative statement or cloze sentence format
- Changing open-ended questions to matching or multiple choice
- Providing a word bank or phrase bank of possible answers
- Creating a graphic organizer for an essay or open-ended question
- Allowing students to draw or illustrate answers
- Using graphics programs, drawings, or stickers to add visuals for students who read at a lower level or for nonreaders
- Providing page numbers or clues as to where answers can be found (e.g., "Check the board")
- Creating a window card (see photo inset) for students to be able to isolate individual questions
- Enlarging the text for students with low vision
- Highlighting directions to draw student attention to key words

Examples

Rob, a student with a learning disability, completed the same worksheet as other students but used a teacher-created word bank to fill in the answers.

In a third-grade classroom, children were writing a story summary on a teacher-created worksheet. A student with autism was reading and writing at a much lower grade level; therefore, he summarized and retold the story by gluing story pictures on an adapted worksheet.

Keep in Mind

The language used on a worksheet should match the reading level of the child. You can provide the meaning of a word in parentheses to teach new vocabulary, if necessary.

References/
Recommended Reading

Downing, J. (2008). *Including students with severe and multiple disabilities in typical classrooms: Practical strategies for teachers* (3rd ed.). Baltimore: Paul H. Brookes Publishing Co.

Hammeken, P. (2000). *Inclusion: 450 strategies for success: A practical guide for all educators who teach students with disabilities.* Thousand Oaks, CA: Corwin Press.

Vendors

Adaptive Worksheets
http://adaptiveworksheets.com
Search by topic or search by grade to find worksheets or create your own materials including schedules, photo cards, and assessments.

EdHelper
http://www.edhelper.com
In addition to carrying a large variety of premade worksheets for different subjects (e.g., language arts, math, science, social studies), EdHelper allows teachers to use templates to set up their own worksheets, which is ideal for those who want to make adapted worksheets or adapt existing worksheets. Users pay an annual subscription.

Enchanted Learning®

http://www.enchantedlearning.com/Home.html

This site contains a large number of teacher resources, including printable books, picture dictionaries, activities, and visuals. Some materials are free; others are available with a subscription.

Web Sites

Access Autism Web Site for the Indiana Resource Center for Autism

http://www.iidc.indiana.edu/irca/education/engaged.html

A link to an informative article titled, "Get Engaged: Designing Instructional Activities to Help Students Stay On-Task"; contains a few examples of adapted worksheets as well as other useful materials.

Project Participate

http://www.projectparticipate.org/CurriculumDisplays.asp?CD=7

This web site of the University of Colorado Health Science Center contains several examples of adapted worksheets for biology and health classes.

More Ideas

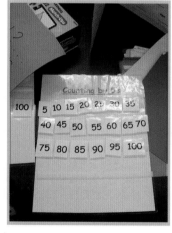

Curriculum Stickers

52

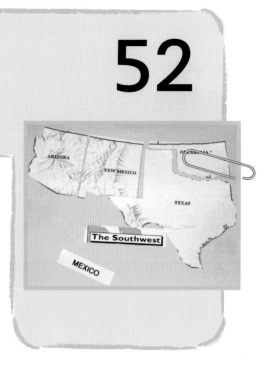

Materials

- Blank white labels or Avery Sticker Project Paper
- Computer graphics program

Description

Teachers often use stickers as curriculum adaptations for students who have fine motor problems. Stickers can be a helpful shortcut for learners who are working on a fill-in-the-blank worksheet, creating drawings, or journaling (Kluth & Chandler-Olcott, 2007). Sometimes, however, the stickers needed for a particular unit or lesson do not exist or are not easy to find. In these instances, teachers can simply print their own curriculum-related stickers.

Directions

To create stickers, simply find an image you want to print (e.g., Japan, plant cell, semicolon), and "paste" in a word processing document (e.g., Microsoft Word). If you are creating images that are very small, you can create your stickers by printing on individual labels (or on a page of labels). An easier way to create homemade stickers, however, is to use sticker project paper. With these sheets, you can create one big (8.5" x 11") sticker or design and cut out shapes and sizes to fit your needs.

Example

Students in a fourth-grade classroom were studying the Southwest region of the United States. At the end of the unit, students took a quiz on the states in the region; they had to draw a rough map of the region and label the four states in it. Riley, a child with cognitive disabilities, could not draw with any accuracy, so he was required to create his map using four stickers of the states that his teacher had printed for this purpose. He practiced this task as a homework assignment in the week leading up to the quiz. This support, along with the stickers, allowed him to succeed in the assessment.

Keep in Mind

To ensure that you always have the images students need, you might have others in the class draw images on sticker paper; the pictures can then be cut out and stored for any learner to use in future projects.

Reference/
Recommended Reading

Kluth, P., & Chandler-Olcott, K. (2007). *"A Land We Can Share": Teaching literacy to students with autism.* Baltimore: Paul H. Brookes Publishing Co.

Vendors

Avery Dennison
http://www.avery.com/avery/en_us/Products/Crafts-&-Scrapbooking/Sticker-Project-Paper/White-Sticker-Project-Paper_03383.htm
Avery sheets of white sticker paper perfect for coloring or printing

Oriental Trading
http://www.orieintaltrading.com/ui/browse/processRequest.do?sku57/6863&requestURI=processProducts Catalog

Although this company is best known for its novelty and holiday items, they also have some unique education products appropriate for both elementary and secondary students. This link takes you to a sticker set of organs of the human body, for instance.

Uncommon Goods
http://www.uncommongoods.com/item/item.jsp?itemId=12365
Elementary teachers and middle school teachers may be interested in the U.S. map sticker set offered on this web site.

Web Site

Circle of Inclusion [Math Adaptation]
http://www.circleofinclusion.org/english/demo/wichitawhite/classroom/math.html
A good example of using money stickers in a math lesson

Hello!
My Name Is_____.

53

Materials

- Labels
- Pen or marker
- "Hello my name is" name tags

Description

Readers may be most familiar with *"Hello my name is _____"* from their own experiences in foreign language classes. Spanish, Chinese, Hebrew, American Sign Language, and other language teachers often give students names from the language being studied and use them all year long. This gives students familiarity with names in other countries and cultures and often adds a bit of fun and humor to the class.

"Hello! My name is _____" is similar to the practice used in foreign language but can be adapted for any content area (in other words—"names" don't have be be names—any label will do) and any grade level. The game simply involves giving students in the classroom new "names" and calling them all by these names for a lesson, a day, a month, or for the entire year!

There are two primary ways to play "Hello! My Name Is _____." The first way is to tell students what category their names represent (e.g., elements in the periodic table, prepositional phrases, Spanish-speaking countries) and simply give each student a label or name from the category. The second way is to try and teach some type of association or relationship. For this version, you would give students a longer name that, in itself, teaches something. For instance, you might give each student a multiplication fact as a name (8 x 8 = 64) and call the student by the problem and the answer.

Directions

Assign students their names by recording them on "Hello my name is _____" tags and distributing them to members of the class. Then, instruct students how you want them to use the newly assigned names. Do you want them to use them just during social studies? All day long? Just for the week? For the first quarter?

Using new names is a good way to inspire laughter in the classroom as well as help students learn and recall facts, information, important people, and associations. You will have to assess as you go to determine if students are learning the content from simply using (and hearing others use) the new names or if they need more structured practice. If practice is needed, consider playing classroom games with student names and identities. For instance, in an art class where the teacher had named all of the students after Impressionist artists, she had a different student introduce him or herself each week with a 5-minute presentation in front of the group. Throughout the semester, then, students not only learned the names of famed Impressionists but also a bit about the lives of each one.

Examples

For a unit on mythology, a middle-school teacher gave all of her students Greek and Roman names of the characters studied.

An eighth-grade teacher gave each of her students names of constellations and used these names for the semester prior to a unit on mapping and observation.

A third-grade teacher gave her students multiplication fact names for just 1 week. Each fact consisted of a digit multiplied by zero (12 x 0 = 0; 66 x 0 = 0) to reinforce the fact that anything multiplied by zero is zero.

Reference/ Recommended Reading

Forsten, C., Grant, J., & Hollas, B. (2002). *Differentiated instruction: Different strategies for different learners.* Peterborough, NH: Crystal Springs Books.

Vendor

PC/NAMETAG
http://www.pcnametag.com
Different products for meetings, including a wide variety of name tags

Web Site

Microsoft Office Online
http://office.microsoft.com/en-us/templates/TC300022091033.aspx?CategoryID=CT101440301033
Print your own "My name is" name tags using this do-it-yourself template from Microsoft.

Whole-Class Response Cards

54

Materials

- Cardstock or tagboard
- Laminate
- Chisel-tip marker
- Mini-wipe boards or chalkboards with dry erase markers or chalk

Description

If one student in the classroom uses augmentative and alternative communication, why not provide opportunities for all students to do so? Whole-class response cards allow you to do just that. When teachers want to elicit information from the group, they usually ask one student at a time for an answer or for feedback. Although this is sometimes quite appropriate, it can be limiting in that it keeps a few students actively engaged (and usually the same few students day after day) and, at times, leaves others to daydream or otherwise disconnect from class (Udvari-Solner, 1996). To avoid this common pitfall, try having all students answer the teacher at the same time by silently holding up a sheet of paper, wipe board, or chalkboard with that person's individual guess, opinion, or idea (Udvari-Solner & Kluth, 2007). By using whole-class cards, students not only have their responses honored and remain more engaged but also the teacher can quickly assess how the class as a whole feels (if the question is an opinion or vote) or how well the group understands the concept being taught or assessed.

Directions

To make cards for one lesson (e.g., a lesson about whether numbers are prime or not; a lesson about pulleys, levers, and wedges), you can use construction paper or even typing paper, but if you are going to use the cards repeatedly across several lessons (e.g., for yes-or-no questions; questions asking students to determine parts of speech), then you may want to use laminated cardstock or tagboard. Mini-wipe boards and chalkboards also work well for this activity. No matter what materials you use, be sure that the cards are clearly legible from the front of the room and are easy for students to manipulate and display to the teacher.

To use the cards, ask a question or seek a response of some kind from the group and then let students know that you want them to respond in a new way. Tell them that instead of raising hands, you will be asking for another indication that they know the answer. Then direct them to construct their answer on their board (or choose a premade card from sets you have distributed) and hold up their answers all at the same time for you to read, comment on, or assess.

Examples

A kindergarten teacher used whole-class response cards to introduce addition and subtraction to his students. He gave each student two laminated cards, one that represented addition (i.e., the card showed a plus [+] sign) and one that represented subtraction (i.e., the card showed a minus [–] sign). As the teacher read various word problems, students had to indicate if the problem called for addition or subtraction and provide their answer by holding up one of the two cards.

A high school physics teacher gave students mini wipe boards and asked a series of questions during his demonstration on momentum. He set up a ramp and rolled different sized soup cans down it several times, each time making the ramp more or less steep. Using the boards, students were asked to make predictions throughout the demonstration (e.g., the can will roll faster; the can will go farther) (Udvari-Solner & Kluth, 2007).

References/ Recommended Reading

Heward, W.L. (1996). Three low-tech strategies for increasing the frequency of active student response during group instruction. In R. Gardner, III, D.M. Sainato, J.O. Cooper, T.E. Heron, W.L. Heward, J.W. Eshleman, et al. (Eds.), *Behavior analysis in education: Focus on measurably superior instruction* (pp. 283–320). Pacific Grove, CA: Brooks/Cole.

Fisher, D., & Frey, N. (2008). *Checking for understanding: Formative assessment techniques for your classroom.* Alexandria, VA: ASCD.

Udvari-Solner, A. (1996). Examining teacher thinking: Constructing a process to design curricular adaptations. *Remedial and Special Education, 17,* 245–254.

Udvari-Solner, A., & Kluth, P. (2007). *Joyful learning: Active and collaborative learning in inclusive classrooms.* Thousand Oaks, CA: Corwin.

Vendor

Learning Resources
http://www.learningresources.com/product/teachers/shop+by+subject/early+childhood/themed+write+-+wipe+boards%3Cbr%3Eset+of+5.do
A variety of themed dry erase boards

Web Site

Education World
http://www.educationworld.com/a_lesson/lesson/lesson251.shtml
A great lesson-planning article titled, "Whiteboards Stimulate Student Learning"

Pocket Sorts

55

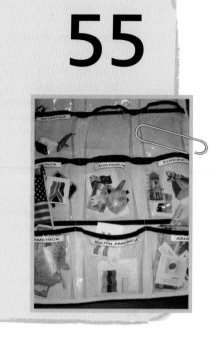

Materials

- Shoe bag, hanging jewelry organizer, or pocket chart
- Objects, cards, or photographs representing key concepts or ideas

Description

A *pocket sort* is an activity that requires students to organize objects or pictures into different categories, thus helping them pay attention to the attributes of the objects or pictures, look for relationships between items, and potentially learn about something abstract (e.g., the alphabet) in a concrete way. Pocket sorts are good alternatives to worksheets or desktop work (especially for students with physical disabilities or motor planning problems), and they often inspire and intrigue students no matter what age they are. In addition, they can be used for many purposes including giving students extra practice, introducing a topic, or assesesing individual learners.

Directions

To create your sort, gather materials from around the classroom or ask other teachers for objects they may have (if you want hard-to-find items, put a list in the staff lounge and let your colleagues help you hunt). Gather enough materials (roughly) to have an equal number of items in each bin or pocket.

Keep items for the activity in a box next to the pocket sort or in any extra pockets in the sorter. Demonstrate the activity before asking students to try it and consider keeping an answer key folded in one of the pockets so learners can check their work.

Give students opportunities to practice sorting on a regular basis and change or add new materials regularly to keep students motivated. For instance, a teacher who created a sort of the continents (see photo inset) kept adding new currency, flags, and souvenirs as students brought them in from family and community members.

Examples

A sixth-grade teacher developed a pocket sort for Wendy, a child with multiple disabilities. The sort consisted of a hanging shoe bag filled with pictures and objects related to the seven continents. Wendy, working with her peers, sorted the items into seven pockets. Some of the items were easy for most of the students (e.g., Beijing Olympics pamphlet for Asia, American flag for North America, miniature pyramid for Africa), but all of the students were stumped by certain items (e.g., a photo and description of the Nile River) and had to search the Internet or use encyclopedias or dictionaries to get more information. The sort helped Wendy participate by allowing her to manipulate objects instead of write on paper. It helped other learners because it made a potentially passive exercise more active and provided plenty of opportunities for discussion among peers and with the teacher.

A kindergarten teacher created a letter sort for all of her students to use during free play. It was particularly helpful for her English language learners and two students with disabilities. Students had fun not only completing the sort but also bringing in new items to add to it. For instance, the letter *T* was represented by a small plastic turtle, a miniature telephone, a plastic number 2, and a man's tie. One of the students brought in a picture of tamales and a table from her doll house.

Keep in Mind

Students need to be able to easily identify the objects or photos in the sort so make sure to choose items with which students are familiar (or you can stick a small label on the objects to avoid confusion altogether). And for students with low vision or for those learners who do not use vision, physical items must be meaningful from a tactile perspective:

> Decisions will need to be made regarding what information can be made meaningful from a tactile perspective. For example, colors, rainbows, extremely large items (airplanes, skyscrapers), and extremely small items (microbes, fleas) will be difficult to adapt for a tactile learner who also has intellectual impairments and limited language skills (Downing, 2005, p. 59)

Reference/ Recommended Reading

Downing, J. (2005). *Teaching literacy to students with significant disabilities.* Thousand Oaks, CA: Corwin Press.

Vendors

Miniatures
http://www.miniatures.com
Miniature everything! Find items for sorts here; categories range from school supplies to appliances to food.

Kaplan

http://www.kaplanco.com/store/trans/productDetailForm.asp?CatID=5%7CLT1020%7C0&CollID =2235

An alphabet sorting tray

Organize.com

http://www.organize.com

Jewelry organizers, shoe bags, and other storage products that will work for sorting activities

Toy Connection

http://toyconnection.com

Lots of little toys that would be useful for sorts

 # Web Sites

kindergarten-lessons.com

http://www.kindergarten-lessons.com/kindergarten-sorting-games.html

An array of sorting games appropriate for small children

Illuminations (Resources for Teaching Math)

http://illuminations.nctm.org/LessonDetail.aspx?ID=L277

A lesson example involving the sorting of polygons

56 Match Games

Materials

- Index cards
- Thick marker

Description

Match games require students to interact in a structured way and assist each other to succeed. They are the perfect antidote to dry and dull drill-and-practice exercises. This activity can be particularly helpful for teaching and reviewing facts, dates, vocabulary, and definitions. Match games get students out of their seats and help even the most struggling learner succeed. If that student cannot find the right answer, the answer may find him or her!

Directions

Begin by making two groups of cards (A and B); each card in one group (A) must have a corresponding card in the other group (B). For instance, you might create one group of questions (A) and one group of answers (B); one group of words (A) and one group of definitions (B); or one group of incomplete sentences (A) and one group of words that complete the sentences (B).

Give each student one index card; then tell the students to walk around the room, talk to other students, and compare their card with the cards of their classmates. Students should also be directed to help each other find their matches.

Once students have found the individual whose card corresponds to their card, they should sit down next to that person and wait for others to find their matches. Once all students have found matches, each pair shares their match with the class. Pairs can simply read their cards to the others or quiz the rest of the class using the information they have learned from their match.

Encourage students to support each other during the game. Remind them that they can give clues to their classmates to help them find matches. You could even demonstrate how learners can give support. Show them, for instance, how to give clues (but not answers) to classmates or how to ask clarifying questions of one another.

Examples

A Spanish teacher had all of her students play match game to introduce the vocabulary for new units. For a unit on clothing, students had to match *falda* to *skirt; zapa* to *shoe;* and *camisa* to *shirt,* for example. Each week, as the new vocabulary was presented, cards from previous weeks were included in the game. So, most students would be finding matches for new words while one or two pairs would get review words from previous weeks.

One teacher used the match game adaptation to showcase the talents of one of her students with autism, Marn, who was interested in trains. During a unit on transportation, Marn created one set of cards that contained concepts, words, and phrases related to trains. On the other set of cards she wrote the corresponding definitions. One card, for instance, had the term *run-through* written on it. The definition of run-through, a train not generally scheduled to pick up or reduce railcars en route, was written on another card. Students had to find matches for terms and phrases that were, in most cases, completely new to them. Students had fun learning the new lingo and were impressed with Marn's expertise in this area. According to the teacher, the game was the first time students in her classroom had to go to Marn to get help and information. This experience changed students' perceptions of their classmate and gave Marn the courage to share more of her specialized knowledge with others. In addition, all students became interested in the activity and were anxious to take a turn designing their own set of cards for the group (Kluth, 2003).

Keep in Mind

To keep students on task once they have found their match, you may want to put related information, trivia, or "brain-buster" questions on the back of the match cards. This way, students can discuss this additional content with their partner while they wait for all other students to pair up.

References/ Recommended Reading

Campbell, L.C., Campbell, B., Dickinson, D. (2003). *Teaching and learning through multiple intelligences* (3rd ed.). Needham Heights, MA: Allyn & Bacon.

Kluth, P. (2010). *"You're going to love this kid!": Teaching students with autism in the inclusive classroom* (2nd ed.). Baltimore: Paul H. Brookes Publishing Co.

Silberman, M. (1996). *Active learning: 101 strategies to teach any subject.* Needham Heights, MA: Allyn & Bacon.

Udvari-Solner, A., & Kluth, P. (2007). *Joyful learning: Active and collaborative learning in inclusive classrooms.* Thousand Oaks, CA: Corwin Press.

Vendor

Office World, Inc.

http://www.officeworld.com

A large selection of index cards, including white, lined, and colored options

Web Site

Kaboose

http://www.kidsdomain.com/brain/read/memorymatchcards.html

Print your own match game cards for elementary learners. Categories include sea life, reptiles, and farm animals.

Loop Games

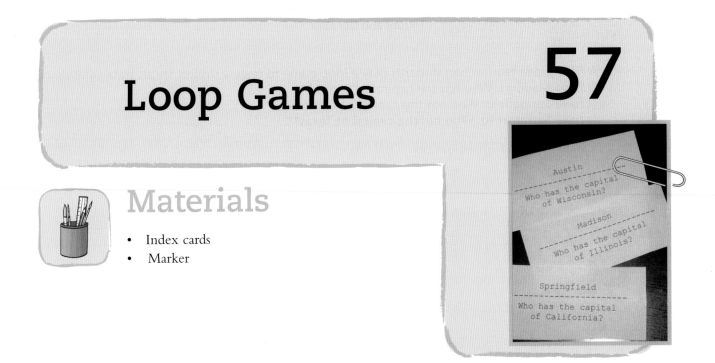

Materials

- Index cards
- Marker

Description

Loop games are a clever way to keep all students attentive and interested and to differentiate for a range of learners (Tilton, 2001). A loop game is a bit like a passing of a baton. One student reads a card, usually with an "I have_____" beginning and a "Who has_____" ending. For example, one person might say, "I have George Washington. Who has the second president of the United States?" and the next person says, "I have John Adams, who has the third president of the United States?" The student who asked the first question should have the answer to the last question on his or her card, thus completing the "loop."

Directions

Hand out one card to each student. Explain the game and watch and listen to see if and how they figure out the sequence.

You can have the loop go around once or you can have students repeat the loop two or three times, perhaps getting faster or more animated each time. Another version is to have students play the game once to get familiar with the content and then collect and redistribute the cards to give them an opportunity to ask and answer a different question while practicing the loop again.

Examples

A first-grade teacher had her students count by fives using a loop game. One student read, "I have 5, who has 5 more than 5?" The student with the 10 then read, "I have 10. Who has 5 more than 10?" and so forth. Ryan, a young man with pervasive developmental disorder, started the game and read his card using a voice output communication device.

A fifth-grade teacher had students play a loop game to review United States state capitals:
"I have Madison. Who has the capital of Illinois?"
"I have Springfield. Who has the capital of California?"
"I have Sacramento. Who has the capital of Texas?"

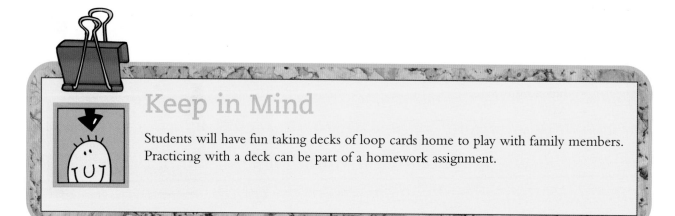

Keep in Mind

Students will have fun taking decks of loop cards home to play with family members. Practicing with a deck can be part of a homework assignment.

References/ Recommended Reading

Kenney, J.M., Hancewicz, E., & Heuer, L. (2005). *Literacy strategies for improving mathematics instruction.* Alexandria, VA: Association for Supervision and Curriculum Development.

Tilton, L. (2001). *Inclusion: A fresh look.* Shorewood, MN: Covington Cove.

Vendors

Loop Writer
http://www.loopwriter.com
A link to purchase software for making loop games as well as dozens of tips for playing games

Mentoring Minds
http://www.mentoringminds.com/motivation-math
Several fun math games including mental math loop games

Staples
http://www.staples.com
A large selection of index cards, including white, lined, and colored cards

Web Site

Super-Gran Puzzle-Maker's Home Page
http://supergran-puzzlemaker.net/T33.htm
Directions for making or downloading your own math loop game

Adapted Board Games

Materials

- Boards and pieces from popular games
- Poster boards
- Markers
- Sticky notes
- Stickers
- Extra pieces from various games (e.g., dice, markers)
- Communication symbols

Description

Most teachers realize that games are motivating and fun for students of any age. They may not understand, however, how much learners can profit from creating their own *adapted board games* or playing teacher-created or teacher-adapted games. Students will surely be excited to engage in this activity and may even surprise the teacher by using their creations outside of the classroom and extending their learning beyond the confines of a particular unit.

Directions

Decide on the objectives, skills, or knowledge you want to teach or reinforce (e.g., adding fractions, speaking in complete sentences, generating adjectives, learning about famous American women). Then, look in your supplies closet for a game you can adapt for this purpose.

Games can be adapted with sticky notes, permanent makers, extra supplies from other games, new cards, or stickers and pictures. Some of the ways games can be adapted include the following:

- Change the rules: Create a different set of rules for all players or just for some.
- Change the format: Draw the game board on a larger piece of poster board or even on a shower curtain to make it easier to see or use for some.
- Make it more accessible: Instead of using a regular pair of dice, use large fuzzy dice (easier to manipulate for some).
- Make it more appealing: Integrate a student's favorite things into the game (e.g., use a Mickey Mouse figurine instead of a colored marker).

Augmentative communication symbols may be used in the construction of the games (e.g., putting a "start" symbol to indicate where markers should be placed) so that learners who use them can better understand the game, their role, and the expectations or directions.

Examples

A first-grade teacher created an adapted Candy Land game to help one of her students work on counting, addition, and subtraction. She created new cards with an addition or subtraction problem on each. If the student drew an addition card, he or she had to figure out the answer and then move forward that number of spaces. If the student drew a subtraction card, he or she had to figure out the answer and move back that number of spaces. The treat cards remained and functioned as they would in a typical game of Candy Land. To respond to the needs of different students, the teacher created two sets of cards: a blue pack, which contained easier questions, and a red pack, which contained more challenging questions. This game adaptation allowed Nathan, a student with significant difficulties in math, to play the game, practice facts, and still be successful.

High school teachers running an after-school board game club created adapted questions to a trivia game for Leslie, a student with cognitive disabilities. Leslie's questions were appropriately challenging and often focused on content the teachers knew she was learning in her classes. Students could then play the game without modifying the rules.

Dixon and Addy (2004), suggest making a three-dimensional game of Snakes and Ladders for students who are dyspraxic. They create drinking straw ladders and rolled-clay snakes on their boards and glue string to the various checkerboard lines on the game to make it easier for students to appreciate the distinction between squares.

References/ Recommended Reading

Dixon, G., & Addy, L.M. (2004). *Making inclusion work for children with dyspraxia: Practical strategies for teachers.* London: Routledge-Falmer.

Moore, L., & White, E. (2000). *Utilizing games and cooperative learning activities in the classroom.* Auburn Hills, MI: Teacher's Discovery.

Vendors

BoardGameDesign.com
http://www.boardgamedesign.com
This unique company specializes in game manufacturing and will make custom pieces for various games. They also make custom games and stock game supplies and components (e.g., blank game boards, blank game boxes, pawns, spinner arrows).

Enabling Devices
http://enablingdevices.com/catalog/toys_for_disabled_children/adapted-games/hungry-hippo
An adapted Hungry Hippo game

Web Sites

Future Reflections (The National Federation of the Blind Magazine for Parents and Teachers of Blind Children)
http://www.nfb.org/Images/nfb/Publications/fr/fr18/fr05sf07.htm
A short newsletter article by Katrilla Martin on adapting games for students who are blind or have low vision

Googol Learning (Math Games to Play at Home)
http://www.googolpower.com/content/articles/math-games-to-play-at-home-adapting-your-favorite-games
A short article by Susan Jarema on creating and adapting card and board games to support math instruction

LoveToKnow Corp. (Board Games for Learning Disabled)
http://boardgames.lovetoknow.com/Board_Games_for_Learning_Disabled
Suggestions for board games for students with learning disabilities

More Ideas

59 "Choose and Learn" Box

Materials

- Any number of toys, activities, print materials, or games
- Box, bin, or basket
- Index cards
- Plastic bags

Description

In an inclusive classroom, there will be times when adaptations and modifications are not practical or possible (especially if creating adaptations requires an on-the-spot response). *"Choose and learn" boxes* (also called other things such as "grab and learn" boxes) are curriculum-related and give paraprofessionals, general educators, and special educators materials to use during times when a learner with disabilities—or any student in the classroom—seems disengaged, bored, or anxious. The boxes may contain several different hands-on items that can be used as a substitute for a planned activity, a filler for times when an activity has not been appropriately planned, or a fidget toy or stay-put support for a learner who needs materials to manipulate during a difficult time period (e.g., a long whole-class discussion).

Although this is a support that is mostly used for students with disabilities, you can create boxes for other purposes as well. Consider creating a "choose and challenge" box filled with tasks for students who need enrichment or have finished their work early. Or, you might make a "choose and create" box for students with extra time who like to spend time crafting, inventing, or developing materials and ideas.

Directions

To create a "choose and learn" box, simply gather a wide range of materials related to your subject area or unit, and design activities that will help your student learn new skills, practice emerging skills, and gain knowledge. After you have gathered the items, place each activity inside a plastic bag and enclose a note card with any directions necessary for doing the activity. As much as possible, these activities should be standards-based and connected to the content being addressed in the classroom.

Examples of activities and materials that can be used in a "choose and learn" box include the following:

- Puzzles
- Math facts or spelling words on a ring

- Card games
- Memory games
- Wipe board and markers
- Pattern blocks and design paper
- Geo boards and rubber bands
- Math manipulatives (e.g., fraction bars, counting bears)
- Books (e.g., photo essays, picture books, content-related comic books)
- Computer games
- Rubber story stamps
- Workbook games (e.g., mazes, word puzzles)
- Books on CD and content-inspired music (e.g., spelling word rap)
- Sorting activities (e.g., things that start with different letters of the alphabet; pictures of liquids, gasses, and solids)
- Letter and number tiles and word tiles

Example

Mr. Fischer, a middle school math teacher, often ended up giving more extensive explanations than he or his students anticipated. J.C., a young man with significant learning disabilities in the classroom, would get very anxious when this occurred. For this reason, Mr. Fischer would often indicate to J.C. that he could get something out of the classroom "choose and learn" box. J.C. would then find a math-related game or puzzle and work at his desk with the chosen materials until it was time to begin the assignment with his cooperative math group. The box included the following materials: fraction bars, calculators, various worksheets, a dry-erase board and mini-chalkboard. brain teaser books, and compact discs of math-related music (e.g., division rap). (Schwarz & Kluth, 2007)

Keep in Mind

These activities and materials should never be the centerpiece of any student's educational program. Rather, "choose and learn" boxes should be used in instructional emergencies to keep learners linked to course content and to prevent periods of frustration and disconnection. In the best cases, watching students work with the different items in the box may inspire ideas for future lessons, curricular adaptations, and learning supports.

References/ Recommended Reading

Schwarz, P., & Kluth, P. (2007). *"You're welcome": 30 innovative ideas for the inclusive classroom.* Portsmouth, NH: Heinemann.

Tilton, L. (1998). *Inclusion: A fresh look.* Shorewood, MN: Covington Cove Publications.

Vendors

Lakeshore Learning Materials
http://www.lakeshorelearning.com/home
Educational materials for every subject area

Oriental Trading
http://www.orientaltrading.com
Already familiar to many teachers, Oriental Trading carries small toys, stickers, and games appropriate for "choose and learn" boxes.

Songs for Teaching
http://www.songsforteaching.com
You will find thousands of songs on this site; you can listen to excerpts and buy CDs about anything from tornadoes to prime numbers to African American history!

Web Site

File Folder Games
http://www.fastq.com/~jbpratt/education/theme/filefolders.html
Go to this site for links to games and activities that can be used across ages and grade levels.

Coloring Book Creations

60

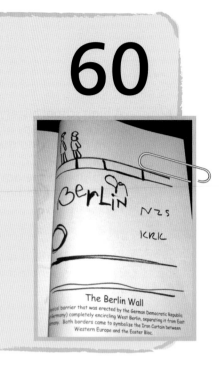

The Berlin Wall

~~~cal barrier that was erected by the German Democratic Republic~~~ ~~~rmany) completely encircling West Berlin, separating it from East~~~ ~~~many. Both borders come to symbolize the Iron Curtain between~~~ Western Europe and the Easter Bloc.

Materials

- Coloring books or coloring pages
- Crayons
- Paper
- Thick, medium, and thin black markers

Description

Coloring is an activity that most small children enjoy. Teachers, therefore, often use it as part of the learning process. A small child might be asked to color "all of the things that are red" or "the things that begin with the letter *B*." Coloring is often part of daily lessons, in fact, it is used in almost every kindergarten and first-grade classroom. As students get older, however, the crayons come out less often and teaching and learning become more serious and less playful.

Students, however, may still enjoy playing with crayons and coloring books after the early primary years. To bring some novelty into the later primary, middle, or high school classroom and to "shake up" your instruction, then, have students move from being consumers of coloring books to creators of them! *Coloring book creations* can be a way to informally review a topic or can even serve as an end-of-unit or end-of-semester assessment.

Directions

Choose some area of content to study that can be illustrated (e.g., explorers, polygons, scenes from the Cold War). This activity can be particularly beneficial when the content chosen is somewhat abstract (e.g., potential energies, hyperbole). Students are then required to have more than a cursory understanding of the material in order to create an appropriate drawing.

Assign either one page of the book to each student to make a class coloring book or ask each student (or each small group of students) to make their own coloring book. Before asking students to create their drawings, pass out coloring books or coloring pages so that they can see the various styles of art and the different ways concepts and ideas are illustrated.

To enhance learning, you can also have students write a short description or explanation on each coloring book page.

When books are completed, they can either be colored by the students themselves, exchanged so that peers can see another interpretation of the materials, "published" at the school or a print shop and distributed to students in other classes or after-school programs, or donated to libraries for distribution in the community.

Examples

A high school history teacher had his students create *The Cold War Coloring Book*. Students worked in groups of three to create 10-page books. Concepts covered in the books ranged from the Domino theory to communism to the Berlin Wall. Students were instructed to create an original drawing for each concept and provide a one- to three-line description or definition at the bottom of each page. Each group was required to bring in three copies of their completed book. Students then traded their books with students in another group and were given time to "read" the other team's book and to color in it as well!

Students in third grade worked as a class to make an endangered species coloring book. They drew simple line drawings of each species and added tips to their books to encourage people to support the different featured animals. The teacher then made several hundred copies and the class gave the books to a local zoo to give away in their education center.

References/ Recommended Reading

Blitz, B. (2001). *Big book of cartooning.* Philadelphia: Running Press Kids.

Clark, G.A., & Zimmerman, E.D. (1987). *Resources for educating artistically talented students.* Syracuse, NY: Syracuse University Press.

Hart, C. (2009). *Humongous book of cartooning.* New York: Random House.

Vendor

Coloringbook.com
http://www.coloringbook.com
This company can create a customized coloring book for your class or for your entire school.

Web sites

Charity Guide (Donate Coloring Books to Hospital Emergency Rooms)
http://charityguide.org/volunteer/fewhours/donate-coloring-books.htm
A short explanation of why hospitals need coloring books donated. Have your students donate their books to a local emergency room and turn a positive educational experience into service learning.

The Coloring Spot
http://thecoloringspot.com
Lots of coloring pages related to various areas of curriculum; students might use these examples to get ideas for their own drawings.

Make Play Dough
http://www.makeplaydough.com/make_your_own_coloring_book-39961.php
A very cute lesson plan for making custom coloring books with and for small children

PhotoshopSupport.com
http://www.photoshopsupport.com/tutorials/jennifer/photo-to-sketch.html
Great tips (from Photoshop pro, Jennifer Apple) on how to turn your own photographs into coloring pages

Literacy

Contents

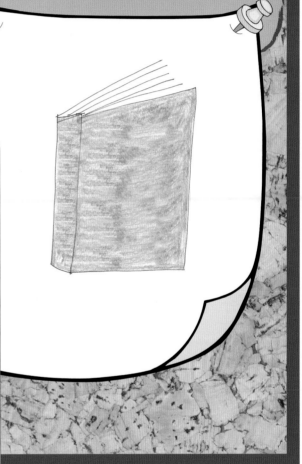

61 Adapted Books

Materials

- Contact paper
- Page protectors
- Binders
- Page tabs
- Index cards
- Paper clips
- Highlighters and Highlighting tape
- Correction fluid
- Communication symbols
- Stickers

Description

Some students will be better equipped to study textbook material or enjoy literature if adaptations are made to these materials (Erickson & Koppenhaver, 2006; Musselwhite & King-DeBaun, 1997). *Adapted books* are simply pieces of literature (Erickson & Koppenhaver, 2006; Musselwhite & King-DeBaun, 1997) or textbooks (Kluth, 2005) that have been modified in some way to increase a student's ability to use, access, or learn from them.

Directions

Decide from what adaptations your student or students could benefit. Create any necessary changes, such as the following:

- Simplifying text
- Enlarging text
- Highlighting key phrases or words
- Adding a personalized glossary
- Adding sticky notes or index cards as reminders
- Adding pictures or taking pictures out
- Adding text or taking text out
- Adding communication symbols
- Translating all or some into another language
- Providing an audio version of the book
- Adding tabs or clips to make sections easier to find
- Adding page "puffers" to make turning pages easier

Examples

In an eighth-grade classroom, five students who were not reading at grade level had their textbooks adapted so they could gain access to the content more easily and study independently. Tabs were added to the pages so these learners could find key sections with ease. A teacher-prepared summary written on a large index card (and at a lower reading level) was clipped to the final page of each chapter. Key words also were covered with highlighting tape.

Zoe, a student with cognitive disabilities and low vision, seemed more interested in literature when her teachers adapted books by making them tactile or interactive in some way. They sometimes added pictures or symbols for Zoe to add or take off (using hook-and-loop tape). Other times they simply pasted materials into the books that Zoe could touch, pull, or trace with a finger. When teachers adapted *Polar Bear, Polar Bear, What Do You Hear* (Martin Jr. & Carle, 1991), for instance, they added cotton balls to the picture of the bear, small pieces of a nylon stocking to the picture of the elephant, and feathers to the picture of the flamingo.

Keep in Mind

Different students will need different adaptations to their books, but once the materials are created, they can be used year after year for other students with similar needs.

References/ Recommended Reading

Erickson, K., & Koppenhaver, D. (2006). *Children with disabilities: Reading and writing the four-blocks way.* Greensboro, NC: Carson-Dellosa.

Kluth, P. (2005). *Rewriting history....and 9 other ways to adapt textbooks.* Retrieved July 26, 2009, from http://www.paulakluth.com/articles/textbookadapt.html

Lindberg, J.A., Ziegler, M.F., & Barczyk, L. (2008). *Common-sense classroom management techniques for working with students with significant disabilities.* Thousand Oaks, CA: Corwin Press.

Martin, Jr., B., & Carle, E. (1991). *Polar bear, polar bear, what do you hear?* New York: Henry Holt & Co.

Musselwhite, C., & King-DeBaun, P. (1997). *Emergent literacy success: Merging technology and whole language for students with disabilities.* Park City, UT: Creative Communicating.

Ohler, J.B. (2007). *Digital storytelling in the classroom: New media pathways to literacy, learning, and creativity.* Thousand Oaks, CA: Corwin Press.

Vendors

Accessible Book Collection
http://www.accessiblebookcollection.org
This web site offers digital versions of high-interest, low-reading-level texts.

Enchanted Learning
http://www.enchantedlearning.com/Home.html
Printable books, picture dictionaries, activities, and visuals are just a few of the resources you will find at enchantedlearning.com. Some materials are free; others are available with a subscription.

Fictionwise
http://www.fictionwise.com
Fictionwise sells e-book titles (fiction and nonfiction) in a variety of formats, such as audio books, and for Adobe Reader, MS Reader, and Palm Reader.

LeveledReader.com
http://www.leveledreader.com
Sets of readers for guided reading programs as well as books that have been individually leveled according to the most up-to-date criteria

Web Sites

AAC Intervention.com
http://www.aacintervention.com
The web site of Julie Maro and Caroline Musselwhite, AAC Intervention.com has many ideas for incorporating Boardmaker symbols into literacy activities and, specifically, into adapted literature selections.

Baltimore City Public Schools
http://www.baltimorecityschools.org/boardmaker/adapted_library.asp
More than 7,000 books adapted using Picture Communication Symbols and Boardmaker for Grades K–6, including suggested questions that connect to a 9-location, 20-location, or 56-location communication topic board

ESL Reading
http://www.eslreading.org
At ESL Reading, teachers will find simplified versions of different texts as well as activities to go along with them.

NYC Department of Education
http://schools.nyc.gov/Offices/District75/Departments/Literacy/AdaptedBooks/default.htm
Adapted books and materials created with Boardmaker picture symbols, Writing with Symbols, and PowerPoint software for students in grades K–6

Personal Word Walls

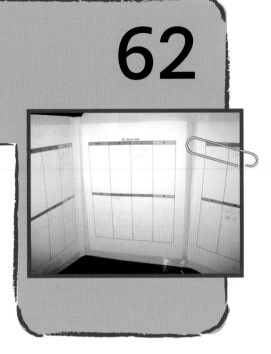

Materials

- 2 manila folders
- Paper
- Stapler or packing tape
- Cookie sheet
- Magnetic words

Description

A classroom word wall is "an interactive, ongoing display…of words and/or parts of words" pulled from meaningful contexts such as class discussions, group viewing of films, and independent reading (Wagstaff, 1999, p. 32). The words may be related to a particular subject, such as science, or tied to a certain unit of study, such as energy. Some teachers even choose to have more than one word wall so that each can address specific purposes.

Word walls can be used in a variety of ways to support vocabulary development. Students may invent cheers and chants for particular words, use the words in games or daily activities, suggest new additions as they read and write, group words for a new purpose, and, of course, use the words as a resource when spelling.

Some students may profit from having a word wall that they can use and manipulate right at their desks. For these students, teachers can create a portable or *personal word wall*. This word wall might be an exact replica of the classroom word wall, or the teacher may add words to a personal word wall that the class is not studying (e.g., words from a communication device), words related to a student's area of interest, or words related to a student's family or home life. A personal word wall allows the teacher to make modifications for a student. For example, if certain words are not critical for the student to learn, these can be omitted on the personal word wall.

To make sure that students get the most from their personal word walls, be sure to remind them to keep them out during all reading and writing tasks.

Directions

To create a personal word wall, simply open up two file folders, put the back of one folder over the top of the second folder, and staple them together so that the student ends up with a standing three-panel "wall" that can be propped up at his or her desk and used as both a writing tool and a mini study carrel to block out distractions.

Then, recreate the categories that you have posted on the classroom wall. If you have categories or walls related to content areas, recreate this on the student's personal wall. If you have an alphabetical word wall, create the personal word wall with one space for each letter. Allow the student to copy the words onto the word wall him- or herself if he or she is able; if not, print the words on the student's word wall for him or her. Or, if a student is somewhat adept at writing, provide a copy of the word wall with some but not all of the words included and leave space for the student to fill in the remainder of the words. You may also add stickers or drawings to help the student read his or her own wall independently.

Example

Ms. Merced, a first-grade teacher, plays a game called Read My Mind with her students. She asks students to number their papers from one to five. Ms. Merced then gives clues about one of the word wall words and has the children write their guess on their paper. "For your first clue," she always states, "It's one of the words on the word wall." She then continues giving clues until, by the fifth clue, all of the students have guessed the word. Michael, a young man with cognitive disabilities, has a difficult time guessing the words, so Ms. Merced has changed his role in the game. Michael studies his portable word wall the night before and chooses two words for Ms. Merced to use in the upcoming game. For his homework assignment, Michael works with his mom to write the clues for these two words. For example, for the word *divide,* some of Michael's clues were the following: "It starts with a *d,*" "It is a math word," and "It rhymes with *ride.*" This homework assignment gives Michael much-needed extra work on reading and spelling skills and allows him to play a valuable role in the classroom activity.

Keep in Mind

Classroom word walls also can be adapted. For example, a picture or symbol can be added to each word on the wall.

References/ Recommended Reading

Lynch, J. (2005). *Making word walls work: A complete, systematic guide with routines, grade-perfect word lists, and reproducible word cards to help all children master high-frequency words.* New York: Scholastic.
Nations, S., & Alonso, M. (2001). *Primary literacy centers: Making reading and writing stick!* Gainesville, FL: Maupin House.

Spann, M.B. (2001). *Scholastic big book of word walls: 100 fresh & fun word walls, easy games, activities, and teaching tips to help kids build key reading, writing, spelling skills and more.* New York: Scholastic.

Wagstaff. (1999). Word walls that work. *Instructor, 110*(5), 32–33.

Vendors

IntaGoal.com
http://www.intagoal.com/teacher-resources/language-arts/portable-word-wall-gr-3-5.html
This site sells an erasable personal word wall. It features alphabet letters A–Z, a prefix and suffix word section, an interesting words section, and an environmental print words section.

Super Duper Publications
http://www.superduperinc.com/products/view.aspx?pid=PWW11
This company offers a great personal word wall that includes 70 magnets that can be written on and wiped clean. The word wall comes with three wet-erase markers.

Web Sites

Bright Hub Inc.
http://www.brighthub.com/education/k-12/articles/7017.aspx
A short and easy-to-follow lesson plan on creating personal word walls, as well as many other plans and tips

Vocabulary.com
http://www.vocabulary.com
A free resource designed to enhance vocabulary mastery and support the development of written/verbal skills; one of the most helpful features is the section of word lists.

63 Picture Directions

Materials

- Pictures, communication symbols, or other graphics
- Computer
- Paper

Description

Directions for tasks, assignments, worksheets, and tests are often very wordy—especially in the higher grades. One way to help a wider range of learners be more independent across these activities is to create picture directions as a replacement for, or as a supplement to, written directions.

Directions

Examine the written directions in your classroom on your assessments and other written work. Determine whether any of your students will need support in reading and understanding them. If you feel that adding graphics will help, consider whether you need to use *picture directions* such as computer-generated images or if using a few small stickers or drawings will be enough. Be aware that no matter what pictures, photos, or symbols you use, you will need to teach your student to read and interpret them.

Examples

In one fourth-grade classroom, students were expected to work without a teacher's aide at a center. In this center, students were supposed to play a probability math game with a partner. The game consisted of 1) making some predictions, 2) shaking a pair of dice 10 times, and 3) recording the results on a large piece of chart paper. The teacher added visual directions for those students with limited reading skills. This allowed Connor, a student with a cognitive disability, to work alongside his peers and follow the directions without needing assistance.

When students in a fifth-grade classroom were getting ready for the science fair, they, along with their teacher, created visual directions for the scientific method. The directions were available in the classroom daily for students to use as a reference.

Schall and McFarland-Whisman (2009) described how Craig, a student with autism, used picture directions to move through the clean-up sequence of activities in his industrial arts class (e.g., PUT YOUR TOOLS IN THE TOOLBOX, PUT YOUR PROJECT IN THE PROJECT BOX). Materials like the picture directions were created to help Craig achieve more independence in the classroom. By using picture supports instead of personal support (i.e., direct cues from a paraprofessional) Craig could achieve more on his own.

References/ Recommended Reading

Cohen, M.J., & Sloan, D.L. (2007). *Visual supports for people with autism: A guide for parents and professionals.* Bethesda, MD: Woodbine House.

Jaime, K., & Knowlton, E. (2007). Visual supports for students with behavior and cognitive challenges. *Intervention in School & Clinic, 42,* 259–270.

Schall, C., & McFarland-Whisman, J. (2009). Meeting transition goals through inclusion. In M. Wehman, M.D. Smith, & C. Schall (Eds.), *Autism & the transition to adulthood* (pp. 95–110). Baltimore: Paul H. Brookes Publishing Co.

Vendors

Attainment Company
http://www.attainmentcompany.com
Boardmaker software and other materials for creating curriculum adaptations

Writing with Symbols
http://www.store.mayer-johnson.com/us/writing-with-symbols.html
This program allows the teacher to type words with the option of having symbols appear with each word.

Web Site

ABC123Kindergarten
http://www.abc123kindergarten.com/boardmaker.html
A great teacher-designed web site that shows several examples of visual supports used for students with unique learning profiles

64 Story Kits

Materials

- Dolls, stuffed toys, or figurines
- Miniatures
- Small props
- Paper bags, shoe boxes, or other small containers

Description

One way to help students plan their writing is to engage them with a *story kit,* a bag or box of items related to a particular text, concept, genre, theme, or even author. A story kit for the popular intermediate-grade novel *Island of the Blue Dolphins* (Dell, 1960), for example, might contain a stuffed dog, a small toy canoe, a rock, some sand or water in a vial, and a dolphin figurine. Student readers and listeners can either participate in creating the kit or use an existing kit to learn about, enrich, or review a story.

The contents of a story kit can give student writers cues about what should be included when they are writing about a story. For example, students who are asked to draft a book review of *Island of the Blue Dolphins* might set the objects from the story kit out in front of them as they write to ensure that they mention each of those important story elements in their summaries. Some students might even sequence the items from the story kit in a particular way, perhaps explaining their choices to a peer or teacher who could take notes on their rationale, before generating text that reflects the order of the items. This combination of visual and verbal cues would provide inexperienced or struggling writers with a good deal of support that students writing without the use of a story kit would not have.

Directions

Skim the story to get ideas of what objects, characters, and ideas could be represented in a story kit. It will probably be easiest to come up with ideas for objects that can be represented (e.g., a story about a circus might prompt you to add miniature animals, a clown toy, and a ticket stub). You may also want to consider how to represent ideas and abstract concepts. A kit for *Romeo and Juliet* could include a heart for love and a band-aid for pain, for example.

To find items for your story kits, look in your own home, in the classroom, inside board games, and in dime and dollar stores. Perhaps the easiest way to find materials for several kits is to create a handout with a short description and photo of a sample story kit and a list of the stories and books for which you are trying to create kits. Post this list in your staff lounge or send the list home to families, and the toys, trinkets, and odds and ends will come pouring in.

Example

A first-grade teacher asked her students to help construct story kits that could be used by all learners in the classroom, but especially one child with Down syndrome who needed help understanding abstract concepts. One story kit that the class spent weeks assembling and modifying was for fairy tales, a theme the class had explored across different areas of the curriculum. The kit contained finger puppets of a princess, a frog, three bears, a wolf, and a grandma; a "magic" wand; a plastic bean stalk; and a red cape. Students then used the kit as the catalyst for writing their own fairytales. Each child chose an item from the kit and wrote a story that was in some way related to that item. One student who chose the red cape developed a story about a flying princess who only had her special powers when she remembered to accessorize her cape with matching shoes or a matching bag (Kluth & Chandler-Olcott, 2008)!

Keep in Mind

Students can help to create the kits and might even be assigned to do so. In fact, you could assign a small group of learners to create a kit for each story or novel the class reads.

References/ Recommended Reading

Dell, S. (1960). *Island of the blue dolphins.* New York: Yearling.

Kluth, P. (2008). "It was always the pictures…": Creating visual literacy supports for students with autism. In N. Frey & D. Fisher (Eds.), *Teaching visual literacy.* Thousand Oaks, CA: Corwin Press.

Kluth, P., & Chandler-Olcott, K. (2008). *"A land we can share": Teaching literacy to students with autism.* Baltimore: Paul H. Brookes Publishing Co.

McGee, L.M., & Morrow, L.M. (2005). *Teaching literacy in kindergarten.* New York: Guilford Press.

Vendors

Cambium Learning Web Store—ReadyMade Story Kits
http://store.cambiumlearning.com/ProgramPage.aspx?parentId=074003436
Thematic units that include printed storybooks and companion interactive storybooks (to be viewed on the computer)

Environments
http://www.eichild.com/moreinfo.cfm?Category=88&Product_ID=5699
Precut felt story kits that go along with popular stories (e.g., Billy Goats Gruff, Three Little Pigs).

Lake Shore Learning
http://www.lakeshorelearning.com
Dolls and props related to popular children's literature selections

Web Sites

Peachtree Publishers' Story Kits
http://peachtree-online.com/storykits.aspx
Story kit ideas for several story books; includes suggestions for props, facts about story elements, songs, and lesson plans/curriculum guides

Storytelling Web Sites and Resources
http://www.courses.unt.edu/efiga/STORYTELLING/StorytellingWebsites.htm
Dozens of links to storytelling web sites with accompanying reviews on many of them

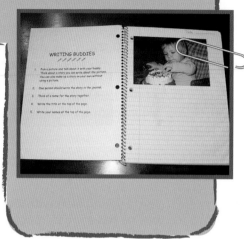

Collaborative Writing Notebook

65

Materials

- Notebook or blank book
- Photographs or magazine photos
- Glue sticks

Description

The *collaborative writing notebook* is a tool that teachers can use to support students who are unable to work independently during writing workshop or journal exercises. Typically, the student with a disability chooses photos or pictures from magazines to use as writing prompts and glues them into a spiral notebook. He or she then invites a peer to write with him or her during workshop or free writing time. Using the collaborative writing notebook as a prompt, the two students then work together to create a poem, story, or essay. To ensure that the students talk about ideas together and remember key components of writing, simple age-appropriate directions are glued right onto the front cover of the notebook.

Directions

Open the front cover of the notebook and paste peer-tutoring directions inside. For instance, the following directions were used for fifth-grade students:

1. Pick a picture and talk about it with your buddy. Think about a story you can write about the picture. You also can make up a story on your own without using a picture.
2. One person should write the story in the journal.
3. Think of a title for the story together.
4. Write the title at the top of the page.
5. Write your names at the top of the page.

On the inside of the back cover of the notebook, you may want to place a tutor sign-up sheet so that the individual can check off names daily and determine who will be his or her next writing partner.

You can add photographs or magazine pictures to the pages if your student cannot select topics on his or her own. However, most individuals—even those with the most significant disabilities—should be able to at least point to favorite pictures from a group of two, three, or four pictures and, therefore, select possible writing topics.

In her book, *"A Land We Can Share": Teaching Literacy to Students with Autism* (2008), Paula and her colleague, Kelly Chandler-Olcott, point out that scribing can be used as a starting point to move learners with disabilities into more opportunities for independent writing. They suggest that teachers who enlist peers to act as scribes for students with disabilities try to fade the level of the scribe's support over time as the students with disabilities gain more control as writers. For example, the teacher may begin by having peers scribe complete stories for students with disabilities. When students' texts get longer and they appear to compose them orally with greater comfort, the peer can scribe just the topic sentences for each paragraph, leaving blank spaces between the paragraphs to cue students about how much text they might include to support those topic sentences. Eventually, the peer might scribe only an outline or just a few key words to serve as a reminder to students as they write independently.

Example

Joe, a young man with Down syndrome, is only able to write a handful of words on his own, but he has a great imagination and the ability to tell elaborate stories. Working with different peer partners and using the collaborative writing notebook, Joe is able to "write" complex stories. His teachers use the notebook as a tool for tracking Joe's progress, assessing his work, and even evaluating the writing fluency of the peer partner. When Joe's special education teacher comes into the classroom during writing workshop, she often asks Joe and his writing partner to choose a story to edit. Together, the students choose a story and work with the teacher to elaborate on ideas, add rich details, and edit for spelling and grammar.

Keep in Mind

Students will need to be taught how to use the notebook; therefore, several weeks in the beginning of the year will need to be dedicated to coaching both participants on how to write as a team.

References/ Recommended Reading

Kalkowski, P. (2001). *Peer and cross age tutoring. Northwest Regional Educational Laboratory.* Retrieved July 27, 2009, from http://www.nwrel.org/scpd/sirs/9/c018.html

Kluth, P., & Chandler-Olcott, K. (2008). *"A land we can share": Teaching literacy to students with autism.* Baltimore: Paul H. Brookes Publishing Co.

Stenhoff, D., & Lignugaris/Kraft, B. (2007). A review of the effects of peer tutoring on students with mild disabilities in secondary settings. *Exceptional Children, 74,* 8–31.

Wiseman, A.M. (2003). Collaboration, initiation, and rejection: The social construction of stories in a kindergarten class. *Reading Teacher, 56*(8), 802–10.

Vendors

Creations by You
http://www.creationsbyyou.com
With this product, young authors write and illustrate a story, send it in to be bound, and receive back a published book they created.

Education 4 Kids
http://edushop.edu4kids.com/product_info.php?s=ghop&products_id=24177
Blank books that work perfectly for student-created journals, dictionaries, and reports

Teacher's Paradise
http://www.teachersparadise.com/c/product_info.php/products_id/3211
Blank books for young authors

Web Sites

Big Universe
http://www.biguniverse.com
A site that allows users to write their own books online

Kids Space
http://storytrain.kids-space.org
A place for kids to post their own stories and read stories written by children around the world

66 Writing Tool Box

Materials

- Pencils
- Markers
- Rubber stamps
- Crayons
- Paintbrushes
- Chalk
- Vibrating pens
- Novelty pens
- Textured pens
- Label maker
- Letter or word magnets
- Chalkboard
- Dry erase board
- Magnetic board
- Paper with raised lines
- Index cards
- Cardboard
- Note pads
- Magazines
- Glue sticks
- Stickers
- Sticky notes
- Etch-a-sketch
- Correction fluid
- Stencils

Description

One way to encourage writing fluency is to use a wide range of materials and allow the learner to choose how he or she would like to complete writing tasks. Some students struggle with using a pencil but can write legibly with a vibrating pen. Some like the feeling of a roller pen or marker. Others may need even more support because of motor problems and may, therefore, need to supplement their writing with a *writing tool box* that could include stamps, stickers, labels, stencils, and magnets. Writing surface choices also can be included in the box.

Directions

Stock your box with any of the suggested materials. Be sure to include any adaptations your student needs for written work (e.g., hand splint, pencil grip). Make sure the box is available to the learner any time he or she needs to write, draw, or mark written materials. To find items for the box, consult with your speech-language and occupational therapists.

Examples

Teddy, a young man with Asperger syndrome, often was much more willing to write longer passages when he wrote with colored makers or when he could use colorful paper.

Rylee did higher quality work when he wrote on a mini-chalkboard instead of on notepaper or the computer.

Keep in Mind

If students work in several different environments (e.g., students in high school), be sure they have a writing box in each one of the classrooms they visit.

References/ Recommended Reading

Downing, J.E. (2005). *Teaching literacy to students with significant disabilities: Strategies for the K–12 inclusive classroom.* Thousand Oaks, CA: Corwin Press.

Erickson, K., & Koppenhaver, D. (1995). Developing a literacy program for children with severe disabilities. *The Reading Teacher, 48,* 676–687.

Koppenhaver, D., Spadorcia, S., & Erickson, K. (1998). How do we provide inclusive early literacy instruction for children with disabilities? In S. Neuman & K. Roskos (Eds.), *Children achieving: Best practices in early literacy* (pp. 77–97). Newark, DE: International Reading Association.

Vendors

Mister Art
http://www.misterart.com
A huge variety of art supplies, writing tools, and crafting materials

Spray Paint Stencils
http://www.spraypaintstencils.com
A large number of free stencils and directions on how to create them

The Pencil Grip
http://www.thepencilgrip.com
A family company offering pencil grips and related office supplies

Web Sites

Occupational Therapy for Kids—Handwriting
http://www.otforkids-handwriting.blogspot.com
This blog by an occupational therapist provides activities that help improve students' handwriting.

School-OT.com—Jennifer's OT Resources
http://www.school-ot.com
Another quality web site created by an occupational therapist that is full of great tips and contains an entire section on recommended fine motor tools

Word
Attack Pack

67

Materials

- Container
- Materials that will help students learn words and hone decoding skills, including the following:
  - Word cards and tiles
  - Game pieces
  - Plastic letters
  - Letter stamps—upper- and lowercase
  - Vowel pattern cards—*cvc, vcv*—for both long and short vowel patterns
  - Consonant digraph and consonant blend cards
  - Prefix and suffix cards
  - Compound word cards
  - Punctuation cards

- Word search books
- File folder games
- Dice featuring different vowel patterns or blends
- Magnets labeled with syllables, consonant blends, and vowel patterns
- Word lists to study or create

Description

Word attack skills give individuals the ability to convert graphic symbols into intelligible language. Examples of word attack skills are as follows:

- Seeing the component parts of words
- Blending those parts into new words
- Recognizing syllable patterns
- Recognizing symbols for consonant sounds
- Recognizing symbols for vowel sounds
- Recognizing capital letters (uppercase) and knowing when to use them
- Recognizing punctuation and how it affects reading for meaning and expression
- Recognizing the use of space to mark word breaks and paragraphs

A *word attack pack* is simply a collection of games and activities that students can use during free time, centers, or even at home to practice these skills. You can make the box available for any learner or you can offer the activities only to certain students who need extra support. Boxes also can be made for families and activities can be assigned as homework.

Directions

Gather games, tools, books, and worksheets that will help struggling learners gain new skills and refine acquired ones. Depending on how many materials are in your pack, you may need to put different activities into individual plastic bags. Place an index card in each bag with directions on how to use the materials. In some cases, it may even be helpful to include a checklist or data-collection tool in the box so you (or the student) can track their performance and progress (e.g., "I matched ___ letters correctly today").

Examples

In a third-grade school classroom, the teacher was reviewing prefixes and suffixes with her students. She made dice using small pieces of cardboard and wrote different prefixes and suffixes on one die and root words on another. The students had to roll the dice and write down as many word combinations as they could in 2 minutes. Then the teacher placed the students in small groups and asked them to think of other, similar activities that they could use to learn about prefixes and suffixes. Each group developed one activity, introduced it to peers, and put it in a whole-class word attack pack.

Price, a student with learning disabilities, needed extra practice with decoding. Ms. Govak, his teacher, made him a word attack pack to use at home, allowing Price to play word attack games for 20 minutes as an alternative to completing all of the required homework. Because Price loved anything related to paleontology, Ms. Govak included plenty of materials—including word finds and word sorts—using the letters from different dinosaur names.

Reference/ Recommended Reading

Walpole, S., & McKenna, M.C. (2004). *The literacy coach's handbook: A guide to research-based practice.* New York: Guilford Press.

Vendors

ClassroomWordGames.com
http://www.classroomwordgames.com
For a small fee, teachers can download software to create word searches, crossword puzzles, and other teaching tools.

Wholesale Board Games
http://www.wholesaleboardgames.com
Popular word games (e.g., Apples to Apples, Boggle, Scrabble) at wholesale prices

Web Sites

Merriam-Webster
http://www.merriam-webster.com
Tools and resources for students and teachers, as well as daily word challenges and a host of word games

Readinga-z.com
http://www.readinga-z.com/more/reading_strat.html
An array of resources related to reading, including a list of word attack strategies

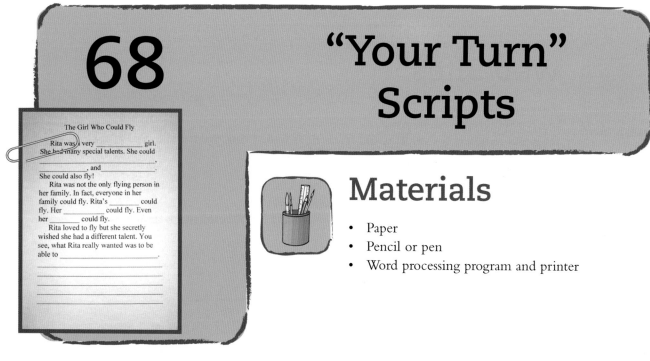

68

"Your Turn" Scripts

Materials

- Paper
- Pencil or pen
- Word processing program and printer

Description

Any seasoned teacher of writing has heard, "I can't think of anything to write" hundreds of times, sometimes just in one day. For some learners with disabilities, getting started on any piece of work is a challenge, but starting a story, poem, speech, letter, or paper in addition to doing the research and planning that accompanies the task of writing is overwhelming.

One way to make the task easier and help students learn the requirements of different genres is to provide a template for writing called a *"your-turn" script* with blank spaces and lines and, in some cases, ideas or content partially developed. Not only does the use of such a tool help students learn the flow or cadence of certain types of writing but also it can provide emerging writers with an opportunity to focus on content or creativity instead of on form.

Directions

After deciding how much support your student needs, create a "your turn" script using pen and paper or any word processing program. Some students may need only a title suggestion or a line to start each paragraph. Others will require that the teacher develop most of the content and provide a few lines here and there for the student to fill in original word choices, a single phrase, or a short sentence. If you have a student who needs a lot of support, you can even add options for word choices, making the learner responsible only for circling or highlighting his or her choices.

Examples

June Downing (2005) writes of a student, Joannie, who profited both from choice activities and from using a form of a "your turn" script during writing exercises. This learner, who, prior to being included in a first-grade classroom, had been in a room for students labeled as "trainably mentally retarded," made gains when she was given materials that allowed her to construct text and participate in typical classroom activities:

When asked to write in her journal, she was given choices of pictures from which to select. She tended to select topics around her classmates, in particular, her friend, Monica. Initially starting with pictures and then fading to word cards alone, Joannie was able to complete sentences by using index cards placed sequentially in separate boxes following the sentence pattern of "Monica is _____." Joannie seemed to take great delight in choosing the adjectives (a choice of three) to complete the sentence, which were then read to her and written in her journal. She held a pencil but used the word cards to put in the sequential boxes to form her sentences about her friend. (p. 68)

Once a week, Mr. King, an earth science teacher, asks all of his students to write two things they learned on an index card and hand it in at end of the class period. Haley, a young woman with multiple disabilities, works with a peer scribe to fill in a few blanks on her card, which is formatted as a "your turn" script (e.g., One thing I learned today is _____ ").

Reference/ Recommended Reading

Downing, J. (2005). *Teaching communication skills to students with severe disabilities* (2nd ed.). Baltimore: Paul H. Brookes Publishing Co.

Vendor

Mad Libs

http://www.madlibs.com

A site from the makers of Mad Libs game books. Not only can you buy Mad Libs products on this site, but you can engage in interactive Mad-Libs-style writing games. If you do want to purchase Mad Libs, you can choose from dozens of options including Star Wars, U.S. presidents, and family tree tablets.

Web Sites

The Fill-In-The-Blank-Story-Generator

http://www.worsleyschool.net/socialarts/generate/astory.html

Part of a Canadian school's web site, this tool is an amusing and somewhat different take on fill-in-the-blank stories. Instead of asking the writer to generate his or her own words, the site features drop-down options for phrases or words at various points in the story. The web site boasts that there are "exactly 9,442,156,179,456,000,000 different possible stories that can be made."

National Geograpic Kids

http://kids.nationalgeographic.com/Games/MoreGames

This link directs you to the Funny Fill-In Game on the National Geographic Kids web site. Here, you will find stories appropriate for elementary school students and early middle school students.

What's Your Story?

http://www.storyfever.com

A blog on writing prompts that integrated language arts (ILA), English, and writing teachers may find useful

69 Comprehension Sticky Notes

Materials

- Sticky notes of various sizes
- Pens and pencils for writing

Description

Comprehension sticky notes are comments that a student attaches to a passage, chapter, or book. They are created as the student reads and are typically reviewed when the reading is completed.

Many students who do not pause to make sense of, record ideas about, and question what they are reading struggle to focus on the text and often do not "store" what they are reading. Comprehension sticky notes can help those students slow down, consider what they are reading, and connect it to their own life experiences.

Directions

Give students a certain number of sticky notes to use during the reading of a story or passage and instruct them to record thoughts and impressions and place notes at key points in the text (Harvey, & Goudvis, 2007; Johnson, 2006) that the students can refer to later. These four types of note-taking strategies are some of the most common:

- *Summaries:* Write down what just happened (e.g., "Troy climbed the tree").
- *Predictions:* Write down what you think is coming next (e.g., "Dorothy will find the wizard!").
- *Questions:* Write down what you are wondering (e.g., "Why doesn't Jo show her mother the letter?" "Why do they keep mentioning swans?").
- *Connections:* Write down some link between you and the text, the text and another text, the text and other media, or the text and the world (e.g., "This reminds me of visiting my own grandmother; my grandmother also is strict but shows love through her cooking").

Examples

In an eighth-grade classroom, all students use comprehension sticky notes to summarize textbook sections. After reading certain sections independently and then completing their comprehension sticky notes, students work with a peer partner to discuss their summaries and create a question about what they have read so far.

Students in a 10th-grade classroom used comprehension sticky notes to mark examples of symbolism in their reading selections. When they found an example, they pasted a note near the passage and jotted down the symbol and what it might represent.

Keep in Mind

There are many novel ways to use comprehension sticky notes, including the following:

- Write the sequence of the story on sticky notes and ask the student to put the sequence together to retell the story.
- Have students leave sticky notes of a certain color on the passages that they do not understand. Have the students form groups to compare their work and ask and answer questions.
- After each page or section, have students draw a picture of what they just read on a sticky note. At the end of the passage, have them put the notes in order and share their interpretation with a peer.

References/ Recommended Reading

Fiene, J., & McMahon, S. (2007, February). Assessing comprehension: A classroom-based process. *The Reading Teacher, 60*(5), 406–417.

Harvey, S., & Goudvis, A. (2007). *Strategies that work: Teaching comprehension to enhance understanding* (2nd ed.). Portland, ME: Stenhouse Publishers.

Jonson, K.F. (2006). *60 strategies for improving reading comprehension in grades K–8.* Thousand Oaks, CA: Corwin Press.

Vendor

3M & Post-It Notes
http://www.3m.com/us/office/postit
3M is the home of the Post-It note and the Post-It note pen (great for students with organizational problems).

Web Site

Sticky-Notes.net
http://www.sticky-notes.net
Electronic sticky notes for students who prefer to work on the computer

Study Support Sentence Factories

70

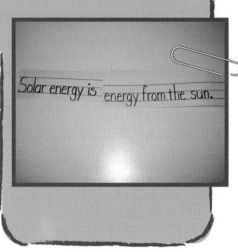

Materials

- Sentence strips
- Thick marker
- Small pieces of comb-style binding

Description

It takes only minutes to create a sentence factory but students can have fun flipping through them and adding on to them all year long. *Study support sentence factories* are essentially a bound stack of sentence strips with one strip being longer than all of the others and containing a complete sentence and the remaining strips cut to fit over the beginning or ending of the sentence. These remaining strips must fit in the sentence and provide a new fact or learning about a given content area.

This activity can be used two ways in a classroom; students can use sentence factories to practice their independent reading and to learn key facts about units of study. Or students can create sentence factories to learn about parts of speech and to research information about any content area including science, social studies, language arts, math, art, physical education, or music.

Directions

On a sentence strip that is approximately 1–2 feet long, write a sentence that, perhaps, is the most important fact you are trying to teach about a specific lesson or unit. Then consider other facts that you could teach using the sentence factory and create either a stack of choices for the subject of the sentence that all create new facts or a stack of choices for the predicate that all create new facts.

Finish by attaching it all together with comb-style binding. Give students opportunities to read sentence factories, to suggest additions to them, or to look up supporting details for the facts provided.

Examples

Ms. Looney, a fourth-grade teacher, made a sentence factory to share with students for a unit on energy. The subject for all of the sentences in her factory was "Solar energy is" and some of the options she created to complete her sentence included "Solar energy is from

the sun"; "Solar energy is renewable"; and "Solar energy is an alternative to fossil fuels."
A few students with learning disabilities took the sentence factory home and read it with
their parents as part of their homework for the unit.

A third grade teacher had students create "Voting is" sentence factories for a unit on elections. Options created by students included "Voting is a right."; "Voting is a privilege";
"Voting is illegal unless you are 18." Students illustrated the factories and took them home
to encourage their parents to vote in upcoming local elections.

Vendors

Augmentative Resources, Inc.
http://www.augresources.com/vindex.html?cat30.htm
If you don't have time to create your own factory, you can order a product called Literacy Flip
Strips from this site to give students opportunities to "write" and read their own sentences.

Full Blast Productions
http://fullblastproductions.mybisi.com
Full Blast makes "factories" (or *flip books* as they call them) with shape, holiday, and compound
word themes.

Intelli-Tunes by Ron Brown
http://www.intelli-tunes.com/music-categories/cdrom-flip-books/flip-books-demo.php
Sentence factory-type books to print on a CD-ROM

Lakeshore Learning
http://www.lakeshorelearning.com/seo
For a tool that allows students to move beyond single sentences, check out the Build-A-Paragraph
Flip Book. It gives students the elements and inspiration needed to write complete paragraphs and
stories.

Web Site

Kids' Wings
http://suzyred.com/flip.html
Several illustrated examples of sentence factories

Mathematics

Contents

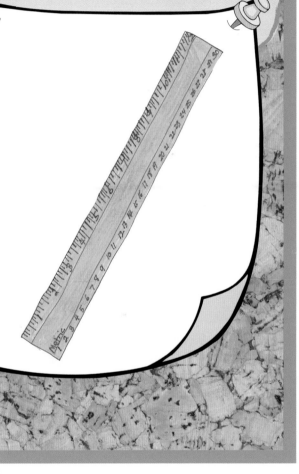

71

Math Helper

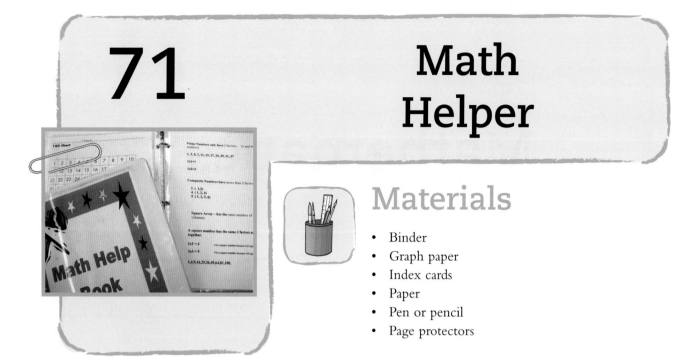

Materials

- Binder
- Graph paper
- Index cards
- Paper
- Pen or pencil
- Page protectors

Description

The *math helper* is a binder filled with math reference materials to help a student during class and assessments and with homework. Students' IEPs often state that they can use visual aids or lists of definitions to complete their work, which makes this an appropriate tool for them to use when completing math assignments. Each year the teacher can add more pages with additional information.

Directions

Personalize the binder for each student. Sample pages in a math binder might include the following:

- Number charts (1–100, counting by 2s, 5s, 10s)
- Addition/subtraction charts (1–100 so that students can use the chart in place of math manipulatives)
- Addition/subtraction template for two- to three-digit numbers, with regrouping
- Place value chart
- Multiplication chart
- Common formulas
- Vocabulary words with definitions
- Conversion charts
- Money-value charts
- Key words/phrases found in word problems
- Lists of words/phrases commonly found in word problems

As students need new information, additional pages can be added to the binder.

Example

Two students with learning disabilities in a fifth-grade classroom use their math helper for classwork and during assessments (including standardized tests). One page contains key words found in math problems, which helps the students remember which method to use when solving a problem. Another page is filled with formulas needed to solve math problems. The math helper puts necessary information right at the students' fingertips and eliminates the need for them to page through their math book or larger reference guides.

Keep in Mind

Math binders should be individualized. Some students will or will not require as many pages of information as others.

Reference/ Recommended Reading

Brunsting, J.R., & Walsh, T. (2007). *Math tools, grades 3–12: 64 ways to differentiate instruction and increase student engagement.* Thousand Oaks, CA: Corwin Press.

Vendors

BnB Home School Store
http://www.bnbhomeschoolstore.com/webstore/pc/Math-Placemats-c43.htm
This vendor sells math-themed laminated placements.

K–3 Teacher Resources
http://www.k-3teacherresources.com/multiplication_table.html
A variety of tables, grids, games, and activities available for an annual subscription fee

Web Sites

Calculate Me
http://calculateme.com
Tools for dozens of calculations and conversions

Free Math Help
http://www.freemathhelp.com
A variety of math help resources, including math lessons, math games, and a math help message board

Math Blog
http://math-blog.com/2008/09/20/13-useful-math-cheat-sheets
Math "cheat sheets," including several for algebra, calculus, and even probability theory

Multiplication.com
http://www.multiplication.com
Techniques, tips, and secrets used by master teachers

Tactile Numbers

72

Materials

- Sandpaper sheets
- Yarn
- Pipecleaners
- Cardstock, cardboard, or manila folders
- Colored glue

Description

Many students with poor fine motor skills or dysgraphia resist writing tasks. A creative way to motivate them to write while giving them a connection between the movement involved in forming numbers and the shape of those numbers is to use *tactile numbers*.

Students can run their hands along the numbers, put a tactile number under paper and do a "rubbing" of it, or use the tactile numbers as a model for writing their own numbers. Another way to use the numbers is to blindfold learners and have them feel a number and guess what it is (Dixon & Addy, 2004). Students can even play this game with one another, competing to see who can identify numbers faster or who can identify the most in a row.

Directions

Start with a stack of sandpaper sheets. Using 10- or 12-inch stencils, trace each number on the sandpaper and cut it out. Numbers can then be glued to squares of cardboard or any other sturdy material.

Colored glue can also be used to outline or create tactile numbers. Simply draw the numbers on cardboard squares and then squeeze the glue on to the squares, creating thick lines and using generous amounts of glue. Let the glue dry for several hours.

Other materials that may be used include hook-and loop-tape, yarn, or pipe cleaners.

Keep in Mind

Colored glue also can be used to teach spatial awareness and writing within the lines on writing paper. Simply highlight the lines on the writing paper using colored glue; when the student starts to write outside the lines, his or her pencil will hit the glue to remind him or her to write smaller.

Reference/ Recommended Reading

Dixon, G., & Addy, L.M. (2004). *Making inclusion work for children with dyspraxia: Practical strategies for teachers.* London: Routledge-Falmer.

Vendors

Nasco
http://www.enasco.com/specialeducation
Tactile numbers and sandpaper numbers

Sense Toys
http://www.sensetoys.com/N4N4B0325751_categoryid;5VEMYAGHAJ
Tactile numbers 1–30

Web Site

eHow (How to Use Montessori Tactile Numbers)
http://www.ehow.com/how_4509971_use-montessori-tactile-numbers.html
Short lesson plan idea on using tactile numbers with young children

Manipulatives Box

73

Materials

- File folder
- Laminated numbers
- Number tiles
- Number puzzles
- Large-number calculator
- Coins (penny, nickel, dime, quarter)
- Number lines
- Base ten blocks
- Attribute blocks
- Counting beads, shapes, and toys
- Plastic or sandpaper numbers
- Math puzzles
- Tangram pieces
- Geoboards
- Box or tray
- Spinners
- Dice
- Legos
- Isometric dot paper
- Graph paper
- Geometric shapes of different colors and sizes

Description

Manipulatives are concrete objects that commonly are used in teaching mathematics. Every math curriculum comes with a set of math manipulatives that can be used with the entire class. Some students, however, will require manipulatives not commonly found in standard sets. One student, for instance, loved dinosaurs, so his teacher found a set of plastic Tyrannosaurus Rex toys and let him use them for counting, adding, and subtracting during math lessons. Although any student may benefit from special materials for any given lesson, students with disabilities, in particular, may need manipulatives (both commercial and teacher-created) to engage in daily lessons and understand abstract concepts.

Many different manipulatives are commercially available (see materials list and vendors for this adaptation), but it is also possible to make manipulatives for almost any purpose using materials you have around the classroom and the home (e.g., craft sticks, beans, straws, pennies, egg cartons, baby food jars, buttons). An excellent way to store and present them is to use a *manipulatives box*.

Directions

Give students time to explore the manipulatives you assign. Then, talk with them about why and how manipulatives will help them learn. You will also need to set ground rules for using the manipulatives. Talk to your students not just about using the manipulatives but also about practicing with them independently, sharing them, and even storing them.

Examples

Since it is difficult for Wylan, a student with cognitive disabilities, to generalize what he learns, his teacher gives him real coins and bills to work with in math class when other students are using play money.

Reggie, a first-grader with autism, uses toy cars from a manipulatives box when his class studies sets, subsets, and addition. Cars are Reggie's special fascination; therefore, he is most motivated when he can use these materials as part of the daily lesson.

While exploring and learning about edges, vertices, faces, or different shapes, Ryan, a student with cognitive disabilities, uses a set of wooden geometric shapes (e.g., sphere, cube, rectangular prism, cone) kept in a manipulatives box to complete his class work. He also takes these materials home so his parents can easily see what and how he is learning new math concepts and can help him more easily with his homework assignments.

In his idea-packed book, *Differentiating Math Instruction,* Bender (2005) shares one teacher's idea for using craft sticks to represent multiplication. In teaching the threes times tables, students use three sticks to make triangles on their desks. Then they count the sides (three). They are then prompted to say, "One triangle with three sides equals three sticks," and then shorten it to "One times three equals three." They continue by adding more triangles and then counting the sides. Students can tackle 4s by building squares, 5s by building stars, and 6s by building hexagons.

Keep in Mind

Just giving students access to manipulatives will not necessarily help them to learn new skills and competencies. Manipulatives should be carefully chosen for different activities. In addition, teachers must be sure to clearly explain (sometimes several times) the relationship between the abstract concept and the math manipulative. Finally, teachers need to carefully observe students and assess their understanding so it can be determined when and how to move from concrete to abstract, when to provide a different type of scaffolding or support, and when to provide more explicit teaching.

References/ Recommended Reading

Bender, W.N. (2005). *Differentiating math instruction: Strategies that work for K–8 classrooms!* Thousand Oaks, CA: Corwin Press.

Moyer, P.S., & Jones, M.G. (2004). Controlling choice: Teachers, students, and manipulatives in mathematics classrooms. *School Science and Mathematics, 104*(1), 16–31.

Moyer-Packenham, P. S. (2005). Using virtual manipulatives to investigate patterns and generate rules in algebra. *Teaching Children Mathematics, 11*(8), 437–444.

Reesnik, C. (2003). *40 easy-to-make math manipulatives.* Jefferson City, MO: Scholastic.

Vendor

Learning Things
http://www.learningthings.com/items.asp?Cc=0113
Hundreds of math manipulatives

Web Sites

Math Playground
http://www.mathplayground.com
Several "virtual" math manipulatives ranging from interactive fraction bars to geoboards to control with a mouse

National Library of Virtual Mathematics
http://nlvm.usu.edu/en/nav/vlibrary.html
Online activities using virtual manipulatives for K–12 students

suite101.com (Math manipulatives for students in special education)
http://specialneedseducation.suite101.com/article.cfm/math_manipulatives
An article by Elizabeth Scott on using math manipulatives

74

Math in Sight

Materials

- Floor tape
- Markers
- Poster board
- Jars
- Beans, marbles, or little toys
- Craft sticks
- Index cards

Description

"Seeing is believing" is a common adage. For many learners who struggle with math learning, seeing is not only believing but understanding, as well! If you want students to understand and gain a working knowledge of concepts such as *mile, million,* or *quart,* it is best to use *math-in-sight* strategies; that is, to illustrate the concepts visually and three-dimensionally, if possible. Math-in-sight strategies also can be used to reinforce concepts and ideas. For instance, numbers can be added around a clock face to help students learn to read the minute hand more accurately, or the classroom schedule can be broken down into thirds and labeled in this manner.

Directions

Search your curriculum for concepts you will be expected to teach during any given period of time. Look for ideas that can be represented visually, and pay particular attention to those that can be illustrated in three dimensions. Consider, at least, the following:

- Measurements of length (e.g., inch, foot, centimeter, meter)
- Measurements of volume (e.g., quart, gallon, liter)
- Measurements of space (e.g., square feet)
- Quantities (e.g., hundred, thousand, five hundred thousand, million, billion)

You can create these models yourself, or you can have students create models with you as part of a lesson or unit.

Examples

A middle school team of teachers asked students to estimate how many grains of salt equaled "a billion." After reading and discussing guesses, they worked with students to estimate grains in small packets, then in shakers, and then in larger containers. Finally, they filled a bathtub-sized container on the playground with salt to illustrate what a billion grains looked like.

When studying tenement housing (and to teach the concept of square feet), Ms. Munoz, a fifth-grade teacher, sectioned the classroom into three areas of about 325 square feet each (the typical size of a tenement house in New York City).

Months before teaching a unit on length and the metric system, Mr. Gordie, a fourth-grade teacher, put colored tape on the floor of his classroom to illustrate the length of a centimeter, a decimeter, and a meter. Next to these lines, he used a different color of tape to illustrate the length of an inch, a foot, and a yard. By the time students studied the metric system, they were very familiar with each of the metric measurements and could visualize how they compared with the English measurements.

Keep in Mind

Many teachers erroneously assume that these models are only appropriate for young students. The truth is, however, that many (if not most) high school students would be hard pressed to explain how big a billion is (beyond "1,000 times bigger than a million") and would struggle to give you a model for understanding it.

Reference/ Recommended Reading

Schwartz, D.M. (1985). *How much is a million?* New York: HarperCollins.

Vendors

Base Ten Blocks.com
http://www.basetenblocks.com/index.aspx
Base ten blocks can help students conceptualize our standard counting system. Many learners can better understand place value when they can touch and see the different units.

Kagan Publishing and Professional Development
http://www.kaganonline.com/Catalog/Mathematics3.html
To share materials easily in a whole-class setting, you can get these Kagan Math Projector Pals. There are sets available to teach fractions, money, place value, patterns, and more.

Lone Star Learning

http://www.LoneStarLearning.com

Target Vocabulary Pictures combine bright colors with illustrations of math vocabulary words. For example, the word *diagonal* is slanted diagonally on the card. The word *cone* is shaped like a cone.

Web Sites

Illuminations (Resources for Teaching Math)

http://illuminations.nctm.org/LessonDetail.aspx?id=L743

A "how much is a million" lesson plan

The MegaPenny Project

http://www.kokogiak.com/megapenny/default.asp

The MegaPenny Project aims to help learners understand big numbers. Using the U.S. penny as a tool, students are invited to ask and answer questions such as, "What would a billion (or a trillion) pennies look like?"

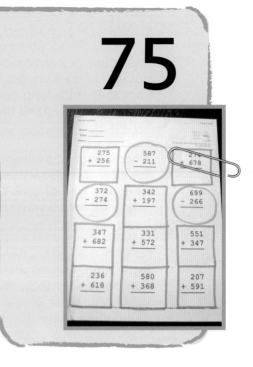

Coded & Cued Assignments

75

Materials

- Highlighter markers
- Different color inks and/or a color printer

Description

One of the easiest adaptations you can provide for students with disabilities is a *coded & cued assignment*. Coded & cued assignments entail creating some type of cue to direct students to the problems, sections, or items they should attend to, avoid, or notice in some way. Although this technique can be used in any subject area for any purpose, it is particularly helpful in mathematics because students can so easily stumble if they do not pay attention to changes in the directions, do not see or attend to the type of problem they are solving, or fail to understand the language used in explanations.

Directions

You will need to use different codes and cues for different students. Assess the difficulties your student is having and determine which elements of his or her written work will need adaptations. You may need to provide a code or cue for any or all of the following:

- The directions
- The language used in the problem
  - To indicate the number or order of steps in a problem
  - To illustrate or indicate the order of operations in a problem

Examples

Ms. Soderberg, a second-grade teacher, added cues and symbols (e.g., a "+" symbol above the words *add* or *sum*) to assignments to help students interpret the directions.

Ms. Philbin, a learning disabilities specialist, codes math tests and assignments for several students in the sixth grade. Using a yellow marker, she highlights key words in the instructions so that students will be assessed on their ability to do the work, not on their ability to read or understand the written directions.

When a page of problems contains both addition and subtraction problems, Mr. Haney circles all of the subtraction problems (or has students do so). He then directs students to complete one type of problem (e.g., all of the addition problems) before tackling the other type (e.g., the subtraction problems).

Early in the year, when two students with autism complete assignments that require regrouping, their teacher places boxes above the problems to indicate that (and where) students should show their work. She also creates boxes for the students to enter the answer for these problems, providing one box for each digit. This helps students assess whether they have the right number of digits in their answer.

Keep in Mind

Instead of creating the cues and codes for your student, you might also try providing a pen or highlighter inscribed with a message that will help your learner create or remember them on his or her own (e.g., "Color important words in the directions"). Or, start by creating the cues or codes for the student and gradually pass the responsibility on to him or her.

Reference/ Recommended Reading

Cohen, M.J. (2007). *Visual supports for people with autism: A guide for parents and professionals.* Bethesda, MD: Woodbine House.

Vendors

Brand Roads
http://www.brandroads.com
Highlighters and markers that can be inscribed with any logo or message

Crystal Springs Books
http://www.crystalspringsbooks.com/teacher-tools.html
Six different colors of highlighting tape

 Web Site

Super Teacher Worksheets
http://www.superteacherworksheets.com
Free, printable worksheets that teachers can use for assignments, practice, homework, games, or class activities

76 Math Communication Board

Materials

- Communication symbols
- Cardboard or board

Description

Increasingly, teachers are focused on the language of math and are encouraging students to talk and write about the meaning behind their work and discuss different ways to solve problems. For students who do not communicate easily or reliably or for those who are just more successful when they have prompts and visuals to support discussions, a *math communication board* may be helpful.

Directions

Math is one of those subject areas in which vocabulary does not change drastically throughout the year and few new terms are introduced from week to week (depending on the grade). For this reason, it is sometimes easier to create a master communication board of all of the math vocabulary and/or symbols that will be needed for the year and make it accessible across activities from the first week of school to the last.

Unlike a board that you are creating for an individual student for a specific purpose, a math communication board may include several symbols that can be used across activities and for different purposes. Make either all of the symbols or just some of the symbols accessible to students during whole-class activities, small-group activities, and even during partner activities. The communication symbols also can be used by the teacher as he or she presents concepts and ideas. Students who do not need the symbols can be encouraged to use them anyway, because frequent use of the symbols across activities will undoubtedly help learners who do need help to learn to communicate faster and in a more complex way.

Example

Eric, a fourth-grade student with multiple disabilities, used a math communication board during all small-group activities. During a probability game, for instance, he used YOUR TURN, MY TURN, SHAKE THE DICE, HIGHER, LOWER, and number symbols to communicate with peers and participate in the game. Other students in his group used the symbols, as well.

Reference/
Recommended Reading

Silbey, R. (2003). Math out loud! Heard the word? Talking and writing about math boosts understanding in a big way. *Instructor, 112,* 24–26.

Vendor

DynaVox Mayer-Johnson
http://www.mayer-johnson.com
DynaVox Mayer-Johnson is the manufacturer of Boardmaker software products. This web site contains descriptions of and information about the Boardmaker family of products. Boardmaker allows a user to create printed materials using Picture Communication Symbols and other graphics.

Web Site

Council for Exceptional Children
http://www.cec.sped.org/AM/Template.cfm?Section=Home&CONTENTID=7015&TEMPLATE=/CM/ContentDisplay.cfm
Ideas for teaching math to students with disabilities

77

Human Calculator

Materials

- Shower curtain or large tablecloth
- Thick marker

Description

Students will have fun with numbers, counting, and calculating when they—not their fingers—do the walking across the keypad. The human calculator, created by drawing calculator keys on a shower curtain or tablecloth, is a novel and motivating activity for students who require extra practice with facts or who simply need more movement than traditional math lessons allow.

Directions

A *human calculator* can be created by taping the curtain or cloth to the floor and drawing (or having students draw) a window for the screen and boxes for numbers 0–9 and the various symbols on the calculator that students are currently using. Because creating the human calculator is so cheap and easy, you may want to create several so that many students can use them at once.

The human calculator can be used in whole-class instruction, small groups, or centers, and can be used for many different purposes, including the following:

- Introducing students to using a calculator
- Teaching new functions of a calculator
- Reviewing addition, subtraction, multiplication, and division facts
- Practicing long number sentences with several steps
- Encouraging students to check their work

Examples

First-grade students in Ms. Hershey's class learned to use their calculators by watching their teacher "push the keys" of the human calculator. As the teacher (or a student) jumped on the various keys, students pushed the same buttons on their handheld calculators.

Ms. Thiel gave one human calculator to each three-person cooperative team in her classroom. In these teams, students played a "hop and add" challenge. One student kept a log of the problems students tackled, another student hopped around the keypad building a three- or four-number addition sentence, and the third student added the numbers in his head and then checked the sum on a real calculator.

Third graders played human calculator games with a partner at a math games center. One student showed a flashcard with a two- or three-digit number on it to another student. The partner had to jump to "keys" on the calculator (including the +, –, x and / signs and the = sign) to create a math problem that would result in the answer printed on the flashcard.

Keep in Mind

A shower curtain can be used to teach other concepts and create other tools, as well. For instance, in his book *Differentiating Math Instruction: Strategies that Work for K–8 Classrooms!*, Bender (2005) suggests making a number grid with a shower curtain. To do so, simply write the numbers 0–9 down the side of the curtain and across the top. Then, call out various problems (e.g., "5 x 5") and have students travel to the answer. For instance, have one student travel down the "5" column and another travel down the "5" row. When they meet, have them confer and shout out the answer to the problem. Students can also play the game individually. To create a game that students can use for practice, you can fill the chart in so learners can see the answers as they travel across the grid.

References/ Recommended Reading

Bender, W.N. (2005). *Differentiating math instruction: Strategies that work for K–8 classrooms!* Thousand Oaks, CA: Corwin Press.
Martin, H. (2007). *Active learning in the mathematics classroom.* Thousand Oaks, CA: Corwin Press.

Vendor

Brand Roads
http://www.brandroads.com
A large selection of school promotional items including pens and highlighters

Independent Living Aids, LLC
http://www.independentliving.com
A selection of large desktop calendars

Web Site

Active Learning Blog Carnival
http://activelearningcarnival.blogspot.com
A great blog on all things related to active learning—great math examples and beyond

Math Snapshots

78

Materials

- Camera
- Existing photographs
- Pictures from web sites, magazines, or books

Description

Many students are visual learners and profit from strategies that capitalize on this strength. Photographs not only appeal to these students but also tend to add a fun and unexpected element to math lessons, and they provide an authentic context for studying new concepts (Allsopp, Kyger, & Lovin, 2007). Students will enjoy not just examining photos but taking and sharing them, as well.

Students who see dry or abstract concepts as challenging or dull will likely find *math snapshots* to be a useful bridge to help them understand some of these concepts. For example, a student who finds it very challenging to describe or create an obtuse angle might be motivated by and interested in finding such angles in photos of architecture. Or, students who seem disenchanted with learning about the Fibonacci Sequence (or the Golden Ratio) may have fun taking photographs of the pattern as it is found in nature (e.g., pinecones, daisies).

Directions

To use photographs in teaching, gather (or have students gather) a range of images that represent concepts you are studying. Incorporate these into various lessons or have the gathering and sharing of photos be a lesson itself. Bull and Thompson (2004) provided readers with a four-step framework for using photos and other images across content areas:

- *Acquire:* Use a search engine like Google Images, or simply take photos.
- *Analyze:* Use of images can involve many kinds of analysis on the part of the student. Software such as the Geometer's Sketchpad can be used to analyze images of natural objects and architectural structures for the presence of ratios such as the golden rectangle.
- *Create:* Many technologies make it easy to incorporate digital images. Mathematical documents can now incorporate multiple representations—numeric, algebraic, graphical, and pictorial.
- *Communicate:* Photos should not just be shared and explored with the teacher but communicated to a larger audience. In this phase, students share their photos and their findings with others (e.g., classmates, visitors to a class web site).

Example

Jason, a young man with autism, loves all things related to garages. Garages are his passion and an interest he likes to share with others. His geometry teacher, therefore, gave him an assignment of taking math snapshots of objects in garages that could illustrate different concepts from class. For example, he took a photograph of a bicycle wheel to illustrate radius, diameter, and circumference. The photos were then shared with his classmates so that they had another way of understanding and seeing these concepts.

References/ Recommended Reading

Allsopp, D.H., Kyger, M.M., & Lovin, L.H. (2007). *Teaching mathematics meaningfully: Solutions for reaching struggling learners.* Baltimore: Paul H. Brookes Publishing Co.

Bull, G., & Thompson, A. (2004). Establishing a framework for digital images in the school curriculum. *Learning & Leading with Technology, 31*(8), 14.

Sharp, B.D., Garofalo, J., & Thompson, A. (2004). Digital images in the mathematics classroom. *Learning & Leading with Technology, 31*(8), 30.

Vendor

Problem Pictures

http://www.problempictures.co.uk

A great CD-ROM with photographs that can be used to teach mathematics as well as puzzles and problems you can use in your lessons

Web Sites

The Fibonacci Numbers and Nature

http://www.mcs.surrey.ac.uk/Personal/R.Knott/Fibonacci/fibnat.html

A look at the Fibonacci numbers and why and how they are seen in nature

Future of Math

http://futureofmath.misterteacher.com/digitalcameras.html

Examples of how photos can be used to teach math and several links to photo sites

My Math Notebook

http://www.mymathnotebook.blogspot.com

This blog, created by a preservice teacher, contains several examples of math in the world.

Stock.xchng

http://www.sxc.hu/index.phtml

A huge variety of stock photos; many are appropriate for classroom use and can be used in the teaching of mathematics

Visual Math Learning
http://www.visualmathlearning.com
Visualization methods for individuals who struggle with math; these lessons help teachers teach and students learn in different, interesting, and inspiring ways.

79

Adapted Ruler

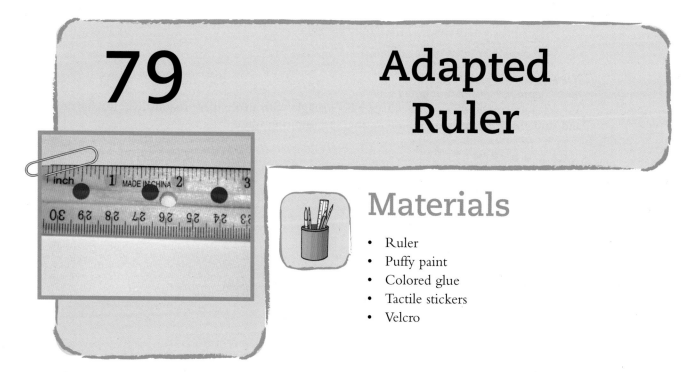

Materials

- Ruler
- Puffy paint
- Colored glue
- Tactile stickers
- Velcro

Description

Measurement is an important part of any math curriculum. Students are required to learn non-standard and metric measurements as well as English customary units (U.S.) and use different measurement tools such as rulers, tape measures, and yardsticks. Some students, however, have difficulty using tools available in the classroom and require teacher-created adaptations.

Directions

Using puffy paint, colored glue, or tactile stickers, highlight the increments on the ruler that are the focus of the lesson (e.g., inches, quarter inches) or that the student will need help finding. These cues can be faded once a student becomes more confident using the ruler and reading measurements accurately.

Examples

Isa's teacher created a ruler for her with Velcro stickers on the inch marks so she could both feel and see the measurements.

Robby, who has Down syndrome and low vision, uses an adapted ruler with green dots on the half-inch marks.

Keep in Mind

For students with physical disabilities, adaptations may be needed to keep the ruler in place. Consider placing a rubber strip on the back or providing a magnetic ruler for lessons involving measuring or drawing (Knight & Wadsworth, 1993).

Reference/ Recommended Reading

Knight, D., & Wadsworth, D. (1993). Physically challenged students: Inclusion classrooms. *Childhood Education, 69,* 211–215.

Vendors

Crystal Springs Books
http://www.crystalspringsbooks.com/index.html?stocknumber=A10065
Folding rulers that are fun to use and help students not only measure but also understand concepts such as odd and even numbers and fractions

Maxi Aids
http://www.maxiaids.com/store/prodView.asp?idproduct=1274
Tactile, braille rulers

Web Sites

Brain Pop Jr.
http://www.brainpopjr.com/math/measurement/inchesandfeet/grownups.weml
Fun activities for teaching inches and feet

The Ruler Game
http://www.rsinnovative.com/rulergame/index.html
Fun, online game that lets students time themselves as they race to find measurements

Teacher Vision
http://www.teachervision.fen.com/measurement/printable/44645.html
Several different printable rulers. Print one for each student in the class and let each learner create his or her own adaptations or cues.

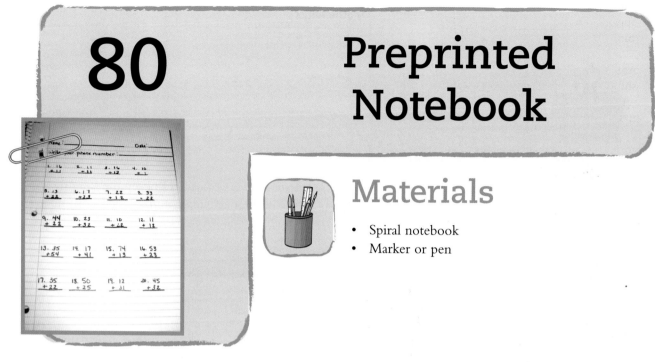

80 Preprinted Notebook

Materials

- Spiral notebook
- Marker or pen

Description

Many students with disabilities will have difficulty using the same instructional materials or engaging in the same work as their peers. To enable students to participate in the same lessons as students without disabilities, written materials—such as the *preprinted notebook*—may be created so that students are still learning the same general concepts as others but with problems or goals that are tailored to their individual learning needs. These notebooks, in essence, are teacher-created workbooks that are personalized for an individual student and used for independent practice and quick reviews. Preprinted notebooks are particularly useful during times when other students are working on textbook problems or on complex work from the chalkboard.

Directions

Look ahead to the upcoming week or month's lessons, and determine which pieces of the lesson or which targeted goals can be adapted. Then, create an entry for each day of the week or for each upcoming lesson. Using a spiral notebook or binder (or whatever materials other students in the inclusive classroom use), enter problems or mini-lessons that are appropriate for your student.

During classroom discussion and presentation of the lesson, students with disabilities can listen to the discussion, work with a teacher on related content, or work with peers to learn new concepts. Then, during periods of independent work, when other students are working on problems from a textbook or problems from the board, the student can address his or her own individual goals by working in his preprinted notebook.

Example

Every day, Ms. Mitchell, a sixth-grade teacher, starts her math lesson with five mental math problems. Students get out their mental math notebooks and scribble down answers to the problems that are presented on the overhead projector as they file into the classroom. Thomas, a young man with Down syndrome, also gets out his mental math notebook as he files into the classroom. He attempts the first problem (usually the easiest problem or a review problem) on the overhead, writing the answer on the first blank line of a page that is already dated, numbered, and filled with other problems tailored to his needs and goals.

Keep in Mind

Preprinted notebooks need not be limited to problems to be solved or information to be recalled. Entries might also direct students to write a journal entry about something they are learning, describe a concept in words or pictures, or complete a math simile or metaphor (Mower, 2003).

References/
Recommended Reading

Fuqua, B.H. (1997). Exploring math journals. *Childhood Education, 74*, 73–77.
Mower, P. (2003). *Algebra out loud: Learning mathematics through reading and writing activities.* San Francisco, CA: Jossey Bass.

Vendor

MathRealm
http://www.mathrealm.com
A host of math resources, including worksheets, books, and CDs; also contains ideas for personalizing instruction

Web Site

Free Math Help
http://www.freemathhelp.com
Free math lessons and games as well as a message board

Study & Review

Contents

81 Human Billboard

Materials

- Thick paper (an old manila folder works well)
- String or ribbon
- Hole punch
- Marker

Description

If you are looking for a fun and memorable way to share information and motivate students, try the *human billboard*. There is so much to love about this quick and easy strategy: It requires nothing more than an old manila folder and a piece of string or ribbon; it can be constructed in less than a minute; and it can be used for just one lesson or for a day, week, month, or year.

The human billboard is simply a sign that a teacher wears around his or her neck to communicate key points, vocabulary, facts, or reminders. It can be worn to signal learners to engage in a certain behavior (e.g., "Don't forget your ending marks!") or to help students learn and remember information (e.g., "The three braches of government are legislative, judicial, and executive").

Directions

Choose the short and simple message you want to "advertise," and print it on a piece of heavy paper. Then, simply punch two holes (one in each corner) at the top of the paper, run a ribbon or string through the holes, and knot it.

Examples

A fifth-grade teacher wore human billboards to represent several of the human body systems (e.g., respiratory system, circulatory system). He wore each sign as he taught the corresponding system. As a review activity, he then asked students to make their own billboards; they each chose one of the five systems to draw and then wrote three facts related to the system they had selected. Learners then walked around the classroom examining the billboards worn by fellow students and reviewing the facts provided.

A kindergarten teacher often wore a human billboard representing a letter of the alphabet and words starting with that letter. The front of the billboard featured the letter (both capital and small letters), and the back included 5 to 10 words beginning with that letter.

Keep in Mind

You can use the human billboard to share more than content. Use this tool for displaying inspirational quotes, advice, words of wisdom, or even jokes.

References/
Recommended Reading

Arwood, E., & Kaulitz, C. (2007). *Learning with a visual brain in an auditory world.* Shawnee Mission, KS: Autism Asperger Publishing Company.

Nelson, R., & Alsina, C. (2006). *Math made visual: Creating images for understanding mathematics.* Washington, DC: The Mathematical Association of America.

Vendors

MathematiciansPictures.com
http://www.mathematicianspictures.com/Shirts_.htm
A variety of math-themed T-shirts, including some featuring famous mathematicians (e.g., Cantor, Descartes)

THE SCIENCE TeeCHER
http://www.scienceteecher.com/index.htm
Pi earrings and phases of the moon T-shirts

Web Site

A Periodic Table of Visualization Methods
http://www.visual-literacy.org/periodic_table/periodic_table.html#
A must-visit site containing examples of dozens of visual support tools including a time line, a mindmap, a cone tree, a story template, and a layer chart

82 Personal Dictionary

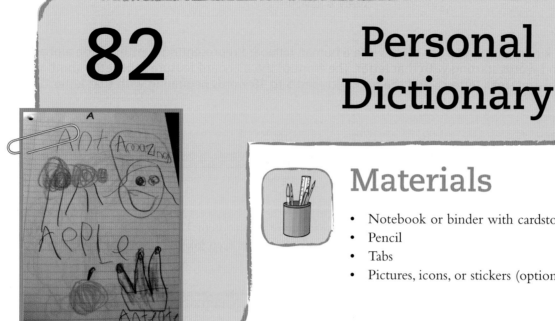

Materials

- Notebook or binder with cardstock pages
- Pencil
- Tabs
- Pictures, icons, or stickers (optional)

Description

For students with learning difficulties, spelling is often a challenge. Having students look up troublesome words in a dictionary, however, can be frustrating for a learner who already is struggling with words. As most of us recall from our school days, it can be hard to find a word in the dictionary if you do not know how to spell it! A *personal dictionary,* a notebook or binder containing only words that are troublesome or meaningful for a particular student, can be a helpful solution to this problem.

Directions

For the dictionary, use a notebook or binder (preferably containing cardstock pages) and designate one page for each letter of the alphabet. Students can then type or write in their personal dictionaries any assigned course words or other words they find problematic; short definitions for the words; and, if they'd like, an example of each word used in a sentence. If the student chooses to type the word, you can keep a file of the dictionary and print out a new one periodically. If the student writes in the entries or a classmate or teacher scribes for him or her, the entries can just be directly added to the blank notebook pages. For older students, we like to use a binder instead of a notebook because the pages grow quickly for each letter.

To help the student find the page he or she needs quickly, letter or section tabs can be created with simple sticky notes or highlighter tape on which the letter is written in marker. In addition to a page for each letter of the alphabet, some teachers devote a section to each content area for commonly used and misspelled spelling words in those areas. For example, the mathematics section might contain mathematical operations terminology; the geography section might contain the names of continents, countries, and states; and a calendar section might contain the days of the week, month names, and holidays. Personal dictionaries can last for years and can travel with students from class to class and grade level to grade level.

Examples

All of the students in an inclusive fifth-grade classroom had personal dictionaries. Each student was responsible for adding new vocabulary words (introduced by the teacher) and their definitions to his or her own dictionary. Cullen, a child with autism, could not write on his own, so his teacher adapted this exercise. She gave Cullen preprinted stickers of individual words and their definitions; Cullen's job was to find the correct section of his notebook and place the sticker inside. He also would draw a picture or stamp an image illustrating the term next to each word to help him find that word more easily.

Thomas, a young man with learning disabilities, created a personal dictionary not only to record unfamiliar vocabulary words but also to keep words he commonly misspelled. For most of the spelling entries (and for all of the vocabulary entries), he included a short definition. His teacher occasionally added in words she saw him using or spelling incorrectly, but Thomas was the one primarily responsible for adding and editing entries.

Keep in Mind

To help students become better spellers, it can be helpful to add a section of instructions dedicated to using word study strategies (e.g., mnemonics, words within words, identifying roots and affixes).

References/ Recommended Reading

Popp, M.S. (1997). *Learning journals in the K–8 classroom: Exploring ideas and information in the content areas.* Mahwah, NJ: Lawrence Erlbaum Associates.

Rupley, W.H., Logan, J.W., & Nichols, W.D. (1998/1999). Vocabulary instruction in a balanced reading program. *The Reading Teacher, 52,* 336–346.

Taylor, R. (2006). *Improving reading, writing, and content learning for students in grades 4–12.* Thousand Oaks, CA: Corwin Press.

Vendors

Franklin
http://www.franklin.com
A good selection of electronic dictionaries

Teachers' Helper
http://catalog.teachershelperonline.com/my_spelling_dictionary_pack_of_25-p-21573.html
Order a pack of 25 paper dictionaries for the entire classroom.

Web Sites

ESL Printables
http://www.eslprintables.com/buscador/buscar.asp?nivel=any&age=0&tipo=any&contents=personal+dictionary&B1=Search
This resource-rich site contains several different templates for personal dictionaries. Although it does not cost anything to download the documents, you do have to contribute resources of your own to use the site.

Read Write Think (International Reading Association)
http://www.readwritethink.org/lessons/lesson_view.asp?id=20
A lesson plan and ideas for using personal dictionaries

Word Central
http://www.wordcentral.com
A web site created by Merriam-Webster; contains great games, a "word of the day," and other features

Beach Ball Review

83

Materials

- Beach ball
- Permanent marker

Description

Liven up your classroom and add some movement to your day by creating a *beach ball review*. Beach balls are big and light, so they are easy to catch and will not hurt anyone or break anything. Here are some examples of how to create a beach ball review in your classroom:

- Write different math facts on the ball with a permanent marker. If the student catches the ball, they have to answer the math fact that is facing them.
- Write different numbers on the ball. The first person who catches the ball shouts out his or her number. He or she passes the ball to another student and that person shouts out his or her number. The second student then adds, subtracts, multiplies, or divides the two digits.
- Write different letters on the ball and have students think of a word that starts with the letter facing them.
- Write different vocabulary words on the ball, and as individual students catch the ball, have them define or give an example of a word they are touching.
- Write different concepts or topics on the ball (e.g., Jim Crow, Montgomery Bus Boycott); as students catch the ball, have them state a fact or question about a topic they are touching.
- Use the beach ball to motivate students during a review session. Have the students hit the ball around as the teacher plays upbeat music. The student who is holding the ball when the music stops must answer the next review question.

Directions

Choose the facts, questions, words, or icons you want to use. With a magic marker, add the content to different sections of the inflated beach ball.

Example

Ninth-grade students play a geography game for the last 10 minutes of the week. A beach ball printed to look like a globe is passed around the room; the student who catches the ball has to name a country, river, or mountain range on one of the continents he or she is touching. The teacher keeps a running list of the answers each week to be sure that, throughout the year, students never repeat an answer.

Keep in Mind

A beach ball is also a nice tool for facilitating a discussion or having a conversation with a student. Sitting down for a face-to-face exchange can feel threatening and overwhelming for some students. For these learners, try tossing a beach ball back and forth as you take turns talking.

References/ Recommended Reading

Armstrong, R. (1994). *Multiple intelligences in the classroom.* Alexandria, VA: Association for Supervision and Curriculum Development.

Bowman, S. (2003). *How to give it so they get it.* Glenbrook NV: Bowperson Publishing.

Cunningham, P.M., & Allington, R.L. (2007). *Classrooms that work: They can all read and write.* Boston: Allyn & Bacon.

Vendors

American Chemical Society

http://acswebapplications.acs.org/portaltools/shopper/productDetail.cfm?prod_cd=1-HS70

The ACS Molar Beach Ball has been specially designed to have a volume of 22.4 liters. It can be used to give students a concrete idea of the size of one mole of gas at standard temperature and pressure.

Education 4 Kids

http://edushop.edu4kids.com

This site sells guided reading beach balls with one question per panel. Some of the featured questions include, "What happened in the story?" and "In the beginning…."

Thumball (Answers in Motion LLC)

http://www.catch32ball.com/

Balls with letters, numbers, animals, categories, and even "getting to know you" questions

Web Sites

Sharon Bowman's Web Site (Teach It Quick & Make It Stick!)

http://www.bowperson.com

Bowman has a great blog about active learning, teaching, and training. The "Try This" section offers a variety of new ideas for educators interested in bringing more novelty and joy to the classroom.

Group Games

http://www.group-games.com

Although the beach ball game is not featured here, this site does contain many other group games and activities appropriate for both younger and older students.

84

Guided Notes

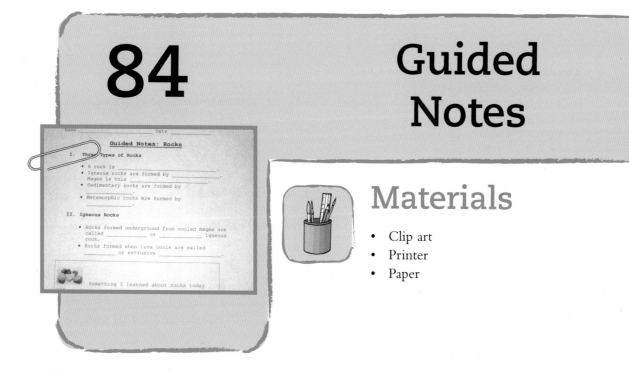

Materials

- Clip art
- Printer
- Paper

Description

Guided notes are teacher-prepared sheets that outline lectures or class discussions but leave blank spaces, lines, and boxes so students can fill in key words, concepts, facts, definitions, or examples. Guided notes help learners follow a lecture, identify key points, and provide opportunities to illustrate or expand on presented ideas. Using guided notes can also increase the chances that learners will capture information that is more accurate than they might on their own.

Guided notes can be prepared for both lectures and assigned readings. Notes can be used for a variety of purposes, such as the following:

- To help students stay interested and connected to lectures
- To preview and teach key concepts
- To summarize stories or chapters
- To prompt class participation
- To set expectations of what the student should be looking or listening for and/or to cue students to the big ideas they should be learning
- To keep the instructor on point

Directions

Guided notes are quite easy to construct, especially for lectures or lessons that are already developed. First, determine the most important elements of the discussion or lecture and arrange these into a set of notes. Keep in mind that less is often more! Then, delete parts of the content leaving partial sentences, blank spaces, and open boxes to provide structure for taking notes. Finally, insert formatting cues such as bullets, asterisks, arrows, and boxes to show students where, when, and how many items to list; how much detail to provide; and what kind of content to add (e.g., a picture, a phrase).

Example

Guided notes were developed for lectures in an earth science class. Initially, these notes were only used by four students with learning disabilities. Eventually, after seeing better test scores and increased attention during lectures, the teacher offered them to all learners. The teacher noted, after two semesters of use, that the most important part of his notes was a box at the top that reminded students what the main idea of the reading or lecture was to be (e.g., "At the end of this lecture, you should know one way to _____").

Keep in Mind

You can develop your own set of codes to use across notes sets. For instance, each page of notes might have a key symbol to indicate "Key idea: _____," a box to show that they should illustrate an idea, and a right-pointing arrow to indicate that students should add an application idea or an example of their own.

References/ Recommended Reading

Boyle, J.R. (2001). Enhancing the note-taking skills of students with mild disabilities. *Intervention in School and Clinic, 36*(4), 221–224.

Heward, W.L. (1994). Three "low-tech" strategies for increasing the frequency of active student response during group instruction. In R. Gardner, D.M. Sainato, J.O. Cooper, T.E. Heron, W.L. Heward, J. Eshleman, et al. (Eds.), *Behavior analysis in education: Focus on measurably superior instruction* (pp. 283–320). Monterey, CA: Brooks/Cole.

Lazarus, B.D. (1993). Guided notes: Effects with secondary and post-secondary students with disabilities. *Education and Treatment of Children, 14,* 272–289.

Montis, K.K. (2007). Guided notes: An interactive method for success in secondary and college mathematics classrooms. *Focus on Learning Problems in Mathematics, 29*(3), 55–68.

Vendor

Spark Notes
http://www.sparknotes.com
Book summaries, notes on a range of topics and subject areas, and many other tools including a "no fear Shakespeare" translation tool that puts Shakespeare's language side-by-side with a facing-page translation into modern English

Web Site

Intervention Central
http://www.interventioncentral.org/htmdocs/interventions/study/gnotes.php
Tips on creating notes and a sample set of guided notes

Pocket Cards

85

Materials

- Index cards (cut in half for small children)
- Thick marker

Description

Pocket cards, like traditional flash cards, are words or concepts written on individual cards for the purpose of independent review or review with a peer or adult. The difference with these cards is that they are designed to fit into a student's pocket and are intended to travel with him or her throughout the day, week, or month.

Teachers can then institute pocket card days where adults in the building know that students will have cards with them. Any student can then be approached by the principal, a cafeteria worker, or parent volunteer to practice their pocket words, definitions, or facts. Students can also work with peers to practice their cards at different points in the day.

Directions

You can make pocket cards for the students or have students make them themselves using index cards or tagboard. Another possibility is to create a sheet of pocket cards with simple typing paper, print them, and have students cut them apart.

Example

An entire sixth-grade unit of a middle school used pocket cards to expand their vocabulary and, eventually, to enhance their writing and improve their reading skills. On Tuesdays and Thursdays, students stuck the cards in their pockets for the day. Teachers then gave students opportunities to work with partners at short intervals throughout the day (e.g., "Take out your pocket cards and quiz your partner"). In addition, staff throughout the building knew about pocket card days and would approach individual students to review words. For example, the lunch monitor might approach five to seven students during lunch and ask them about their words. Parents also knew about the cards and were asked to practice at home either at dinnertime, in the car, or as part of that day's homework.

Keep in Mind

Pocket cards can be used class- or schoolwide or can be used for just a few students who need extra practice with certain concepts or skills. Easy concepts for cards include spelling words, vocabulary words, or math facts. Other skills also can be honed with this strategy, however. For example, one card might feature an individualized education program (IEP) objective: "Ask me to tell you the number to call in an emergency," or "Ask me to spell my name."

References/ Recommended Reading

Junn, E.N. (1995). Empowering the marginal student: A skills-based extra-credit assignment. *Teaching of Psychology, 22,* 189–192.

Provost, M.C., Rullo, A., & Buechner, M. (2000). 20 ways to make spelling sizzle. *Intervention in School and Clinic, 36*(1), 45-46.

Utley, C.A., Reddy, S.S., Delquadri, J.C., Greenwood, C.R., Mortweet, S.L., & Bowman, V. (2001). Classwide peer tutoring: An effective teaching procedure for facilitating the acquisition of health education and safety facts with students with developmental disabilities. *Education & Treatment of Children, 24*(1), 1–27.

Vendors

Flash My Brain
http://www.flashmybrain.com
This is a unique web site and product; it includes both resources for making and printing your own set of flashcards as well as software for loading words and review games onto your iPod, cell phone, or PDA.

Sam's Club
http://www.samsclub.com/shopping/navigate.do?dest=5&item=146715&pid=_Froogle&ci_src=141109 44&ci_sku=351603
Inexpensive blank note cards

Web Site

Free Printable Flashcard Maker
http://www.kitzkikz.com/flashcards
A user-friendly resource for both parents and teachers—simply type in the information you want on the front and the back of each card, and this site will design the cards for you.

Walk-It-to-Know-It

86

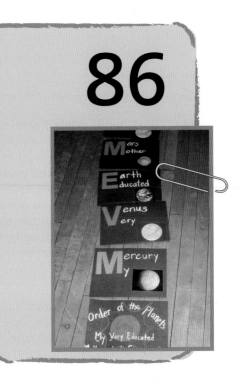

Materials

- Poster board or butcher paper
- Markers
- Clear packing tape

Description

Although teachers routinely use bulletin boards, easels, and of course, the chalkboard for displaying important information, they often forget the untapped canvas of the classroom floor! The entrance of the classroom, the path from the door to the students' desks, and even the tiles underneath student desks can feature images, words, or concepts that will promote student learning. Teachers might make a floor chart (or what we call *walk-it-to-know-it*) (Kluth, 2003; Udvari-Solner & Kluth, 2007) to teach any number of concepts, including the scientific method, steps to solving a binomial equation, or the parts of a business plan. This structure is especially helpful for visual and kinesthetic learners.

Directions

To prepare for the walk-it-to-know-it structure, you (or your students) will need to design flow charts or series-of-events chains on paper and then transfer each square to a separate piece of poster board or butcher paper. The squares can then be laid out and taped onto the classroom floor in a pattern that will help you communicate the concepts. If the content you are teaching is a chronology of events (e.g., time line of the U.S. Civil War), the pattern will likely be a straight line, but if the content is a cycle (e.g., water cycle), the paper can be arranged in a circle or in any other shape that will help the learner understand and remember the information. As the students enter the classroom each day or during a lesson in which the concepts are introduced, have all of the students stand and walk through the sequence. Have students chant each step as they walk over it, or even add a gesture or motion to each to make the learning more memorable. Any walk-it-to-know-it may be used for a single day, a unit, or an entire semester or year.

Examples

A ninth-grade health teacher used the walk-it-to-know-it technique to teach her students the steps used in cardiopulmonary resuscitation (CPR). The first day CPR was introduced, the entire class spent 20 minutes moving through the steps repeatedly. For the rest of the year, the teacher asked students to enter her classroom by stepping individually on each square. Furthermore, she assigned a short movement to each step of the process and occasionally asked students to act out each of the steps using the actions she had shared with them as they stepped on the squares. For example, for step one, which is to call out to the person, she had students wave their hands and yell, "Are you okay? Are you okay?" During class, she periodically quizzed students on the steps to be sure they were retaining the information.

Sixth-grade students strolled over a solar system walk-it-to-know-it every day during their 10-day unit. Every day, every student walked on each planet, chanting the names as they passed over each one.

Keep in Mind

You can ask students to construct their own version of walk-it-to-know-it. This structure can even be part of your assessment of student learning at the end of a unit or used as a review for an upcoming quiz. Students can print the text on the computer or write it by hand and embellish each square with clip art, photographs, or drawings.

References/ Recommended Reading

Campbell, L., Campbell, B., & Dickinson, D. (1996). *Teaching and learning through multiple intelligences.* Boston: Allyn & Bacon.

Kluth, P. (2010). *"You're going to love this kid!": Teaching students with autism in the inclusive classroom* (2nd ed.). Baltimore: Paul H. Brookes Publishing Co.

Udvari-Solner, A., & Kluth, P. (2007). *Joyful learning: Active and collaborative learning in inclusive classrooms.* Thousand Oaks, CA: Corwin Press.

Van Tine, E., Lee, S., Cooper, C., & White, B. (1999). *Super social studies! Quick and easy activities, games, and manipulatives.* New York: Scholastic Teaching Resources.

Vendors

3M
http://www.3m.com/us/office/postit/products/prod_poster.html?gnID=8
These sticky notes in poster form can be attached and reattached to any surface.

Instructional Images
http://www.instructionalimages.com
A wide variety of educational posters and prints, including maps, science posters, history posters, and more

Web Sites

Articlesbase (Free Online Articles Directory)
http://www.articlesbase.com/printing-articles/visual-learning-tools-using-poster-prints-in-the-classroom-713098.html
Download and print this short but useful article on using visuals in the classroom. This piece may be especially helpful for secondary teachers because the author has included examples for foreign language, history, math, and literature.

History.com (The History Channel)
http://www.history.com/wt.do
A fantastic resource for teachers of social studies; includes time lines of every era in history along with detailed descriptions of events

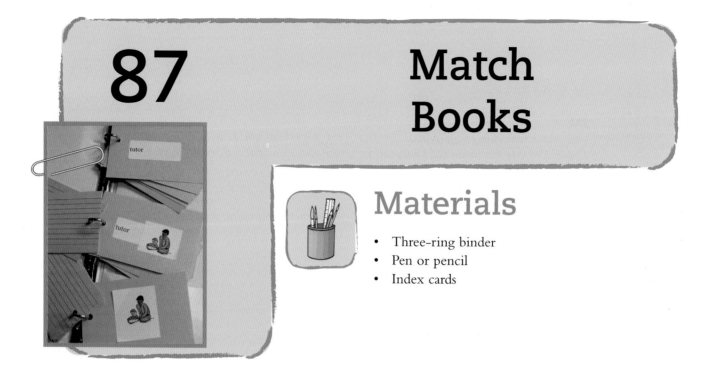

87 Match Books

Materials

- Three-ring binder
- Pen or pencil
- Index cards

Description

Match books are tools that students can access for independently reviewing spelling or vocabulary words. These "books" consist of three sets of hole-punched flashcards stored in a 3-ring binder. One set of cards features both a printed word and a picture of the word; the second set of cards includes the same words but no pictures; the third set of cards includes the same pictures and no words.

Students can play several different games with their books; initially, they can just find 3-card matches as they learn how to use the book, then they can test themselves by matching a word with the picture and checking to see if they have the correct answer by flipping to the middle card and checking to see if they have matched correctly. Students can also take the cards out of the book and play a 3-card "memory" type game (Bender, 2002; Blachowicz & Ogle, 2007) by flipping all of the cards over and trying to recall where the three related cards are placed.

These simple, teacher-created resources are useful as "sponges" (activities to use when there are a few extra minutes of class time that can be "absorbed"), self-checking homework, or as homeroom or free time games.

Directions

To create a match book, you will need three index cards for each vocabulary or spelling word. On one card, you will write the word and include a picture. On a second card, you will add words only. The third set of cards features only pictures. Once the cards are made, you can punch a hole in the left side of each card and add them to the binder with one ring holding all of the photo cards, one ring holding all of the word cards, and one ring holding all of the cards that feature both pictures and words. When you add the cards, be sure to shuffle each group so that the three cards on top, for example, are not matches for one another.

Example

Dante, a third-grader with cognitive disabilities, uses his match book to get extra practice learning spelling and vocabulary words. He uses it at the word-learning table during the weekly stations-teaching lesson. He also occasionally practices with his book when the assigned spelling activities are too difficult or not appropriate for him. In addition, the word match book travels home with Dante on weekends so he can practice new words as part of his homework assignment.

Keep in Mind

Flip books can be created for math concepts (e.g., one card with an acute angle described, one card with a picture of an acute angle, and one card featuring both the picture and the description) and for learning science or social studies facts (e.g., one card with a picture of a U.S. state, one card with the name of the capital of that state written on it, and one card with a picture of the state with the capital labeled).

References/ Recommended Reading

Bender, W. N. (2002). *Differentiating instruction for students with learning disabilities: Best teaching practices for general and special educators.* Thousand Oaks, CA: Corwin Press, Inc.

Blachowicz, C., & Ogle, D. (2007). *Reading comprehension: Strategies for independent learners* (2nd ed.). New York: Guilford.

Vendors

Beyond the Blackboard
http://www.beyondtheblackboard.com/Word-Games-2.aspx
Games that help students learn spelling, word families, and vocabulary

Science Kit & Boreal Laboratories
http://sciencekit.com/tools-of-science-memory-game-flashcards-teacher-developed%2C-classroom-tested/p/IG0031877
This link will take you to a great set of oversized flash cards of science tools, materials, and concepts. You can use the cards as visual supports for a lab activity or give them to students to create their own games and activities.

Office Depot
http://www.officedepot.com/browse.do?N=201439
Customizable binders for any project

Web Sites

Vocabulary.com

http://www.vocabulary.com
Vocabulary-building games and activities

Quia

http://www.quia.com/cc/1312.html
An online algebra vocabulary matching game as well as dozens of other related games and activities

Study Stack

http://www.studystack.com
A host of study tools for students to use for independent practice and review. Users simply choose content from a menu, select a study tool (flashcards, crossword puzzles) and either print materials or study online.

Card Game Curriculum Review 88

Materials

- Index cards
- Marker
- Blank playing card paper (see vendors)
- Graphics program and/or clip art
- Color printer

Description

This idea comes from a fun, resource-packed book, *Teaching by Design,* by Kimberly Voss (2005), the mother of a young woman with a disability. Voss made card games featuring the faces and names of family members for her daughter; we have adapted this idea to incorporate standards-based content into common card games. Games can be used within the context of a lesson, during free time, or even after school.

Although you could use or create a deck of cards for any game, we have most often created a game that functions like Go Fish!, where the players pick cards from one another to make matches. We create 11 categories based on a theme that we are teaching and make a set of four cards for each of these categories.

Directions

To make a customized card game, it is possible to use index cards and draw or paste your images onto the cards. To give your game a more polished look, however, you can use the computer. Simply replace your computer paper with some type of card paper (such as Avery #5371) and use your graphics program to find and print images.

Examples

A seventh-grade teacher had her students create their own Go Fish! games using concepts and vocabulary from their unit on the Great Depression (e.g., Hoovervilles, Dust Bowl, Black Tuesday, fireside chat, New Deal). Students chose terms to illustrate and define and then spent a class period playing a game of Go Fish! with their peers. When students requested a card (e.g., "Do you have Black Tuesday?"), they also had to read the definition or explain it in their own words.

Dustin, a second-grade student with cognitive disabilities, was learning the names of his classmates. The teacher made two sets of a Go Fish! game with all of the students' pictures on the cards. One set remained at school for students to play during indoor recess. Dustin took the other game home to play with his family.

Reference/ Recommended Reading

Voss, K.S. (2005). *Teaching by design: Using your computer to create materials for students with learning differences.* Bethesda, MD: Woodbine House.

Vendors

Creative Kidds
http://www.creativekidds.com/index.cfm/page/cat/cat/Game%20Accessories/cid/16.htm
A variety of blank game pieces and parts (e.g., money, game boards, cards) that can be used to create your own games and activities

Elementeo
http://www.elementeo.com
A 14-year-old boy made headlines when he introduced this card game in 2008. In the game, two or more players wage a war of chemistry with just one goal in mind—to destroy their opponent's electrons to zero! This is a great game to both inspire reluctant students and challenge advanced learners.

Plaincards
http://plaincards.com
Perforated blank card templates for your computer

Web Site

The United States Playing Card Company
http://www.bicyclecards.com/pages/game_rules/2.php
Includes an illustrated list of card games appropriate for children

Graphic Organizers

Materials

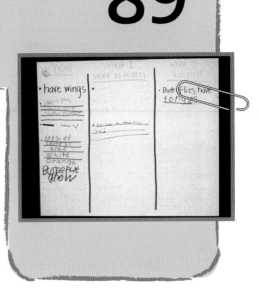

- Poster board, construction paper, drawing paper, or typing paper
- Markers or computer graphics programs

Description

Graphic organizers, also known as *concept maps* or *diagrams, advance* or *cognitive organizers, flow charts,* or *story maps,* are visual displays of knowledge that structure information by arranging important aspects of an idea, term, or topic into a pattern and by showing relationships between related concepts (Bromley, 1996; Bromley, DeVitis, & Modlo, 1999). Graphic organizers are effective teaching tools in that they help students store and recall information, demonstrate relationships among facts and concepts, and organize ideas (Billmeyer & Barton, 1998; Bromley, DeVitis, & Modlo, 1999).

When the class is studying a novel, the teacher might provide students with a pictorial time-line of the events in the story. Or, he or she might use a Venn diagram to show learners how to compare and contrast two time periods in history. Such applications of graphic organizers can help all students better understand the content, connect the new learning to concepts they already understand, and make abstract concepts more concrete. Graphic organizers may be especially useful in supporting the literacy development of students with disabilities because these visual tools reduce the cognitive demands on the learner. In other words, the student does not need to process as much semantic information to comprehend the content (Ellis, 2004).

Directions

Teachers can use graphic organizers in a variety of ways. They can use them to illustrate points in a lecture, give them to students to fill in or create to keep them engaged in a whole-class lesson, or model how they can be used for note taking. Examples of organizers that might be employed include Venn diagrams, cause-and-effect frameworks, semantic webs, series-of-events chains, network trees, cycle maps, and flow charts.

When using graphic organizers in the inclusive classroom, educators may want to consider the following adaptations, ideas, and implementation tips:

- If some students in the classroom are emerging readers, then icons, images, or pictures should be paired with words whenever possible.

- Students should have many opportunities to see the teacher develop and use a range of different graphic organizers before they are asked to use them as learning tools. Because it is sometimes hard for a teacher to talk and illustrate her discussion at the same time, many teachers rely on another adult to co-teach this type of lesson with them. A general educator might work with a special educator, paraprofessional, speech-language therapist, or even another student to "show and tell" about graphic organizers.

- Graphic organizers can be used to teach more than reading. When students are taught to read and develop graphic organizers, they also learn critical thinking, organization, and communication skills. Consider the needs of individual students in the classroom. Can individual goals (e.g., IEP objectives) be taught through the use of graphic organizers? If a student with a disability is working on note-taking skills, for example, he or she might be taught how to do so using a graphic organizer such as a semantic web.

Examples

Glenn, a student with autism, used visual notes to track his understanding of the texts he chose for independent reading. While he read, he drew illustrations of notable pieces of the story. When he read *The Devlin Affair* (Marlowe, 1987), a mystery story about a private eye who is assigned to take a suitcase to Mexico City, Glenn tracked his reading by drawing a map and illustrating the events as they unfolded. In his drawing, Glenn included arrows to mark Dev's travels, several of the settings of the book, and the FBI building. He also drew the suitcase with the false bottom, though this is a detail that might be missed by those who can't "read" Glenn's drawing easily. On a separate sheet of paper, Glenn listed the names of the main characters and a story summary. His sketch and related text then became a tool that was remarkably effective in guiding him through the reading. Though it was simple, it helped him as he read later chapters, answered questions about the story, and completed related classroom projects.

Ms. Wendt creates a cycle chart to show students the life cycle of a flowering plant. She fills in the main categories (seed, germination), and students are expected to fill in details about each piece of the cycle as well as provide an illustration for each.

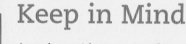

Keep in Mind

A student with more significant disabilities may not be able to construct or fill in the components of a graphic organizer. For this type of learner, alternative materials can be used that would allow the student to create or manipulate a diagram without being able to write or draw. For instance, a student can be given cards or magnetic pieces to assemble for a timeline. Or, this same learner may be able to use a program such as Kidspiration (software that helps students build graphic organizers by combining pictures, text, and spoken words) to create a visual representation of ideas (http://www.inspiration.com/productinfo/kidspiration/index.cfm).

References/ Recommended Reading

Billmeyer, R., & Barton, M. (1998). *Teaching reading in the content areas: If not me, then who?* Aurora, CO: Mid-Continent Regional Educational Laboratory.

Bromley, K.D. (1996). *Webbing with literature: Creating story maps with children's books* (2nd ed.). Needham Heights, MA: Allyn & Bacon.

Bromley, K., Irwin DeVitis, L., & Modlo, M. (1999). *50 graphic organizers for reading, writing & more: Reproducible templates, student samples, and easy strategies to support every learner.* New York: Scholastic Professional Books.

Drapeau, P. (1998). *Great teaching with graphic organizers.* New York: Scholastic.

Ellis, E. (2004). *Q&A: What's the big deal with graphic organizers?* Retrieved October 20, 2008, from http://www.graphicorganizers.com/Sara/ArticlesAbout/Q&A%20Graphic%20Organizers.pdf

Griffon, C., Malone, L., & Kame'enui, E. (2001). Effects of graphic organizer instruction on fifth-grade students. *The Journal of Educational Research, 89*(2), 98–107.

Hibbing, A., & Rankin-Erickson, J.L. (2003). "A picture is worth a thousand words": Using visual images to improve comprehension for middle school struggling readers. *The Reading Teacher, 56,* 8.

Marlowe, D. (1987). *The Devlin affair.* Belmont, CA: Fearon.

Vendors

graphicorganizers.com
http://www.graphicorganizers.com
Software to create a range of graphic organizers, as well as many free downloads

Kidspiration
http://www.inspiration.com/Kidspiration
Created for K-5 learners, Kidspiration software develops thinking, literacy, and other skills. Students can create elaborate organizers with Kidspiration as well as use it to express themselves and create stories with words, pictures, and other tools.

Smart Draw
http://www.smartdraw.com/exp/mim
This software can be used to create mind maps, flowcharts, organizational charts, time lines, bar graphs, and more.

Web Sites

CAST (Graphic Organizers)
http://www.cast.org/publications/ncac/ncac_go.html
CAST offers a nice outline of research related to graphic organizers as well as several different examples of organizers.

edHelper.com
http://edhelper.com/teachers/graphic_organizers.htm
Organizers for storytelling, graphs, charts, and KWL forms

90 Graffiti Recall

Materials

- Adding machine tape
- Markers
- Pencils or pens
- Label maker
- Stickers

Description

Graffiti recall, or what Forsten, Grant, and Hollas (2002) call "personal-learning time lines," involves having students summarize a lesson, unit, day, week, or even month on a long roll of paper that can hold many (perhaps several dozen) entries. Using these small rolls of paper is less daunting for students than having to fill a page in a notebook, and using rolls that are long enough to store several entries creates opportunities for learners to go back to previous sections at any point for the purpose of review or to embellish any drawing or add details to their notes, in general.

Many students need repeated opportunities for practice of new skills and require reviews of newly introduced content. Graffiti recall is not only appropriate for this purpose but can also be lots of fun for learners who are accustomed to didactic methods of review, but prefer more responsive and even creative ways to show what they remember. Having students draw instead of write notes will be especially appealing to artistic students and will serve as a more accessible way to take notes than any traditional format or method.

Directions

Give each student his or her own personal roll of adding machine paper and a small box in which to store it (or keep all of the rolls in one big classroom box). During a few minutes of the school day or during the last 20 minutes of each week, have students get their roll out and start to "graffiti." Notes can include pictures, symbols, phrases, and words. Have them keep the roll intact so that learners can review a week or month or even year at a glance.

Examples

Seventh graders in Mr. Crane's classroom create graffiti during the last 20 minutes of class each Friday. The students can include anything from the week but are encouraged to include something from each subject area and must feature at least one solved math problem from their homework as well as the "word of the week."

In a ninth-grade social studies classroom, students are occasionally asked to get out their "recall tape" either at the beginning of class or at the end. In the beginning of a class period, they are used as a tool for review; students find a partner and "read" their notes from beginning to end to that person. If they are used at the end of class, students create new notes, illustrating one main theme from the day's class and three details. Saul, a young man with physical disabilities, works on his time line with a peer partner and uses stickers and a label maker to add words and pictures to his notes.

References/ Recommended Reading

Fisher, D., Schell, E., & Frey, N. (2004). "In your mind and on the paper": Teaching students to transform (and own) texts. *The Social Studies Review, 44*(1), 26–31.

Forsten, C., Grant, J., & Hollas, B. (2002). *Differentiated instruction: Different strategies for different learners.* Peterborough, NH: Crystal Springs Books.

Golon, A.S. (2008). *Visual-spatial learners.* Austin, TX: Prufrock Press.

Vendors

ArtSuppliesOnline.com
http://www.artsuppliesonline.com/catalog.cfm?cata_id=2284
Large rolls of easel paper and other supplies

PaperJack.com
http://www.paperjack.com
Rolls of adding machine paper in bulk

Web Sites

LD Online (Teaching Students to Take Notes in Class)
http://www.ldonline.org/article/12855
A short article with tips and examples about teaching students to take notes in class

Maximize the Power of Your Brain (by Tony Buzan)
http://www.youtube.com/watch?v=MlabrWv25qQ
This YouTube video may be helpful for teachers who are interested in teaching mind mapping (a graphic way to represent concepts, ideas, and words). Depending on the age of your students, it could also be shown to students themselves.

Time Lapse Mural Creation High Speed Art

http://www.youtube.com/watch?v=eK0IGfKuRCQ

High school students, in particular, may enjoy this video from a company called Chrysalis Studios. Through the miracle of time lapse photography, the viewer can see an artist create a massive set of graphic notes in just a few minutes.

Visual-Spatial Resource

http://www.visualspatial.org

Research, articles, tips, and note-taking advice, all related to visual-spatial learners

Assessment

Contents

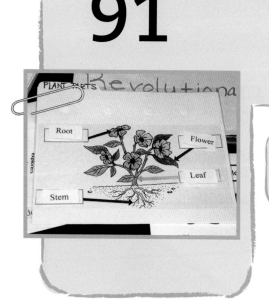

91 Adapted Standards

Materials

- Copy of national, state, or district standards
- Copy of grade-level standards
- Student's individualized education program (IEP) or individual goals

Description

Another differentiation technique that we advocate is the *adaptation of goals and standards*. This means simply that teachers in the inclusive classroom should feel comfortable creating objectives *based on* those targeted for students without disabilities but appropriate for individual learning needs. Reigeluth (1997) is one of many scholars who cautioned against standards-based learning that does not allow for individualization:

> Uniform standards may be appropriate for business—a manufacturer wants all microwave ovens to meet specified standards of quality. That's good. But to what extent do we want all students to be alike? Of course, there are certain skills we want all students to master, but should all students be required or expected to attain them at exactly the same age or grade level? To use a travel analogy, standards for manufacturing are comparable to a single destination for all travelers to reach, whereas standards for education are more like milestones on many never-ending journeys whereby different travelers may go to many different places. We must be careful not to overgeneralize what works well for business. (p. 204)

Clearly, all students cannot or should not be able to do the same thing at the end of a school year. For this reason, standards must be viewed as developmental. This approach allows students to work at different levels based on their individual abilities, skills, and interests.

Directions

Examine the standards and curriculum for any given subject area and determine when and how your students will meet these goals. If you have students who need alternate objectives, look at the IEPs of those learners and look for any intersections between the curriculum and the individual's goals. Two primary types of adaptations might be made. The first way to adapt a standard is to focus on one piece of it. For instance, if the standard is to "Describe the major conflicts and outcomes of World War II, including Pearl Harbor, El-Alamein, Stalingrad, D-Day, Guadalcanal, and the Philippines," you might focus on one of these pieces (e.g., having the student describe the attack on Pearl Harbor). A second method is to adapt the standard altogether to meet the needs of the learner. If the standard is "Write clear, coherent laboratory reports related to scientific investigations," it might be adapted to "Use augmentative communication device to ask a question related to a scientific investigation" or "Write a hypothesis given a cloze statement, such as "I predict _____ will turn _____.""

Consider the following additional examples:

- The standard "The student will write a complete paragraph" can be adapted to "Given three sentence strips arranged into a paragraph, the student will correctly 'write' a topic sentence by selecting the correct sentence strip from a field of three choices."
- The standard "The student will be able to explain causes of the U.S. Civil War" can be adapted to "The student will explain how slavery played a role in the U.S. Civil War."
- The standard "The student will know that the earth is a planet" can be adapted to "Given a picture of all of the planets, the student will identify the earth," or even "Given a picture of the solar system, the student will identify a planet."

Examples

Students in a middle school science class were asked to explain the role that the parts of a plant play in its growth and development. Sam, who has multiple disabilities, was, instead, expected to identify at least four parts of a plant. Using a diagram of a plant, Sam was assessed on his ability to correctly place four labels on the diagram—the leaf, stem, flower, and the root.

In a fifth-grade classroom, students had to "write for multiple audiences" by the end of the year. Ross, a student with autism, had the same goal; however, instead of having to demonstrate that he could write for six different audiences, like his peers, Ross had to write for just three audiences: his family, his friends, and a local business. Furthermore, Ross's writing consisted of either creating a document using Writing with Symbols software or arranging sentence strips created by his peers.

Students in a middle school computer class are expected to "Demonstrate and explain correct spacing for punctuation keys" and "Demonstrate proper keyboarding techniques for keying all letters." Ty is in the same class as his same-age peers and engages in many of the same exercises as they do (e.g., typing sentences, playing keyboarding games), but he is working on adapted objectives such as "Identify and use the question mark key" and "Demonstrate proper keyboarding techniques for keying four letters."

References/ Recommended Reading

Beam, A.P. (2009). Standards-based differentiation: Identifying the concept of multiple intelligence for use with students with disabilities. *TEACHING Exceptional Children Plus, 5*(4), 1–13.

Kluth, P., & Chandler-Olcott, K. (2007). *"A land we can share": Teaching literacy to students with autism.* Baltimore: Paul H. Brookes Publishing Co.

Kluth, P., & Straut, D. (2003). Toward standards for diverse learners. In P. Kluth, D. Straut, & D.P. Biklen (Eds.), *Access to academics for ALL students: Critical approaches to inclusive curriculum, instruction, and policy* (pp. 33–48). Mahwah, NJ: Lawrence Erlbaum Associates.

Reigeluth, C.M. (1997). Educational standards: To standardize or to customize learning? *Phi Delta Kappan, 79,* 202–206.

Vendor

National Professional Resources
http://www.nprinc.com/inclusion/vsin.htm
NPR carries a huge assortment of books on disability, differentiation, and inclusion, but they also publish their own materials including this videotape, *Standards & Inclusion: Can We Have Both?* by Dorothy Kerzner Lipsky and Alan Gartner. A great staff development tool.

Web Sites

Education World: National Standards
http://www.education-world.com/standards
Links to state and national standards across content areas and grade levels

National Center on Educational Outcomes
http://www.cehd.umn.edu/NCEO
The National Center on Educational Outcomes provides national leadership in the participation of students with disabilities in national and state assessments and in standards-setting efforts. On this site, you will find an extensive list of links (including regional resources) and an updated selection of teleconferences.

Adapted Tests

92

Materials

- Paper
- Sticky notes
- Stickers
- Stamps
- Thick marker
- Highlighters
- Correction fluid

Description

Adapting a test is very similar to adapting a worksheet or other written assignments. The most important elements to keep in mind are the reading level of the student, his or her expressive ability, the goals or objectives targeted for the person, and any physical needs that the person may have (e.g., inability to read small print, difficulties holding a pencil). After assessing the student's challenges and skills in each of these areas, appropriate supports can be implemented. If the student is in sixth grade but reads at a second-grade level and has mild cognitive disabilities, for example, then simplified language and a modification of key concepts may be needed. If a student has difficulty writing or is a nonreader, then paper-and-pencil assessments might be avoided.

Directions

Consider these different ways to adapt a test:
- Allow the student who has difficulty with writing to dictate his answers or record them.
- Reduce the number of items.
- Create less complex questions (e.g., fewer multiple-choice items).
- Cut apart the answers and allow students to glue or paste them on the answer sheet.
- Allow students to answer all or some items verbally.
- Take the test "off the page" and allow some answers to be performance-based (e.g., have students match flash cards instead of matching items).
- Allow students to draw or illustrate answers instead of writing their response.
- Allow students to use notes or an open book for tests (and possibly provide the page number on which to find an answer).
- Allow the use of crib notes or a "cheat sheet."
- Allow students to write all or some of the test questions.
- Provide examples (with answers) of each type of question.

- Add icons, pictures, or other visuals to help students understand the directions or the content.
- Use highlighters to draw students' attention to the directions in each section and to any key words or phrases (e.g., "Show your work") that they should notice throughout.
- Enlarge the text for students with low vision.
- Put larger spaces in between sections to allow the student to identify where a new one begins and a previous one ends.
- Circle the items the student needs to complete.
- Change the format of questions from open ended to fill in the blank, multiple choice, or matching.

Examples

Cinco, a fifth-grader with autism, had such a hard time with penmanship that he began to dread spelling tests. He was an excellent speller but often performed poorly on assessments because not only did his writing need to be neat on these tests but also he had to work quickly. Instead of having Cinco spell out each word, Cinco's teacher gave him a choice of eight different spellings for each word. Cinco simply had to circle the correctly spelled word. After the adaptations were offered, Cinco scored nearly 100 percent on each test.

Jamal, a student with fragile x syndrome, took an adapted test after every social studies unit. Adaptations that were made to these unit tests included the following:

- Simplified language
- Addition of graphics and illustrations
- Changing multiple-choice options from four choices to only two choices
- Opportunity to verbally answer one of the questions on the test

References/ Recommended Reading

Casbarro, J. (2005). *Text anxiety & what you can do about it: A practical guide for teachers, parents, and kids.* Port Chester, NY: National Professional Resources.

Wormeli, R. (2006). *Fair isn't always equal: Assessing & grading in the differentiated classroom.* Portland, ME: Stenhouse Publishers.

Vendors

Bic Wite-Out Brand Correction Fluid
http://www.wite-out.com
Correction fluid is a must-have for on-the-spot adapting. Bic's site features every kind of fluid you might need, including smooth, extra coverage, and quick dry.

Dyslexiacure.com (National Reading Styles Institute)
http://www.dyslexiacure.com
For some students, reading the test is as challenging as answering the questions on it. Colored overlays help students with certain learning disabilities conquer headaches and eye fatigue that may be associated with reading black print on white paper.

Highlighter Tapes
http://www.highlightertapes.com
This translucent highlighter tape allows text to show through clearly. The tape can be removed easily and will not cause any damage to the document.

Web Sites

Authentic Assessment in Mathematics
http://mathforum.org/sum94/project2.html
Several links to assessment options for math teachers

The Authentic Assessment Toolbox
http://jonathan.mueller.faculty.noctrl.edu/toolbox
A how-to site that will help you create authentic tasks, design rubrics, and improve student learning

Discovery School's Kathy Schrock's Guide for Educators (Assessment and Rubric Information)
http://school.discoveryeducation.com/schrockguide/assess.html
Tons of information on creating quality assessments

Paula Kluth.com
http://www.paulakluth.com
Visit Paula's web site to see a number of photographs of adapted tests.

93 Crib Sheets

Materials

- Large index cards
- Highlighters
- Pencil

Description

Students often need to reference facts, formulas, or strategies to succeed on formal and informal assessments. A *crib sheet* that they have created in their own language or learning style is the best tool for these students. The creation of a crib sheet gives the student the opportunity to revisit key concepts from class and from the text, review and succinctly summarize the content, and identify areas that need more attention. This support is, of course, highly personalized because it is created by students themselves.

Directions

You can create crib sheets for students or you can have them create their own crib sheets. The latter is better than the former in most cases because students get support in two ways: 1) they get practice with concepts, facts, or information by perusing the textbook or course materials and deciding what to put on the sheet; and 2) they get support during the assessment so that they can participate using the same format as their peers.

Some examples of what to put on cheat sheets include the following:

- Vocabulary words with definitions
- Drawings or pictures that help students remember information
- Steps or sequences of steps
- Strategies to use during a test
- Ideas for relieving stress during a test

Examples

Celeste, a student with learning disabilities, uses a crib sheet for chapter tests in her physical science class. Other students are allowed to use a sheet of paper to add any information they deem relevant. Celeste can also fill the page, but her crib sheet has reminders from her teacher to include certain formulas, definitions, or illustrations.

Students in a ninth-grade algebra class created crib sheets for each exam. Per their teachers' instructions, they filled in a table with four columns (see Figure 10.1).

Concept	In my own words	Sample problems	Other hints/notes

Figure 10.1.   Sample crib sheet.

Keep in Mind

Teacher-created crib sheets also are an option for students who cannot create such a tool on their own. You can either give the student a template to complete or create the entire tool for him or her.

References/
Recommended Reading

Mower, P. (2003). *Algebra out loud: Learning mathematics through reading and writing activities.* San Francisco: Jossey–Bass Teacher.

Wormeli, R. (2005). *Summarization in any subject: 50 techniques to improve student learning.* Alexandria, VA: American Association of Supervision and Curriculum Development.

Vendors

Avery

http://www.avery.com/avery/en_us/Products/Cards/Index_Cards/_/Ns=Rank

Index cards for the printer; create your crib sheet online and print for a neater and easier to navigate study tool.

The Daily Planner

http://www.thedailyplanner.com/graph-index-cardslarge-p-9190.html

Graph index cards with grids instead of lines—especially helpful for math and science crib sheets.

Web Sites

Math Blog

http://math-blog.com/2008/09/20/13-useful-math-cheat-sheets

Links to 13 different crib sheets including ones for calculus, probability theory, and abstract algebra

Scribd

http://www.scribd.com

On Scribd, anyone can publish, discover, and discuss original writings and documents. Although much of the site is dedicated to sharing creative writing, people also publish many other types of documents including crib sheets and study guides.

Data Forms

Materials

- Sticky notes
- Graph paper
- Clipboards
- Pen or pencil
- Three-ring binders

Student: Teri

Objective: reading w/ switch

	Given Ms. Henry's gestural cue, T. "read" ___ out of 3 sentences using her switch (without additional prompts or cues).	comments
9/1	1 /3	hit switch on last attempt - smiled!
9/8	2 /3	
9/15	3 /3	(")
9/22	1 /3	had to be cued verbally - but was sick yesterday so...
9/29	3 /3	actually 4 times w/o prompts from me

Description

Data collection is an essential task for both general and special educators, and a wide range of forms including checklists, graphs, tables, and anecdotal record sheets can be used or created in order to track progress in academic skills, behavior, communication competencies and abilities, and social skills. Data may be collected hourly, daily, weekly, monthly, or even annually depending on the student, the goal, and the targeted behaviors or skills.

Data forms can be used to track progress toward specific goals and are helpful in seeing change or progress that is small or hard to see on other assessments, communicating a student's skills and abilities to multiple stakeholders, and teaching students to monitor their own goals and accomplishments.

Directions

You will want to create a different data form for every type of skill, competency, or ability you want to assess. Some of the questions you might consider when designing your sheet are the following: What type of information do I need (e.g., qualitative, quantitative)? Who is taking data? Where is the data going to be taken (e.g., on a bus, in a classroom)? What is the easiest way to get the information I want? You may make different choices in different situations depending on the answers you generate to each of these questions. For instance, if you have little time to record data, anecdotal records probably won't work well for you. Instead, you may want to put a few phrases on the form (e.g., "Worked without any support," "Got a few cues," "Worked with several cues from peers") and have the person collecting data circle an option instead of writing one out.

Every data form will be different but, in most cases, all should include a place for recording the date and a small area for including comments that are not obvious or detectable from the data itself. You also can add pictures to data sheets for nonreaders to assess and self-monitor.

Examples

Teri, a student with autism, was learning to use a switch to read a book with a peer. Every day, Teri had four opportunities to read sentences using her switch. The data sheet in Figure 10.2 was constructed to assess Teri's progress.

Date	Given Ms. Henry's gestural cue, T. "read" ___ out of 3 sentences using her switch (without additional prompts or cues).	Comments
9/1	___/3	
9/8	___/3	
9/15	___/3	
9/22	___/3	
9/29	___/3	

Figure 10.2.   Teri's reading data form.

Brent, a student with Asperger syndrome, used the data form in Figure 10.3 to keep track of his goal of "greeting one peer per class every day." He also used the same sheet to help him keep aware of and committed to his goal of "handing in all homework without being reminded."

Goal/Objective	Date	Algebra	English/ILA	Media	Lunch	Science	Social Studies	Speech
Greeting one peer per day								
Handing in home-work without being reminded								

Figure 10.3.   Brent's data form.

Anisa, a student with ADHD, used the data form in Figure 10.4 to follow her own progress on math assignments. This data form was designed to help her become more organized with materials as well as to motivate her to get the highest possible points and to observe the point totals from week to week.

Date	Assignment	Points earned	Comments
12.1	Tuesday's homework	10	
12.2	Wednesday's homework	6	
12.3	Quiz	25	

Figure 10.4. Anisa's grade tracking sheet.

References/ Recommended Reading

Bender, W.M., & Larkin, M.J. (2003). *Reading strategies for elementary students with learning difficulties.* Thousand Oaks, CA: Corwin Press.

Wagner, J.E. (2007). Using spreadsheets to assess learning. *The Physics Teacher, 45,* 34–37.

Vendor

Sandbox Learning Education Tools
http://www.sandbox-learning.com/default.asp?page=34
A variety of checklists and data sheets for young children

Web Sites

Math Milestones Checklist
http://ethnicpublications.com/math_skills.htm
A math chart that suggests some milestones for the primary grades

National Center for Education Statistics (Create a Graph)
http://www.nces.ed.gov/nceskids/createagraph
Designed for kids, this site allows the user to choose a design, enter data, and create their own graph.

Postively Autism
http://www.positivelyautism.com/links.html
Free data sheets and data graphs

Polyxo.com
http://www.polyxo.com/documents
Several click-and-print data sheets that can be used for students of different ages and for different purposes (e.g., math skills, communication goals)

95 Portfolios

Materials

- Expandable file folders
- Three-ring binders
- Spiral notebooks
- Photo albums

Description

Portfolios are "a purposeful selection by a student of work/artifacts that represent the student's pursuits, explorations, and projects as a way of evidencing the student's progress, effort, achievements, and growth" (Tierney & Clark, 2002, p. 443). Portfolios are a tool that teachers often choose in a differentiated classroom because they validate all kinds of learning and encourage varying modes of expression—the written, the oral, the graphic, the three-dimensional model, the video, and the audio. And they allow students to demonstrate their preferred way of knowing as well as gain expanded awareness of other ways of knowing (Clagett, 1996).

Portfolios are a unique assessment because they serve many different purposes. For example, they can be used to show the progress of a student's work over time, help teachers see a student's abilities across activities and tasks, and enlarge the teacher's and the student's view of what and how much is being learned. Portfolios are ideal in inclusive classrooms because, unlike tests or other traditional assessments, they require no "right answer," allow for different contributions from different learners, and provide students with opportunities to show off the skills, abilities, and competencies they have that may not be target skills for assessment. Finally, portfolios create a "marriage" between instruction and assessment; they allow students to see that assessment can be collaborative and even enjoyable; and that evaluation does not necessarily come at the end of some predetermined learning period but, ideally, happens regularly and is part of the process of learning and teaching.

Some of the most commonly used portfolios include the following:

- *Showcase models:* This approach contains samples of the student's best work and is usually used for the purpose of summative evaluation.
- *Evaluative models:* This model contains work by the student that has been evaluated using a certain criteria.
- *Documentation models:* Known as the "working" portfolio, this approach contains a collection of work over time showing growth and improvement and reflecting students' learning of identified outcomes. For this reason, it is perfectly acceptable to show both the best of the student's work and the worst.
- *Process models:* This approach documents all facets or phases of the learning process. It can show how students integrate specific knowledge or skills and progress toward both basic and

advanced mastery. In addition, the process portfolio inevitably emphasizes students' reflection on their learning process. Specific materials may be included to this end (e.g., journals, think logs) (Kluth & Chandler-Olcott, 2007).

Directions

You can assemble the portfolio, or the student can assemble it. Products for a student's portfolio can include any or all of the following:

- Work samples
- Any artifact that represents student learning or success (e.g., drawing, diagram, sheet music from a song that has been mastered, note from a teacher about working well with classmates)
- Photographs of the student engaging in a task or pictures of completed work
- Photographs, drawings, or graphics that the student has created him- or herself
- Videotapes or audiotapes of the student demonstrating a task, performing, or explaining learning
- A list of learning materials that the student shows interest in
- Photographs of the student engaged in learning activities, especially if his or her participation looks different than that of neurotypical learners
- Multimedia files such as PowerPoint presentations, web sites, or video created by the individual, either independently or with support
- Student data sheets

Examples

Fourth graders in an inclusive classroom demonstrate their emerging writing skills using a portfolio approach. Students are required to keep sloppy copies, drafts, and final copies to show their teacher their work on each piece of writing. By the end of each quarter, students are expected to prepare their three best samples for formal grading. Isabel, a student with cognitive disabilities, also is expected to have three samples and to demonstrate her writing process, but her products are much shorter (only a few sentences each), and the skills teachers are targeting for her to develop are slightly different. For example, other students have to demonstrate how they can identify sentences with grammatical errors and make necessary corrections. Isabel has to demonstrate how she consistently spelled 10 words (i.e., *Isabel, dad, mom, is, was, the, my, I, went, saw*) correctly.

Students in a high school Family and Consumer Education class have to create a showcase portfolio for half of their final grade. They must show how they have mastered more than a dozen different standards and, using captions and written descriptions, explain their learning process and growth.

References/ Recommended Reading

Belgrad, S., Burke, K.B., & Fogarty, R.J. (2008). *The portfolio connection: Student work linked to standards* (3rd ed.). Thousand Oaks, CA: Corwin.

Chen, Y.-F., & Martin, M.A. (2000). Using performance assessment and portfolio assessment together in the elementary classroom. *Reading Improvement, 37*(1), 32–38

Cole, D.J., Ryan, C.W., Kick, F., & Mathies, B.K. (1999). *Portfolios across the curriculum and beyond.* Thousand Oaks: Corwin Press.

Klein-Ezell, C., & Ezell, D. (2005). Use of portfolio assessment with students with cognitive disabilities/mental retardation. *Assessment for Effective Intervention, 30*(4), 15–23.

Kleinert, H.L., & Kearns, J.F. (2001). *Alternate assessment: Measuring outcomes and supports for students with disabilities.* Baltimore: Paul H. Brookes Publishing Co.

Kluth, P., & Chandler-Olcott, K. (2007). *"A land we can share": Teaching literacy to students with autism.* Baltimore: Paul H. Brookes Publishing Co.

Tierney, R., & Clark, C. (2002). Portfolios. In B. Guzzetti (Ed.), *Literacy in America: An encyclopedia of history, theory, and practice* (pp. 443–445). Santa Barbara, CA: ABC-CLIO.

Vendors

MisterArt
http://www.misterart.com/g26/Cachet-Classic-Student-Portfolio.htm
For older students, in particular, using actual artist portfolios may be an option. These sturdier folders may be especially appropriate for portfolios that will be used across subject areas.

Paper Mart
http://www.papermart.com/Search_20Pages/CombinedSearch.aspx?SearchStr=pizza_20boxes
Teachers often use pizza boxes to store student portfolio artifacts. Several different sizes are available from this vendor.

Web Sites

TeacherVision
http://www.teachervision.fen.com/assessment/teaching-methods/20153.html
Many short articles, links, and descriptions of every aspect of portfolio assessment

Using Technology to Support Alternative Assessment and Electronic Portfolios
http://electronicportfolios.org
Dozens of links to help teachers explore the use of technology to support alternative assessment

Audio/Video Assessment

96

Materials

- Video camcorders
- Flip video cameras
- Tripod
- Cell phones
- Tape recorders
- Digital recorders

Description

Audio- or videotaping student performance is an ideal way to capture learning over time. Taping can be used to track student progress or illustrate mastery of a skill or learning standard for families, other teachers, or the student him- or herself. Using recording devices may be especially helpful for students who have moderate and significant disabilities and may, therefore, demonstrate progress very gradually. For example, a student may learn to "run" in physical education by moving his or her wheelchair 1–2 inches, then 6 inches, then a foot, and finally a few feet. This progress may not seem significant or even detectable to a person observing the progress over time; someone watching these clips on videotape, however, will see the individual's growing ability.

Audio- or videotaping at regular intervals can help a teacher notice things he or she simply does not notice in the moment due to distractions or the subtlety of the event. For example, a teacher listening to an audiotape of one of her students reading a picture book noticed that he kept stopping and babbling to himself, saying things such as, "Julius is a baby" and "admiring his little eyes." Because the young man had an autism label, the teacher had written this off as self-talk or echolalia that was not necessarily functional or purposeful. After listening to the tape, however, she clearly understood that he was retelling a different story she had read to another boy days before. She was, therefore, not only able to use the tape to get information about the young man's reading fluency but also she ended up with data on his memory and attention skills.

Directions

Determine how you might use taped assessment. Consider, at least, the following areas:
- Social skills
- Organizational skills
- Speech and language skills and goals
- Occupational and physical therapy skills and goals

- Independent functioning skills (e.g., moving around school independently, purchasing items in the cafeteria)
- Study and work skills (e.g., remaining on task, working independently)
- Group projects and group behavior (e.g., asking questions, sharing materials)
- Reading fluency
- Reading comprehension

After you have decided on which skills to focus, consider what intervals will be appropriate for the type of information you need. For example, some abilities such as increasing reading fluency might not change much day to day but probably will be worth assessing every month.

You also will want to make some decisions about what to do with the data once it is collected. Videotapes and audiotapes can, of course, be used to assess learners and provide evidence of growth, learning, or difficulties, but they can also be used to design other assessments, plan instruction, or create more appropriate adaptations.

Tools that might be used for your recordings include traditional video cameras and tripods or small, hand-held cameras such as Flip cameras that allow you to capture the action then connect to the USB port on your computer and upload the video (no tapes to buy or fuss with later). Flip cameras can hold 30 to 60 minutes of video at a time. Some cell phones can also hold short video clips, and many computers will allow you to record and store video footage as well.

For audio recording, the easiest materials may still be cassette tapes and recorders (because the technology is outdated, unused machines and tapes often can be found in back closets of school offices or classrooms). Digital recorders are also an option.

Examples

Independent transitions and participation in certain classes were target goals for Kevin, a young man with cognitive disabilities. In particular, Kevin was working on participating in his music class without any support from a paraprofessional. To do so, he needed to enter the classroom with a peer, find his seat independently, listen to the directions from his music teacher, and participate in the various exercises and activities. This sequence was very hard for him to master early in the year. In September, he was only able to participate for about 6 minutes without cues from the paraprofessional. His team videotaped him four times throughout the course of the year and found that he gained new skills and functioned more independently each quarter. By taping the classes and watching the videos, the team was able to see that Kevin was able to do a lot of the work independently and that the paraprofessional and the music teacher often stepped in too early to give him cues or to correct him. The tape thus functioned as both an assessment tool for the student and as a teaching tool for staff.

All of the students in the high school orchestra class were assessed on their improvement over several weeks. Students were audiotaped playing a piece of music chosen by the teacher. They were taped again each week for a month and were instructed to use the tapes to assess their own progress and critique their own performance. Rich, a student with Asperger syndrome, loved participating in this assessment and not only used his own tapes for self-assessment but also used the tapes of more capable cello players to improve his performance.

References/
Recommended Reading

Doering, N. (2000). Measuring student understanding with a videotape performance assessment. *Journal of Physical Education, Recreation & Dance, 71*(7), 47–51.

Kingore, B. (2007). *Developing portfolios for authentic assessment, PreK–3*. Thousand Oaks, CA: Corwin Press.

Vendors

Flip Video
http://www.theflip.com
A tiny, stripped-down video recorder the size of a small digital camera

Just Recorders
http://www.justrecorders.com/digitalrec.htm
A selection of digital voice recorders

Web Site

Teacher Tap
http://eduscapes.com/tap/topic78.htm
Ideas for using handheld devices in the classroom

97 Sticky Note Record Book

Materials

- Notebook
- Pen or pencil
- Sticky notes

Description

For many students with disabilities, classroom assessments are hard to perform. This is especially true of students with the most significant disabilities. For these learners, physical, communication, sensory, and social differences impede their ability to show what they know. Because most of these learners cannot use traditional assessment materials or formats, their knowledge and abilities are often unseen, unmeasured, or not assessed at all.

The *sticky note record book* is one attempt to capture the learning and abilities of these students. Using such a record book simply involves jotting weekly (or more frequent) anecdotal notes about what you are seeing, hearing, and experiencing with your student. Add anything to the notebook that will help you see or understand not just what the student knows but also how he or she learns. We call it the sticky note record book because we often jot down observations across environments and do not have the notebook handy. Therefore, it is not uncommon to write notes on a sticky pad to adhere to the notebook at the end of the day.

This record book reminds us of the idiom, "If the mountain will not come to Mohammed, Mohammed will go to the mountain!" In other words, students may not be able to "come" to your assessment and perform, so you may have to go to them, observe, be alert, and look for signs of ability, growth, and knowledge.

Directions

Keep the notebook in an area that is very accessible, or keep a batch of sticky notes near at all times so you are ready to record "findings" at any point during the day. Include any information that will help in understanding the student's ability and progress. For example, if the student starts paging through a book he has not touched before, that might be helpful to know. If he becomes suddenly fascinated with an abacus in the classroom, write a note about what he does with it. If she takes some papers off your desk that happen to have her name on them, you might jot a note to yourself about the possibility that she can read her name.

Example

Ms. Thiel, a second-grade teacher, uses a sticky note record book for Jon, a student with multiple disabilities. She has primarily used this book for taking down information, observations, and thoughts about Jon's literacy learning, including the following:

- 1/15: Jon sat by Simon as Simon read two books. Did not sit down but stayed near him and looked down at the pages.
- 1/16: Jon played the "Songs That Teach Phonics" tape today and danced. Showed me that he could play it by himself.
- 1/30: Jon sat by Simon during groups and gave him "A Fish Out of Water." (Is this a request?).
- 2/2: Jon has been carrying around "A Fish Out of Water" today and yesterday.
- 2/13: Jon used the switch to read with G.G.—he started the book by "reading," "Once there was a little mouse…" but then walked away.

Keep in Mind

Some teachers may want to use different color notes for different types of observations or behaviors. For instance, observations on a student's communication goals might be written on blue notes while data on social skills could be written on pink notes.

References/ Recommended Reading

Boyd-Batstone, P. (2004). Focused anecdotal records assessment: A tool for standard-based, authentic assessment. *The Reading Teacher, 58*(3), 230–239.

Klingner, J.K., Vaughn, S., & Boardman, A. (2007). *Teaching reading comprehension to students with learning difficulties.* New York: Guilford Publications.

Vendor

3M & Post-It Notes
http://www.3m.com/us/office/postit
3M is the home of the Post-It note and the Post-It note pen.

Web Sites

University of Saskatchewan: School of Education (Anecdotal Records Form)
http://www.usask.ca/education/coursework/mcvittiej/bio30unit1/evaluation/anecdotal.htm
A helpful anecdotal record form

Prekinders
http://www.prekinders.com/anecdotal.htm
Tips and forms related to anecdotal assessment

The United Federation of Teachers
http://www.uft.org/chapter/teacher/special/anecdotal_recor
Information on anecdotal records and a link to a record-keeping form

Strengths & Strategies Profile

98

Materials

- Computer and printer paper or pen and paper
- Strengths and strategies template

Description

The way that we, as teachers, talk, think, and write about our students affects our practice. In addition, our perceptions of learners and the ways in which we communicate about them can serve to strengthen or damage our relationships with families (Kluth, 2010). A parent of a fifth-grade student once shared that she was in the education system for 6 years before any teacher said anything kind or positive about her daughter. When the teacher off-handedly shared that Rachel, her daughter, had "a beautiful smile and great energy," the mother burst into tears, startling the teacher. After learning of the reason for the mother's reaction, the teacher made it a point to keep sharing information about Rachel's abilities, gifts, skills, and accomplishments throughout the school year.

Clearly, as we assess students, we should be focusing not only on what students need and where they struggle but also on what is going well, what works, and what their strengths are. For this purpose, we recommend a simple document called the *Strengths & Strategies Profile* (Kluth Dimon-Borowski, 2003). This document can help educators focus on the abilities of learners instead of only on their difficulties and areas of need. One list (*strengths*) contains a student's strengths, interests, gifts, and talents. The other list (*strategies*) answers the question, "What works for this student?" This list should contain strategies for motivating, supporting, encouraging, helping, teaching, and connecting with the learner.

Although this tool is not complex and does not necessarily provide a team with new information, it can help teachers organize the information they have and understand it in a new way. The focus on positive language and abilities can prompt educators to think and talk about students in a more proactive way. It also can help teachers make changes in their planning and in their daily practice. Specifically, educators may be able to use these forms to do the following:

- Assess progress from year to year
- Plan curriculum and instruction
- Create curricular adaptations
- Develop student goals and objectives
- Design supports for challenging situations
- Work more collaboratively with and elicit concrete ideas from families
- Collaborate and communicate with each other

The Strengths & Strategies Profile can be used anytime for any purpose. Often, it is used to begin IEP meetings, but it can also be used as an attachment to a positive behavior plan or as a communication tool for teams who are transitioning a student from teacher to teacher or school to school.

Directions

To create your lists, gather your team together and explain the process. Better yet, pass out a blank template and an example of a completed form (one can be found on Paula's web site at http://www.paulakluth.com/articles/strengthstrateg.pdf) to let them see what they will create. Then, designate one or two recorders and have people shout out items until at least 50 items are collected. If you want to run the process in a more orderly fashion, each person around the table can take a turn at adding a few items to each list.

Be aware that it is important that the profile be completed by the entire team. If just one teacher or parent fills in the pages, the other team members do not have an opportunity to contribute to and feel invested in the assessment. Furthermore, we feel strongly that when it comes to this tool, the process is often more powerful than the product itself.

Example

Maeve's team used a Strengths & Strategies Profile to make her transition from elementary school to middle school more smooth and successful. The elementary team completed the assessment during a transition meeting so the new team could both become familiar with the tool and hear all about Maeve's strengths and abilities as they began planning her seventh-grade year.

Keep in Mind

The theory of multiple intelligences (Gardner, 1983) is a good tool for framing both strengths and strategies. A student who might be seen by some as "struggling with seat work" or as "hyperactive" might be seen as kinesthetic or as profiting from active learning (Armstrong, 2009).

References/
Recommended Reading

Armstrong, T. (2009). *Multiple intelligences in the classroom* (3rd ed.). Alexandria, VA: Association for Supervision and Curriculum Development.

Gardner, H. (1983). *Frames of mind.* New York: Basic Books.

Kluth, P. (2010). *"You're going to love this kid!" Teaching students with autism in the inclusive classroom* (2nd ed.). Baltimore: Paul H. Brookes Publishing Co.

Kluth, P. & Dimon-Borowski (2003). *Strengths & strategies profile.* Retrieved December 2, 2009, from http://www.paulakluth.com/articles/strengthstrateg.pdf

Vendor

PEAK Parent Center (The IEP: A Tool for Realizing Possibilities)
http://www.peakparent.org/product.asp?id=115
This innovative new toolkit created by Christi Kasa-Hendrickson, Barb Buswell, and Julie Harmon holds all of the resources you need for a successful IEP meeting. The kit includes a training script, a PowerPoint presentation, resource handouts, and other resources including a complete copy of the *Strengths & Strategies Profile.*

Web Sites

Paula Kluth's web site (Strengths & Strategies)
http://www.paulakluth.com/articles/strengthstrateg.html
Go to this link to get an article on using the Strengths & Strategies tool, and then click on the PDF hyperlink to get a blank template to use and reproduce.

Multiple Intelligences for Adult Literacy and Education
http://literacyworks.org/mi/assessment/findyourstrengths.html
To learn more about a student's strengths, have them fill out this inventory focused on Howard Gardner's multiple intelligences theory.

99 Luck-of-the-Draw Jar

Materials

- Small jar or coffee can
- Index cards
- Marker

Description

In this game, students take turns providing short summaries of the content from the previous day. A *Luck-of-the-Draw jar* (Saphier & Haley, 1993) helps students stay on their toes, inspires them to come to class prepared, and provides them with opportunities to remember content from days passed.

Directions

To prepare for the game, put every student's name on an index card or slip of paper and place these in a jar or coffee can. Introduce the activity by modeling what a quality summary looks like and sounds like. Ask students to give you feedback on your summary. Coax them to comment on and notice the length of the summary and the type of information provided. Then, have students practice summarizing a lesson with a partner. Stress that summaries should 1) be brief (about 3–5 minutes); 2) be cogent, or clear; and 3) include specific key points. Then, place all student names on cards and put them in a container. You are now ready to play Luck of the Draw every day or every week or whenever you feel a summary is in order.

To play the game, reach into the container, pull out a name, and announce who has won the Luck of the Draw! This student will begin the following day's class with a summary. On the next day, after summarizing, this student will select the next person to win Luck of the Draw.

Examples

In a high school Family and Consumer Education class, the teacher used Luck of the Draw several times a week. Raven, a young woman with emotional disabilities, did not like to be surprised or get short notice on assignments, so she wrote a short, two-sentence summary in her notebook every day. Students, therefore, often consulted with Raven when it was their turn to share.

Ms. DiDomenico, a sixth-grade teacher, uses a slightly longer version of Luck of the Draw weekly. A different student presents 5 to 10 key points from the previous week. The drawing takes place on Friday, and the summary is shared on Monday morning. All students are encouraged to write a few summary points on Friday afternoon before the name is drawn. This way, everyone has an opportunity to review and the person who is responsible for summarizing has some class time to do so. Even though the summary is supposed to take 10 minutes or less, the student summarizing is encouraged to incorporate humor, use a visual, or engage the group in some way.

Reference/ Recommended Reading

Saphier, J., & Haley, M.A. (1993). *Summarizers: Activity structures to support integration and retention of new learning.* Acton, MA: Research for Better Teaching, Inc.

Vendors

National School Products
http://nationalschoolproducts.com/nsp/product_info.php?pid=13847
Convenient locking-lid storage jars in four sizes: 16 oz., 24 oz., 32 oz., and 40 oz.

Container & Packaging Supply
http://www.containerandpackaging.com
Any type of jar, can, or container you need for the classroom

Web Site

Teachers Network (Adjust Your Teaching Style to Your Students' Learning Style)
http://www.teachnet.org/ntol/howto/adjust/c17207,.htm
Several ideas for debriefing and summarizing across grade levels and subject areas from author James E. Dallas

100   Exit Cards

Materials

- Sticky notes
- Scraps of paper
- Pen or pencil
- Box to place exit slips

Description

It is important for teachers to assess students' learning to provide further instruction in an effective way. *Exit cards* may be used as part of ongoing assessment and may be used in daily routines or lessons as a closure activity.

Exit cards (also called *quick checks* or *tickets out*) are a simple way for teachers to assess how well students grasped the key concepts of the day's lesson. They take no more than 5 minutes for students to complete and are often a good indication of how well the content was understood, what material still needs to be reviewed, and what topics might be good to explore in greater detail.

Exit cards can consist of any of the following:

- Multiple-choice questions (students write one choice on paper)
- Fill-in-the-blank questions
- Sentence starters (e.g., "Today I learned _____"; "My favorite line from the poem was _____"; "I would nominate _____ for the Supreme Court")
- A problem to complete or an equation to solve

Directions

Distribute a slip of paper or an index card to each student and direct students to put their name on the card. Then, provide the question or prompt and give students a few minutes to respond. As students leave the classroom, have them turn in their cards. Once you have the cards, they can be used in a variety of ways. For instance, you might

- Put a ★ on three cards and give them back to their owners the next day; have these learners put their responses on the board and use them as a quick review
- Choose three cards randomly and examine as a quick "How did they do?" assessment of student learning to use in your own planning
- Do a quick scan of all of the cards and create discussion questions or lesson extensions based on responses

Examples

Pagnano-Richardson and Henninger (2008) use exit cards in physical education to help students assess their tactical decision-making abilities. Examples of exit-card questions they suggest include the following:

- What did you think about when you were hitting the ball?
- What were you thinking about when the ball did not come to you?
- What did you think about during game play today?

Students in an 11th-grade expository writing class need to provide their teacher with an exit card each Friday as they file out. Every week, she provides them with a new challenge related to language, writing, and expression. One week, for instance, she asked for an example of hyperbole related to the upcoming Superbowl. Another week, she asked students to develop a metaphor about their development as a writer. She read the cards, giving each student a point for completing the assignment, and then shared three favorite cards with the class on Monday.

A third-grade teacher, Ms. Boise, used exit cards to keep math concepts fresh in her students' minds. Whenever she had 5 or more minutes to spare at the end of her math lesson, Ms. Boise gave students a math problem to solve. The problem, however, was seldom one from the current unit. Typically, she chose content from earlier units so that students would have opportunities to continually revisit the concepts they had learned weeks and even months earlier. Anthony, a student with cognitive disabilities, had difficulty participating in this exit card exercise; therefore, it was designed so that Ms. Boise always gave Anthony the same type of problem (i.e., a multiplication problem or a clock fact to read) for his exit card.

References/ Recommended Reading

Kryza, K., Stephens, S.J., & Duncan, A. (2007). *Inspiring middle and secondary learners: Honoring differences and creating community through differentiating instructional practices.* Thousand Oaks, CA: Corwin Press.

Pagnano-Richardson, K., & Henninger, M.L. (2008). A model for developing and assessing tactical decision-making competency in game play: This framework will help teachers develop age-appropriate instruction and assessment tools. *JOPERD—The Journal of Physical Education, Recreation & Dance, 79*(3), 24–29.

Strickland, C.A., & Tomlinson, C.A. (2005). *Differentiation in practice: A resource guide for differentiating curriculum, grades 9–12.* Alexandria, VA: American Association for Supervision and Curriculum Development.

Vendors

GreenLine Paper Company
http://www.greenlinepaper.com/filing-school/index-cards/cat_22.html
Recycled index cards

Staples
http://www.staples.com
A variety of cards in different colors, sizes, and brands

Web Sites

Constructivism (Strategies)
http://www.saskschools.ca/curr_content/constructivism/how/strategies.html
Several strategies, including exit cards, that can be used across K–12 classrooms

Montgomery County Public Schools (Summarizing Strategies)
http://www.montgomeryschoolsmd.org/departments/development/resources/strategies/index.shtm
Several summary techniques as well as links to related web sites